Communications
in Computer and Information Science　　1827

Rationale

The CCIS series is devoted to the publication of proceedings of computer science conferences. Its aim is to efficiently disseminate original research results in informatics in printed and electronic form. While the focus is on publication of peer-reviewed full papers presenting mature work, inclusion of reviewed short papers reporting on work in progress is welcome, too. Besides globally relevant meetings with internationally representative program committees guaranteeing a strict peer-reviewing and paper selection process, conferences run by societies or of high regional or national relevance are also considered for publication.

Topics

The topical scope of CCIS spans the entire spectrum of informatics ranging from foundational topics in the theory of computing to information and communications science and technology and a broad variety of interdisciplinary application fields.

Information for Volume Editors and Authors

Publication in CCIS is free of charge. No royalties are paid, however, we offer registered conference participants temporary free access to the online version of the conference proceedings on SpringerLink (http://link.springer.com) by means of an http referrer from the conference website and/or a number of complimentary printed copies, as specified in the official acceptance email of the event.

CCIS proceedings can be published in time for distribution at conferences or as post-proceedings, and delivered in the form of printed books and/or electronically as USBs and/or e-content licenses for accessing proceedings at SpringerLink. Furthermore, CCIS proceedings are included in the CCIS electronic book series hosted in the SpringerLink digital library at http://link.springer.com/bookseries/7899. Conferences publishing in CCIS are allowed to use Online Conference Service (OCS) for managing the whole proceedings lifecycle (from submission and reviewing to preparing for publication) free of charge.

Publication process

The language of publication is exclusively English. Authors publishing in CCIS have to sign the Springer CCIS copyright transfer form, however, they are free to use their material published in CCIS for substantially changed, more elaborate subsequent publications elsewhere. For the preparation of the camera-ready papers/files, authors have to strictly adhere to the Springer CCIS Authors' Instructions and are strongly encouraged to use the CCIS LaTeX style files or templates.

Abstracting/Indexing

CCIS is abstracted/indexed in DBLP, Google Scholar, EI-Compendex, Mathematical Reviews, SCImago, Scopus. CCIS volumes are also submitted for the inclusion in ISI Proceedings.

How to start

To start the evaluation of your proposal for inclusion in the CCIS series, please send an e-mail to ccis@springer.com.

Daniel Vasić · Mirela Kundid Vasić
Editors

Digital Transformation in Education and Artificial Intelligence Application

First International Conference, MoStart 2023
Mostar, Bosnia and Herzegovina, April 18–20, 2023
Revised Selected Papers

 Springer

Editors
Daniel Vasić 🆔
University of Mostar
Mostar, Bosnia and Herzegovina

Mirela Kundid Vasić 🆔
University of Mostar
Mostar, Bosnia and Herzegovina

ISSN 1865-0929 ISSN 1865-0937 (electronic)
Communications in Computer and Information Science
ISBN 978-3-031-36832-5 ISBN 978-3-031-36833-2 (eBook)
https://doi.org/10.1007/978-3-031-36833-2

This Springer imprint is published by the registered company Springer Nature Switzerland AG
The registered company address is: Gewerbestrasse 11, 6330 Cham, Switzerland

Preface

We are proud to present the proceedings of the inaugural International Conference on Digital Transformation in Education and Artificial Intelligence Applications (MoStart 2023), which took place from April 18–20, 2023, in the historic city of Mostar. The conference, organized by the University of Mostar, aimed to provide an international forum for researchers, academicians, and practitioners to collaborate, exchange ideas, and showcase their research findings related to state-of-the-art advancements in digital transformation and artificial intelligence applications within the educational sphere.

The conference covered a diverse range of topics, including Artificial Intelligence and Robotics in Education, Games and Simulations, Intelligent Tutoring Systems, Augmented and Virtual Reality, Natural Language Processing, Computer Vision, IoT and Metaverse Applications, Learning Analytics, Deep Learning, and Ethical Issues in AI applications in Education and Law.

For this first edition, we received a total of 30 high-quality submissions. Our esteemed program committee members, comprising experts in digital transformation, artificial intelligence, and education, meticulously reviewed each submission. After extensive deliberations, 12 exceptional papers were selected for presentation and are included in this proceedings volume. Additionally, the conference program featured two illuminating invited talks delivered by distinguished experts in the field.

We extend our gratitude to the program committee members for their invaluable contributions in the review and selection of the papers, and to the authors for their diligent research efforts and participation. Our special thanks go to our keynote speakers for imparting their knowledge and insights during the conference.

As we reflect on the success of the inaugural MoStart conference, we hope that the attendees found the event intellectually stimulating, fostering new connections and collaborations, and contributing to the ongoing growth and development of digital transformation and artificial intelligence applications in education.

Thank you for your participation in MoStart 2023, and we look forward to welcoming you to future editions of the conference!

May 2023   Daniel Vasić
                                                                Mirela Kundid Vasić

Organization

General Chair

Mirela Kundid Vasić   University of Mostar, Bosnia and Herzegovina

Program Committee Chair

Daniel Vasić   University of Mostar, Bosnia and Herzegovina

Steering Committee

Boris Crnokić	University of Mostar, Bosnia and Herzegovina
Tomislav Volarić	University of Mostar, Bosnia and Herzegovina
Mirela Kundid Vasić	University of Mostar, Bosnia and Herzegovina
Krešimir Rakić	University of Mostar, Bosnia and Herzegovina
Davorka Topić Stipić	University of Mostar, Bosnia and Herzegovina
Daniel Vasić	University of Mostar, Bosnia and Herzegovina
Damir Vasilj	University of Mostar, Bosnia and Herzegovina
Marin Bošnjak	University of Mostar, Bosnia and Herzegovina
Tin Brdar	Ministry of Science, Education, Culture and Sports, Herzeg-Bosnian Canton, Bosnia and Herzegovina
Emil Brajković	University of Mostar, Bosnia and Herzegovina
Krešimir Čavar	University of Mostar, Bosnia and Herzegovina
Željko Ćorić	Institute of Education, Mostar, Bosnia and Herzegovina
Snježana Damjanović	School Center Martin Nedić (OFM), Orašje, Bosnia and Herzegovina
Josip Doko	University of Mostar, Bosnia and Herzegovina
Goran Dujak	Ministry of Education, Science, Culture and Sports, Posavina Canton, Bosnia and Herzegovina
Ana Kordić	Ministry of Education, Science, Culture and Sports, West Herzegovina Canton, Bosnia and Herzegovina
Hrvoje Ljubić	University of Mostar, Bosnia and Herzegovina

Maja Marić	University of Mostar, Bosnia and Herzegovina
Anton Martinović	University of Mostar, Bosnia and Herzegovina
Petar Matić	University of Mostar, Bosnia and Herzegovina
Vedran Mihalj	University of Mostar, Bosnia and Herzegovina
Manlio Napoli	University of Mostar, Bosnia and Herzegovina
Ivan Ostojić	University of Mostar, Bosnia and Herzegovina
Tomislav Papac	University of Mostar, Bosnia and Herzegovina
Ana Pinjuh	University of Mostar, Bosnia and Herzegovina
Karlo Popović	University of Mostar, Bosnia and Herzegovina
Robert Rozić	University of Mostar, Bosnia and Herzegovina
Jelena Skoko	Institute for Upbringing and Education, Bosnia and Herzegovina
Robert Slišković	University of Mostar, Bosnia and Herzegovina
Goran Škvarč	Croatian Academic and Research Network – CARNET, Croatia
Valentina Vidović	Ministry of Science, Education, Youth, Culture and Sports, Bosnia and Herzegovina
Franjo Vučić	University of Mostar, Bosnia and Herzegovina

Program Committee

Sanja Bijakšić	University of Mostar, Bosnia and Herzegovina
Mirjana Bonković	University of Split, Croatia
Ivo Čolak	University of Mostar, Bosnia and Herzegovina
Juan Manuel Fernández Luna	University of Granada, Spain
Irena Galić	University of Osijek, Croatia
Sven Gotovac	University of Split, Croatia
Tamara Grujić	University of Split, Croatia
Rainer Herpers	Bonn-Rhein-Sieg University of Applied Sciences, Germany
Branko Katalinić	Vienna University of Technology, Austria
Zdenko Klepić	University of Mostar, Bosnia and Herzegovina
Goran Martinović	University of Osijek, Croatia
Pedro Miguel Moreira	Polytechnic Institute of Viana do Castelo, Portugal
Vladan Papić	University of Split, Croatia
Marko Rosič	University of Split, Croatia
Slavomir Stankov	University of Split, Croatia
Zoran Tomić	University of Mostar, Bosnia and Herzegovina
Drago Žagar	University of Osijek, Croatia
Boris Crnokić	University of Mostar, Bosnia and Herzegovina

Malik Čabaravdić	University of Zenica, Bosnia and Herzegovina
Ani Grubišić	University of Split, Croatia
Tonćo Marušić	University of Mostar, Bosnia and Herzegovina
Jonathan Schler	Holon Institute of Technology, Israel
Jan Snajder	University of Zagreb, Croatia
Danijel Topić	University of Osijek, Croatia
Tomislav Volarić	University of Mostar, Bosnia and Herzegovina
Branko Žitko	University of Split, Croatia
Krunoslav Žubrinić	University of Dubrovnik, Croatia
Elisabete Cunha	Polytechnic Institute of Viana do Castelo, Portugal
Bárbara Cristina Dos Santos Gaspar Cleto	Polytechnic Institute of Porto, Portugal
Angelina Gašpar	University of Split, Croatia
Janez Gotlih	University of Maribor, Slovenia
Miroslav Grubišić	University of Mostar, Bosnia and Herzegovina
Timi Karner	University of Maribor, Slovenia
Mirela Kundid Vasić	University of Mostar, Bosnia and Herzegovina
Nikola Ljubešić	University of Ljubljana, Slovenia
Željko Marušić	University of Mostar, Bosnia and Herzegovina
Mirza Oruč	University of Zenica, Bosnia and Herzegovina
Ivan Peko	University of Split, Croatia
Krešimir Rakić	University of Mostar, Bosnia and Herzegovina
Višnja Simić	University of Kragujevac, Serbia
Suzana Tomaš	University of Split, Croatia
Daniel Vasić	University of Mostar, Bosnia and Herzegovina
Josip Vasilj	University of Split, Croatia

Additional Reviewer

Maleta, Nikolina

Contents

Evaluating Text Summarization Using FAHP and TOPSIS Methods in Intelligent Tutoring Systems

Emil Brajković[(✉)] [ID], Daniel Vasić [ID], and Tomislav Volarić [ID]

Faculty of Science and Education, University of Mostar, Mostar,
Bosnia and Herzegovina
{emil.brajkovic,daniel.vasic,tomislav.volaric}@fpmoz.sum.ba

Abstract. The objective of this study is to suggest a fuzzy decision-making model that can help in choosing the most suitable text summarization technique for e-learning systems based on the subjective evaluations of decision makers. The criteria used for selecting the ideal text summarization method in this research are derived from the common features of the available text summarization techniques. Since there are multiple criteria involved in the assessment of text summarization techniques, multi-criteria decision-making methods (MCDM) need to be employed. Our proposed method involves the use of the FAHP (fuzzy analytic hierarchy process) and TOPSIS (Technique for Order of Preference by Similarity to Ideal Solution) methods. Initially, FAHP is used to calculate the weightage of each criterion, and the preference of one criterion over another is evaluated using triangular fuzzy numbers in the FAHP method. Then, the TOPSIS method is utilized to rank the text summarization techniques, and the one that is farthest from the negative ideal solution and closest to the positive ideal solution according to the TOPSIS method is considered the best method. The integration of FAHP and TOPSIS methods ensures an efficient selection of the most suitable text summarization method based on one's requirements.

Keywords: Text summarization · Multi-criteria decision-making methods · Fuzzy AHP · TOPSIS

1 Introduction

This paper introduces a fresh method for automatic document summarization that employs multicriteria decision-making techniques. With the explosion of digital data, there is a growing problem of information overload, which necessitates a tool that can create a condensed version of a digital document, interpreting a large amount of textual information. Text summarization is crucial for generating a summary of a document by highlighting important information. Automatic text summarization involves using a machine to generate a summary from the source text without human intervention, condensing the most significant information into a shorter format. Text summarization is useful for people who need to comprehend large amounts of information quickly, and exploring this area further or improving these techniques is an attractive technological prospect [17]. Automatic summarization is a computer-based process that condenses a written document with the aim of producing a summary that captures the key points of the original source. To create an accurate summary, technology must take into account the length, writing style, and syntax of the text [22]. Machine learning techniques and data analysis are used to identify a subset of data that is representative of the entire document [13]. Key sentences are selected to create a summary, making the task similar to finding keywords within the document. There are two main categories of automatic summary generation: extraction and abstraction [22]. Extraction involves selecting important sentences from the original document based on certain criteria. This approach is more common than abstraction because it is simpler and easier to achieve [16]. Abstraction, on the other hand, creates a semantic representation from which sentences are generated, resulting in a summary that may use different words and phrases than those present in the source document. Abstraction requires advanced natural language processing and is therefore less commonly used in practice [17].

There are numerous approaches to this problem, and most of them treat it as a classification task. The first part involves generating pairs or triples of words that are classified based on binary classification. For most feature extraction approaches, keywords are used that are assumed to be available [8]. There are numerous criteria by which a sentence can be classified in this process. Some of these criteria include the use of morphosyntactic features of the text, the use of pragmatic markers in the text such as capitalization, punctuation marks, sentence length, and numerous others [12]. Most approaches assume equal importance of these features in the classification process. In this paper, we propose six evaluation criteria for summaries that we rank using the FAHP method. After ranking, we use the TOPSIS method to evaluate the importance of each text summarization method based on the predefined criteria. We selected criteria based on the ROUGE procedure [22] (Recall-Oriented Understudy for Gisting Evaluation) on the DUC (Document Understanding Conference) 2007 dataset. The ROUGE procedure proposes six different methods for evaluating text summarization. It is difficult to find which method gives the most accurate results in these evaluation methods. Therefore, we propose a new method of combining the existing six text summarization evaluation methods. In the second chapter, we provide an overview of types of text summarization. The third chapter discusses the problem of text summarization in e-learning systems. The fourth chapter provides a description of the multicriteria methods we used. The fifth chapter describes the criteria that will be used in the previous chapter. In the sixth chapter, we define our own method and illustrate its application with an example. In the final chapter, we provide a conclusion with ideas for future research.

2 Types of Text Summarization

This chapter covers various text summarization techniques, including extractive and abstractive methods, multiple document and web-based summarization, personalized summarization, etc. In the following subsections, we will discuss many of these techniques in detail.

2.1 Summarizing One or More Documents

A summary can be created from either one or multiple documents. In the case of multiple documents, summarizing them is more challenging than summarizing a single document, as redundancy is a significant problem [11,38]. To address redundancy, some systems select sentences at the beginning of a paragraph and only include additional sentences if they provide new, relevant content [28]. The Maximal Marginal Relevance (MMR) method has also been proposed as a way to reduce redundancy. Researchers worldwide are investigating various techniques to achieve optimal results when summarizing multiple documents [2]. Researchers around the world are exploring various methods to achieve the best results in summarizing multiple documents [31,34].

2.2 Extractive or Abstractive Text Summarization

Extractive summarization involves selecting multiple relevant sentences from the source document to create a summary, with the length of the summary being determined by the degree of compression. This is a straightforward and reliable approach to text summarization, where sentences are assigned significance scores and highly ranked sentences are chosen for the summary. Abstractive summarization, on the other hand, includes words and concepts that are not present in the source document, resulting in a summary that presents ideas or concepts in a different form. Abstractive summarization is much more complex than extractive summarization as it requires extensive natural language processing. Extractive summarization has become the norm for document summarization due to its straightforward approach.

2.3 Generic and Query-Focused Text Summarization

Text summarization can be categorized as generic or query-focused [36]. Query-focused summaries, also known as topic-based or user-focused summaries, include content that is relevant to a specific query, while generic summaries aim to capture the overall essence of the data in the document.

2.4 Supervised and Unsupervised Text Summarization

There are two methods for text summarization: supervised machine learning and unsupervised machine learning [25]. Supervised machine learning systems for text summarization require training data to identify important content in documents. A significant amount of labeled data is needed for these techniques. These systems operate at the sentence level, where sentences that are included in the summary are labeled as positive samples and sentences that are not included in the summary are labeled as negative samples [3]. The process of sentence classification in text summarization involves the use of popular classification methods like Support Vector Machine (SVM) [36] and neural networks [11] . However, unsupervised systems do not require any training data and can generate summaries by accessing selected documents. These systems are suitable for processing new data without requiring modifications. Unsupervised systems apply heuristic rules to extract relevant sentences and generate a summary [11]. Clustering is the method employed in unsupervised systems.

2.5   Indicative and Informative Text Summaries

The two types of summaries based on their output style are indicative and informative. Indicative summaries provide information about the topic of the document, while informative summaries offer complete information in a detailed form. Critical evaluative summaries are similar to informative summaries and contain the author's opinions, feedback, reviews, and recommendations about a particular topic. An example of critical evaluative summaries is the reviews provided by reviewers for research papers, which include feedback such as acceptance, rejection, or acceptance with revisions.

2.6   Language-Based Summaries

The classification of summaries can be based on language, and there are three types: monolingual, multilingual, and language-independent summaries. A monolingual system generates a summary in the same language as the source document. On the other hand, a multilingual system generates a summary in multiple languages when the source document is in multiple languages. A language-independent system, however, generates a summary in a language other than the language of the source document, for example, generating a summary in German when the source document is in English.

2.7   Text Summarization on the Web

In today's era, the internet contains an abundance of information, and the number of web pages available on the internet is constantly increasing. Some search engines like Google and Alta Vista help users find the required information, but they provide a long list of web pages for a single query. Due to this, users have to go through multiple pages to determine which pages are relevant and which are not, which makes them abandon their search after the first attempt. Therefore, text summarization techniques are used to compress important information present on web pages. An introduced search engine is capable of generating condensed versions of associated documents, which may assist users in systematically examining search outcomes [24].

2.8   Text Summarization Based on Email

Text summarization applied to emails is a type of summary that condenses email conversations. Due to its rapid delivery and low cost, email has become an efficient communication method. However, a large number of emails can accumulate in the inbox, leading to email overload issues and taking up a significant amount of time for reading, sorting, and archiving incoming messages. Email summarization has other potential applications as well. For instance, it can serve as a corporate memory in the business world, where summaries contain all the decisions made in the past.

2.9   Personalized Summaries

Personalized summaries cater to individual users' preferences by selecting specific information that the user wants to read. These systems determine the user's profile and then choose relevant content for summary creation. On the other hand, updated summaries assume that users have basic knowledge about the topic and only require current updates. The emergence of Web 2.0 has led to the development of new types of websites such as social networking sites, forums, and blogs where users share their opinions or provide reviews about products, entities, services, or topics. This has resulted in the emergence of sentiment-based summaries.

2.10   Sentiment Analysis and Surveys

Opinion mining involves both text summarization and sentiment analysis to create summaries that contain opinions. These summaries detect and classify opinions based on subjectivity and polarity, which includes positive, negative, or neutral [21]. Survey summaries are general overviews of a particular entity or topic and can be quite lengthy since they contain essential information about the subject. This category includes biographical summaries, survey summaries, and Wikipedia articles. Table 1 provides an overview of different summary types and the factors that influence their classification.

3   Problems of Automated Evaluation of Summaries in Intelligent Tutoring Systems

The writing of summaries is an essential part of English language exams, but grading them manually can be a time-consuming task. To solve this issue, computer-assisted evaluation has been suggested, as it could provide a more effective and efficient way of grading summaries. However, this problem is still present in today's computerized world, and many teachers reduce the number of summaries given to students to avoid the burden of manual grading. Unfortunately, this also limits the students' opportunities to practice and develop their writing skills. To address this problem, researchers have been working on automatic evaluation of summaries using techniques from e-learning, information

Table 1. Overview of different summary types

Type of Text Summarization	Factors
Summarization of one or multiple documents	Number of documents
Extractive or Abstractive	Output in extractive or abstractive form
Generic and Query-Based Purpose,	Generally or query-related data
Supervised and Unsupervised	Availability of training data
Monolingual, Multilingual and Language-independent	Language
Web Summarization	For summarizing text on web pages
Email Summarizing	Email messages
Personal	Specific information for personal use
Updates	Current updates on required topics
Opinions and Sentiments	Detection and classification of opinions and sentiments
Surveys	Important facts about people, places, or other entities

extraction, and natural language processing. Summaries are typically evaluated based on content and style criteria, and intelligent tutoring systems [29] can be used to provide adaptive knowledge acquisition by delivering summary information to students initially. The main focus of this paper is on determining the quality of summaries using computer-assisted evaluation.

4   Application of Multicriteria Decision Making Methods

4.1   Multicriteria Decision Making Methods

MCDM (Multiple Criteria Decision Making) is a field that addresses various decision-making problems, such as selecting one option from multiple alternatives that are distinguished by different criteria. It is essential to identify the appropriate criteria for a particular domain to make an informed decision. Many methods and approaches are available in the MCDM field. The most commonly used are AHP (Analytic hierarchy process) [27], TOPSIS (Technique for Order of Preference by Similarity to Ideal Solution) [35], ELECTRE (Elimination and Choice Expressing Reality) [26], PROMETHEE (Preference Ranking Organization Method for Enrichment of Evaluations) [1], GRA (Grey relational analysis) [4], and others. Certain MCDM methods incorporate fuzzy set theory [14,37], and when modified in this way, they are referred to as fuzzy AHP [5], fuzzy TOPSIS [6], and similar variations. In complex decision-making problems, fuzzy AHP and TOPSIS methods can be employed in conjunction with one another, as demonstrated in references [7]. The selection of a suitable method can also be resolved by combining these methods. In reference [33], the possibilities of applying the fuzzy AHP method in natural language processing are presented. Applications such as evaluation and assessment, quality assessment, and selection of an optimal set of features are mentioned [32]. The article presents a new method for choosing the best text summarization technique from four options. This method combines two MCDM approaches, namely fuzzy AHP and TOPSIS. Fuzzy AHP evaluates the criteria of the techniques using fuzzy sets and compares them to one another. The TOPSIS method is then used to rank the techniques and select the most optimal one.

4.2 Fuzzy Logic

The process of designing a fuzzy logic system generally involves selecting membership functions and fuzzy rules, and the performance of the system will depend on these choices. Fuzzy logic has four main components: fuzzifier, inference engine, defuzzifier, and fuzzy knowledge base. The fuzzifier translates inputs into linguistic values using membership functions, which are then used as inputs for the linguistic variable. The inference engine uses fuzzy IF THEN rules from a base to determine linguistic values for the output. The defuzzifier then converts the output linguistic variables into final values using a membership function. The output membership function is divided into three function members: insignificant, average, and significant, which are used to produce the final output for each sentence. Fuzzy logic is an extension of classical propositional logic, allowing for partial truth and values ranging from 0 to 1 [37]. In fuzzy set theory, elements can partially belong to a set, and fuzzy numbers generalize real numbers within the interval of 0 to 1, with triangular and trapezoidal fuzzy numbers being commonly used [37].

Triangular Fuzzy Numbers. A triangular fuzzy number is described by three real numbers: l, m, and u, which correspond to the minimum, most probable, and maximum values of the fuzzy number. The membership function $\mu(\frac{x}{m})$ of a triangular fuzzy number takes a value of 0 when x is less than l or greater than u. When x is between l and m, the membership function is $\frac{x-l}{m-l}$, and when x is between m and u, the membership function is $\frac{u-x}{u-m}$. If two positive triangular fuzzy numbers (l_1, m_1, u_1) and (l_2, m_2, u_2), are defined, certain rules apply.

$$(l_1, m_1, u_1) + (l_2, m_2, u_2) = (l_1 + l_2, m_1 + m_2, u_1 + u_2) \tag{1}$$

$$(l_1, m_1, u_1) - (l_2, m_2, u_2) = (l_1 - l_2, m_1 - m_2, u_1 - u_2) \tag{2}$$

$$(l_1, m_1, u_1) * (l_2, m_2, u_2) = (l_1 * l_2, m_1 * m_2, u_1 * u_2) \tag{3}$$

$$(l_1, m_1, u_1)/(l_2, m_2, u_2) = (l_1/l_2, m_1/m_2, u_1/u_2) \tag{4}$$

$$(l_1, m_1, u_1)^{-1} \approx (1/l_1, 1/m_1, 1/u_1) \tag{5}$$

4.3   Analytic Hierarchy Process (AHP) Method

The Analytic Hierarchy Process (AHP) technique was developed in the 1970s s by Thomas Saaty as a solution to MCDM issues. AHP is a commonly used method for decision-making, where alternatives are chosen and ranked based on several criteria with different measures and meanings. The AHP approach ensures that both quantitative and qualitative aspects of the decision are taken into account, and flexibility is maintained. MCDM methods are generally used to handle complicated issues. Breaking down these problems into simpler ones is the goal, which is done during the problem structuring and priority-setting stages through pairwise comparisons. The classical AHP method employs precise values to express the decision-maker's viewpoints during pairwise comparisons of alternatives. However, Chang introduced a new approach called the Fuzzy Analytic Hierarchy Process (fuzzy AHP), which uses fuzzy logic, fuzzy sets, and fuzzy numbers to extend the classical AHP method. The fuzzy AHP approach uses triangular fuzzy numbers instead of specific numerical values, making it easier to comprehend and manage quantitative and qualitative data used in MCDM problems. Let X be a set of objects and U be a set of goals according to [5].

$$X = \{x_1, x_2, ..., x_n\} \tag{6}$$

$$U = \{u_1, u_2, ..., u_m\} \tag{7}$$

For every item, the range analysis for each objective is conducted utilizing Chang's range analysis technique.:

$$M_{gi}^1, M_{gi}^2, ..., M_{gi}^m, i = 1, ..., n \tag{8}$$

The Eq. (8) involves triangular fuzzy numbers for all $M_{gi}^j, j = 1, 2, ..., m$. The fuzzy synthetic value concerning the ith object is determined as follows:

$$S_i = \sum_{j=1}^{m} M_{gi}^j \otimes \left[\sum_{i=1}^{n} \sum_{j=1}^{m} M_j^{gi} \right]^{-1} \tag{9}$$

To obtain $\sum_{i=1}^{n} \sum_{j=1}^{m} M_j^{gi}$, the fuzzy addition operation of $\sum_{j=1}^{m} M_{gi}^j, j = 1, 2, .., m$ values needs to be performed as follows:

$$\sum_{i=1}^{n} \sum_{j=1}^{m} M_j^{gi} = \left(\sum_{j=1}^{m} l_j, \sum_{j=1}^{m} m_j, \sum_{j=1}^{m} u_j \right) \tag{10}$$

The degree of likelihood that M_1 is greater than M_2 can be established if M_1 and M_2 are both triangular fuzzy numbers:

$$V(M_1 \geq M_2) = sup_{x \geq y} \left[min \left(\mu M_1(x), \mu M_2(x) \right) \right] \tag{11}$$

If there exists a pair x, y such that $x \geq y$ and $\mu M_1(x) = \mu M_2(y)$, then we have $V(M_1 \geq M_2) = 1$. If M_1 and M_2 are triangular fuzzy numbers, then $V(M_1 \geq M_2) = 1$ if $m_1 \geq m_2$ 0 if $l_2 \geq u_1$, and otherwise it is equal to $\frac{l_2 - u_1}{(m_1 - u_1) - (m_2 - l_2)}$.

$$V(M_1 \geq M_2) = hgt(M_1 \cap M_2) = \mu M_1(d) \tag{12}$$

The ordinate value of the highest point of intersection D between the membership functions of $\mu(M_1)$ and $\mu(M_2)$ (as illustrated in Fig. 1) is referred to as d.

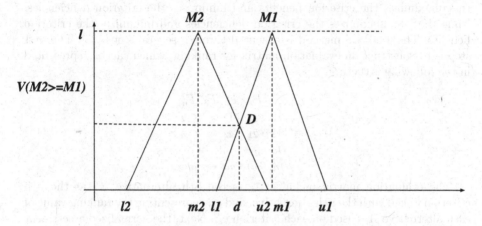

Fig. 1. Intersection of fuzzy numbers

The equation to determine the degree of probability that a fuzzy number M is greater than k other fuzzy numbers $M_i, i = 1, 2, ..., k$ is expressed as follows:

$$V(V \geq M_1, M_2, ..., M_k) = minV(M \geq M_1), i = 1, 2, 3, ..., k \tag{13}$$

The weight of each vector can be determined if we make the assumption that $d(A_i) = minV(S_i \geq S_k), k = 1, 2, ..., n, k \neq i.$:

$$W' = (d'(A_1), d'(A_2), ..., d'(A_n))^T \tag{14}$$

The set A_i is made up of n elements. The resulting priority vector is denoted by W'. Once normalized, the weight vectors become:

$$W = (d(A_1), d(A_2), ..., d(A_n))^T \tag{15}$$

where is not a fuzzy number.

The fuzzy AHP method was utilized to establish the weight of the criteria, with the comparisons of criteria being conveyed through triangular fuzzy numbers.

4.4   Technique for Order Preference by Similarity to Ideal Solution (TOPSIS) Method

Hwang and Yoonfirst introduced the TOPSIS method in 1981 to tackle various MCDM problems [6]. This method requires only a minimal input data set, and the output data set is easy to comprehend. The only subjective parameters of the method are the criterion weights. The basic concept of the method is that the best alternative is the one that is closest to the Positive Ideal Solution (PIS) and farthest from the Negative Ideal Solution (NIS) [1]. The PIS is the solution that maximizes thé criterion benefits and minimizes the criterion deficiencies, while the NIS maximizes the criterion deficiencies and minimizes the criterion benefits. The TOPSIS method is executed through several steps [23]. The first step is to construct an evaluation matrix for ranking, which can be represented in the following structure:

$$
D = \begin{array}{c} \\ A_1 \\ A_2 \\ A_3 \\ A_m \end{array} \begin{array}{cccc} F_1 & F_2 & F_3 & F_n \\ c_{11} & c_{12} & \cdots & c_{12} \\ c_{21} & c_{22} & \cdots & c_{2n} \\ \cdots & \cdots & \cdots & \cdots \\ c_{m1} & c_{m2} & \cdots & c_{mn} \end{array} \qquad (16)
$$

The evaluation matrix includes A_i as the i-th alternative, F_j as the j-th criterion linked with the i-th alternative, and c_{ij} representing the ranking value of each alternative A_i based on each criterion c_{ij}. Next, the normalized assessment matrix is determined by computing the normalized vector as follows:

$$
r_{ij} = \frac{w_{ij}}{\sqrt{\sum_{j=1}^{J} w_{ij}^2}} \qquad (17)
$$

where $i = 1, 2, ..., n$ and $j = 1, 2, ..., J$.

Multiplying the normalized evaluation matrix with the corresponding criterion weights yields the weighted normalized evaluation matrix. The weighted normalized value v_{ij} is calculated as follows The process of obtaining the weighted normalized evaluation matrix involves multiplying the normalized evaluation matrix by the respective criterion weights. The calculation of the weighted normalized value r_{ij} is performed by multiplying the normalized value of each criterion by its corresponding weight w_{ij}:

$$
v_{ij} = w_{ij} * r_{ij}, i = 1, 2, ..., n, j = 1, 2, ..., J \qquad (18)
$$

where w_j represents the weight of the jth criteria.

The Positive Ideal Solution (PIS) and Negative Ideal Solution (NIS) are obtained through the following procedure:

$$
A^+ = v_1^+, v_2^+, ..., v_n^+, maximum \; values \qquad (19)
$$

$$
A^- = v_1^-, v_2^-, ..., v_n^-, minimum \; values \qquad (20)
$$

The separation measures were determined using Euclidean distance in an m-dimensional space [20]. The distance between each alternative and the PIS and NIS is computed as follows:

$$d_i^+ = \sum_{j=1}^{n}(v_{ij} - v_i^+)^2, j = 1, 2, ..., J \qquad (21)$$

$$d_i^- = \sum_{j=1}^{n}(v_{ij} - v_i^-)^2, j = 1, 2, ..., J \qquad (22)$$

The method calculates the relative proximity of each alternative to the ideal solution, and the alternatives are then ranked in a descending order based on this proximity coefficient. The calculation of the proximity coefficient for each alternative is as follows:

$$CC_i = \frac{d_i^-}{d_i^+ + d_i^-}, i = 1, 2, ..., J \qquad (23)$$

The values of CC_i range between 0 and 1, and the alternative with a higher value is considered superior. To determine the ranking of alternatives, values are compared.

5   Criteria for Evaluating Text Summarization Techniques

Evaluating the effectiveness of text summarization is a critical task within the field of automatic text summarization. Evaluating summaries not only helps improve the development of resources and infrastructure that can be used, but also enables comparison and replication of results, thus increasing the potential for improving results. However, manually evaluating multiple documents for an unbiased representation is practically impossible. Therefore, reliable automatic measurement data is needed for fast and consistent evaluation. Summarization evaluation is a complex task because humans may not be sure about the relevant information that should be included in a summary. The information needed in a summary may differ based on the intended purpose of the summary, and automatic extraction of this information is a daunting task. Two methods can be used to evaluate the quality of text summarization:

Extrinsic evaluation: One approach to evaluating the quality of a summary is to measure how well it aids in solving other tasks such as text classification, information retrieval, or question answering. A good summary is one that helps in achieving these tasks effectively. A variety of techniques are employed for extrinsic evaluation, including relevance assessment, which measures the significance of the topic covered in both the summary and source document. Additionally, comprehension reading evaluation determines whether a user can successfully answer multiple-choice questions based on the summary they have read.
• Intrinsic evaluation: The evaluation of the summary quality is based on the

extent of agreement between the summary generated by a machine and the summary produced by a human. The two main aspects on which the summary is assessed are quality and informativeness. To assess the informativeness of the summary, it is usually compared with a reference summary that has been created by a human. Another approach to evaluate the summary is fidelity to the source, which determines whether the summary captures the same or similar information as the original document. However, determining which concepts in the document are relevant and which are not poses a challenge.

The criteria used to evaluate automatic text summarization methods are based on specific metrics. These metrics are defined by ROUGE, which stands for Recall-Understudy for Gisting Evaluation. They measure the quality of a summary by comparing it to other summaries written by humans. The comparison is done by calculating the number of overlaps of units such as n-grams, word sequences, and word pairs between the computer-generated summary and the ideal human summary. There are four ROUGE measures - ROUGE-N, ROUGE-L, ROUGE-W, and ROUGE-S, which are included in the ROUGE evaluation package for summarization and its evaluations. Six criteria have been defined based on these measures as important indicators of system performance for automatic text summarization. These criteria were used at the Document Understanding Conference (DUC) in 2004. We define a total of six criteria that are important indicators of system performance according to ROUGE for automatic text summarization:

ROUGE 1 - refers to the overlap of a single word in a sequence between the summarized text and the manually created summary. (C1) ROUGE 2 - refers to the overlap of two words in a sequence (bigram) between the automatically generated and manually created summaries. (C2) ROUGE L - the longest common subsequence method that looks for the number of overlaps of the largest common subsequence. (C3) ROUGE W - this approach uses weighting values that validate the values of the largest common subsequence. (C4) ROUGE S - is based on the statistics of co-occurrence. Skip-bigrams are constructed from sentences on which the similarity of two summaries is evaluated. (C5) ROUGE SU - combines ROUGE S word pairs with single words and based on that builds the statistics of co-occurrence. (C6)

In this research, a selection is made among four text summarization methods, according to the aforementioned criteria, which will be labeled C1 to C6. The first method is TextRank [18], which uses an unsupervised approach to text summarization. This approach uses the PageRank algorithm to select important sentences. The second method is the LexRank [10] algorithm, which is very similar to TextRank but combines PageRank with other methods. The third method is LSA (Latent Semantic Analysis) [15,30], which uses statistics to model words based on their context. This LSA approach considers the semantics of words and generates a summary of sentences by excluding those sentences that are similar, based on a certain similarity threshold. These word and document representations can be used in various tasks for representing words as vectors. SVD (Singular Value Decomposition) is used to reduce the dimensionality of data while retaining the structure of similarity. LSA uses a sparse matrix of word occurrences, where words are rows of the matrix and columns are documents or paragraphs. After constructing the matrix, a lower rank approximation is made. There are numerous reasons for this approximation, one of which is that larger matrices require more resources, while another reason is that matrices in natural language processing often tend to be sparse, and SVD preserves the main features of the matrix. There are numerous applications of LSA, ranging from document comparison and finding similar documents in multiple languages to expanding feature spaces for machine learning systems. The fourth method is EDM [9], which takes into account various heuristics based on manually defined rules described in the work. The weight of each criterion is determined using multi-criteria decision-making methods. Based on this, the methods of the summarization system are ranked, taking into account various evaluation techniques. All the methods described in this work were evaluated based on the DUC 2007 corpus using the ROUGE measure, as previously described.

6 Evaluating Text Summarization Methods Using Combined Results

The selection of the method that shows the best results considering the importance of all measures is illustrated with a numerical example and test data. Our method is defined in three steps. The first step in text summarization involves text preprocessing, which aims to clean up unclear text containing grammatical and typographical errors. One of the challenges in text summarization is the undefined size of the document, resulting in high-dimensional vector representations of every word in the document. Preprocessing plays a crucial role in reducing the dimensions passed to summarization algorithms. This study follows preprocessing methods for framing, fitting end words, removing punctuation and extra white spaces, identifying stop words and key phrases, sentence segmentation, and tokenization. Converting all capital letters to lowercase is also essential for equalizing different variations of the same word. Stop words, which have little meaning, are removed from the text, and root words are produced by removing suffixes and prefixes. Identifying important phrases involves finding the occurrence of word pairs using the relative frequency approach. Sentence segmentation detects paragraph breaks in a sentence, and tokenization breaks down the text into individual words. In the second stage of our approach, we utilize the fuzzy AHP technique to determine the weight values of the criteria. The linguistic scale, as presented in Table 2, was used for comparing the criteria C1 to C6. The comparisons between criteria were carried out by evaluating ci, j, which represents the assessment of the comparison between criterion Ci and criterion Cj. This evaluation was based on the agreement of three experts [19].

After creating a matrix for comparing fuzzy criteria, the weights of each criterion are determined using the fuzzy AHP method. The initial step is to compute the degree of synthesis using the same method [19]. An example of the calculation of the fuzzy degree of SC1 for criterion C1 according to Eq. 24 is

Table 2. Linguistic scale

Linguistic scale	Explanation	Triangular fuzzy number	Reciprocal value
Completely equal	Two traits have equal importance	(1, 1, 1)	(1, 1, 1)
More important	One trait is more important than another	(0.5,1,1.66)	(0.66, 1, 2)
Moderately more important	One trait is moderately more important than the other	(1,1.5,2)	(0.5, 0.66, 1)
Much more	Important One trait is significantly more important than another	(1.5,2,2.5)	(0.4, 0.5, 0.66)
Much more important	One trait is dominant over the other	(2,2.5,3)	(0.33, 0.4,0.5)
Distinctly more important one trait	Completely outweighs another in importance, which can be ignored	(2.5,3,3.5)	(0.28, 0.33, 0.4)

shown below (Table 3).

$$sc_1 = (2.81, 3.23, 3.97) \otimes (34.77, 44.21, 55.64)^{-1} = (0.051, 0.073, 0.114) \quad (24)$$

Table 3. Unexpressive synthetic values for each criterion

Criterion	SC_i
C1	(0.051, 0.073, 0.114)
C2	(0.064, 0.101, 0.163)
C3	(0.086, 0.14, 0.225)
C4	(0.117, 0.189, 0.302)
C5	(0.155, 0.249, 0.403)
C6	(0.153, 0.249, 0.393)

Next, the imprecise synthesized values were compared using Eq. (13), and the priority vector was obtained using Eq. (15). The resulting priority weights are presented as a vector $W' = (0.30, 0.05, 0.39, 0.71)$.

After the values are calculated, they are normalized, and the priority weights regarding the primary objective are determined using Eq. (16)

$$W = (-0.106, 0.018, 0.137, 0.249, 0.351, 0.351) \quad (25)$$

The third step in our method involves using the TOPSIS method to establish the final ranking of text compression methods. We have created a decision matrix

Table 4. Decision matrix

	C1	C2	C3	C4	C5	C6
LexRank	0.93	0.93	0.94	0.87	0.91	0.87
TextRank	0.95	0.93	0.93	0.92	0.89	0.90
LSA	0.95	0.92	0.94	0.91	0.90	0.87
EDM	0.95	0.94	0.85	0.88	0.81	0.85

M that considers the six selected criteria for ranking the text summarization methods, and it is shown in the table below (Table 4).

In this stage, the TOPSIS technique is applied, wherein the highest and lowest values for each criterion are identified using Eq. (19) and Eq. (20) to determine the positive and negative ideal solutions:

$$A^+ = (-0.048, 0.007, 0.054, 0.101, 0.133)$$ (26)

$$A^- = (-0.045, 0.008, 0.063, 0.116, 0.165)$$ (27)

Table 5 displays the rankings, proximity coefficients, and distances from the PIS and NIS for each text summarization method, which were calculated using Eq. (23) in conjunction with Eqs. (21) and (22). Specifically, the distance of each alternative from the PIS and NIS is calculated for each criterion.

Table 5. Final ranking of methods for text summarization

Methods	d_i^+	d_i^-	CC_i	Rank
LexRank	0.079	0.002	0.03	4
TextRank	0.074	0.002	0.04	2
LSA	0.073	0.003	0.05	1
EDM	0.065	0.003	0.04	3

The preferred text compression method is LSA, given the ranking in Table 5.

7   Conclusion

This paper proposes a method for selecting text summarization techniques in e-learning systems that utilizes both the fuzzy AHP and TOPSIS methods. First, the fuzzy AHP method is employed using triangular fuzzy numbers to determine decision weight criteria. Next, the TOPSIS method is used to rank text summarization methods based on important evaluation indicators and commonly used metrics. These evaluation criteria are established using de facto standards for text summarization found in databases. Our research focuses on developing a fuzzy decision-making model that relies on subjective judgments made by decision-makers to select the optimal text summarization method. We conducted an empirical study and presented a tool for evaluating text summarization methods. In future research, other multi-criteria methods such as fuzzy TOPSIS, PROMETHEE, and ELECTRE may be utilized to enhance the selection process of the optimal text summarization method.

References

1. Brans, J., Vincke, P., Mareschal, B.: How to select and how to rank projects: the PROMETHEE method. Eur. J. Oper. Res. **24**(2), 228–238 (1986). https://doi.org/10.1016/0377-2217(86)90044-5
2. Carbonell, J.G., Goldstein, J., Carbonell, J.: The use of MMR and diversity-based reranking for reodering documents and producing summaries, pp. 335–336 (1998)
3. Chali, Y., Hasan, S.A.: Query-focused multi-document summarization: automatic data annotations and supervised learning approaches. Nat. Lang. Eng. **18**(1), 109–145 (2012). https://doi.org/10.1017/S1351324911000167
4. Chan, J.W., Tong, T.K.: Multi-criteria material selections and end-of-life product strategy: grey relational analysis approach. Mater. Des. **28**(5), 1539–1546 (2007). https://doi.org/10.1016/J.MATDES.2006.02.016
5. Chang, D.Y.: Applications of the extent analysis method on fuzzy AHP. Eur. J. Oper. Res. **95**(3), 649–655 (1996). https://doi.org/10.1016/0377-2217(95)00300-2
6. Chen, C.T.: Extensions of the TOPSIS for group decision-making under fuzzy environment. Fuzzy Sets Syst. **114**(1), 1–9 (2000). https://doi.org/10.1016/S0165-0114(97)00377-1
7. Chen, M.F., Tzeng, G.H.: Combining grey relation and TOPSIS concepts for selecting an expatriate host country. Math. Comput. Model. **40**(13), 1473–1490 (2004). https://doi.org/10.1016/J.MCM.2005.01.006
8. Díaz, A., Gervás, P.: User-model based personalized summarization. Inf. Process. Manage. **43**(6), 1715–1734 (2007). https://doi.org/10.1016/J.IPM.2007.01.009
9. Edmundson, H.P.: New methods in automatic extracting. J. ACM **16**(2), 264–285 (1969). https://doi.org/10.1145/321510.321519
10. Erkan, G., Radev, D.R.: LexRank: graph-based lexical centrality as salience in text summarization. J. Artif. Intell. Res. **22**, 457–479 (2004). https://doi.org/10.1613/jair.1523
11. Fattah, M.A., Ren, F.: GA, MR, FFNN, PNN and GMM based models for automatic text summarization. Comput. Speech Lang. **23**(1), 126–144 (2009). https://doi.org/10.1016/j.csl.2008.04.002
12. Ferreira, R., et al.: Assessing sentence scoring techniques for extractive text summarization. Exp. Syst. Appl. **40**(14), 5755–5764 (2013). https://doi.org/10.1016/j.eswa.2013.04.023
13. Kirmani, M., Manzoor Hakak, N., Mohd, M., Mohd, M.: Hybrid text summarization: a survey. In: Ray, K., Sharma, T.K., Rawat, S., Saini, R.K., Bandyopadhyay, A. (eds.) Soft Computing: Theories and Applications. AISC, vol. 742, pp. 63–73. Springer, Singapore (2019). https://doi.org/10.1007/978-981-13-0589-4_7
14. Klir, G.J., Yuan, B.: Fuzzy Sets and Fuzzy Logic: Theory and Application. Prentice Hall, New Jersey, USA (1995)
15. Landauer, T., Foltz, P., Laham, D.: An introduction to latent semantic analysis. Discourse Process..**25**, 259–284 (1998)
16. Lloret, E.: Text summarization: An overview. Special Issue III (2021)

17. Mani, I., Maybury, M.: Advances in Automatic Text Summarization. MIT Press, Mass (1999). https://books.google.ba/books?id=YtUZQaKDmzEC
18. Mihalcea, R., Tarau, P.: TextRank: bringing order into texts, pp. 404–411 (2004)
19. Ishizaka, A., Nemery, P.: Multi-criteria Decision Analysis: Methods and Software, 1st edn. Wiley (2013)
20. Olson, D.: Comparison of weights in TOPSIS models. Math. Comput. Model. **40**(7–8), 721–727 (2004). https://doi.org/10.1016/J.MCM.2004.10.003
21. Pang, B., Lee, L.: Opinion mining and sentiment analysis. Found. Trends Inf. **1**(2), 91–231 (2006). https://doi.org/10.1561/1500000001
22. Patel, S.M.: Extractive based automatic text summarization. J. Comput. **12**, 550–563 (2017). https://doi.org/10.17706/jcp.12.6.550-563
23. Personal, M., Archive, R., Wulf, D., Bertsch, V.: A natural language generation approach to support understanding and traceability of multi-dimensional preferential sensitivity analysis in multi-criteria decision making. Exp. Syst. Appl. **2017**(83), 131–144 (2017)
24. Radev, D.R., Fan, W., Zhang, Z., Arbor, A.: WebInEssence: a personalized web-based multi-document summarization and recommendation system. In: NAACL 2001 Workshop on Automatic Summarization, pp. 79–88 (2001)
25. Riedhammer, K., Favre, B., Hakkani-Tür, D.: Long story short - global unsupervised models for keyphrase based meeting summarization. Speech Commun. **52**(10), 801–815 (2010). https://doi.org/10.1016/j.specom.2010.06.002
26. Roy, B.: Classement et choix en présence de points de vue multiples. RAIRO - Oper. Res. - Recherche Opérationnelle **2**(V1), 57–75 (1968)
27. Saaty, T.L.: The Analytic Hierarchy Process. McGraw Hill, New York (1980)
28. Sarkar, K.: Syntactic trimming of extracted sentences for improving extractive multi-document summarization. J. Comput. **2**, 177–184 (2010)
29. Slavomir, S., Marko, R., Andrina, G., Lada, M., Ani, G., Branko, Z.: Paradigma e-učenja i inteligentni tutorski sustavi (2004)
30. Steinberger, J., Ježek, K.: Using latent semantic analysis in text summarization and summary evaluation. Technical report (0)
31. Tao, Y., Zhou, S., Lam, W., Guan, J.: Towards more effective text summarization based on textual association networks, pp. 235–240 (2008)
32. Tofighy, S.M., Raj, R.G., Haj, H., Javadi, S.: AHP techniques for Persioan text summarization. Malays. J. Comput. Sci. **26**(1), 1–8 (2013)
33. Volaric, T., Brajković, E., Sjekavica, T.: Integration of FAHP and TOPSIS methods for the selection of appropriate multimedia application for learning and teaching. Int. J. Math. Models Meth. Appl. Sci. **8**(1), 224–232 (2014)
34. Wang, D., Zhu, S., Li, T., Chi, Y., Gong, Y.: Integrating document clustering and multidocument summarization. ACM Trans. Knowl. Discov. Data **5**, 14:1–14:26 (2011)
35. Xu, L., et al.: Multiple Attribute Decision Making: Methods and Applications (2011). https://doi.org/10.1007/978-3-642-48318-9
36. Ouyang, Y., Li, W., Li, S., Lu, Q.: Applying regression models to query-focused multi-document summarization. Inf. Process. Manag. **47**, 227–237 (2011)
37. Zadeh, L.A.: Fuzzy sets. Inf. Control **8**(3), 338–353 (1965). https://doi.org/10.1016/S0019-9958(65)90241-X
38. Zajic, D.M., Dorr, B.J., Lin, J.: Single-document and multi-document summarization techniques for email threads using sentence compression. Inf. Process. Manag. **44**, 1600–1610 (2007). https://doi.org/10.1016/j.ipm.2007.09.007

Overview of Tools for Programming and Virtual Simulation of Robots Within the STEM Teaching Process

Boris Crnokić[1]([✉]) [ID], Perica Topić[2] [ID], Marko Divković[2] [ID], and Emanuel Prgić[2] [ID]

[1] Faculty of Mechanical Engineering, Computing and Electrical Engineering, University of Mostar, Matice hrvatske b.b., 88000 Mostar, Bosnia and Herzegovina
boris.crnokic@fsre.sum.ba

[2] Faculty of Science and Education, University of Mostar, Matice hrvatske b.b., 88000 Mostar, Bosnia and Herzegovina
{perica.topic,marko.divkovic,emanuel.prgic}@fpmoz.sum.ba

Abstract. Robotics has proven to be a powerful learning tool, not only as a subject of study and an engineering branch, but also for general aspects of studying STEM disciplines. There are numerous areas of engineering technique and science that are included in the STEM concepts of education based on the application of robotics, such as: sensors and actuators, voice recognition, image processing, new technologies in general, the Internet of Things, smart devices, the digital world as a whole, Industry 4.0/5.0, etc. The inclusion of virtual programming environments and simulators in the teaching of robotics can eliminate many limitations, and enable a larger number of students to simultaneously have access to quality teaching at the same level. This paper presents an overview of several robotics programming environments and simulators, which can be an excellent tool for teaching STEM disciplines through programming, modeling and simulating different robots.

Keywords: Virtual simulation · Robot programming · Robotics in education · STEM education

1 Introduction

A central aspect of STEM education is problem solving, thus robots are excellent tools for teaching problem-solving skills in group settings. Based on the growing success of education programs that use robotics as a teaching tool, more and more work is being done to develop robot hardware and software that will be exclusively at the service of education, starting from the youngest ages and elementary school, all the way to adult education [1]. Robotics and STEM disciplines share some common characteristics, such as: opportunities to arouse and activate students' emotional engagement and interaction with physical devices, to refine ways of acquiring knowledge with learning through work and multidisciplinary learning, and to stimulate creative thinking through constructivist access [2]. Virtual simulators are already used for educational robotics. Given that in some cases physical robots are very difficult to acquire, install or transport,

D. Vasić and M. Kundid Vasić (Eds.): MoStart 2023, CCIS 1827, pp. 18–32, 2023.
https://doi.org/10.1007/978-3-031-36833-2_2

virtual software platforms represent an ideal replacement by providing opportunities to simulate robots in different environments [3]. In addition, this concept allows students to join robotics classes from any location at any time [4]. Also, in the recent COVID-19 pandemic, it has been shown that there is a great need for such ways of teaching robotics. Various studies have shown that virtual robotics can also be a powerful tool for enhancing personalized learning, making computing and engineering problems accessible to students with a wider range of experience and schools with fewer resources [5]. Many studies compare the effectiveness of teaching robotics in real-world and virtual environments. It has been proven that in some cases the virtual class showed different advantages, such as time reduction because students would finish the course about a month earlier compared to physical classes, but without a negative impact on their overall learning and output competencies [6]. This suggests that working with virtual robots enabled students to learn more effectively [7]. However, this way of teaching can keep students too busy, because virtual platforms are available to them in an unlimited time interval, and it is necessary to properly design syllabi and lesson plans [8]. There are also practical market reasons for the increasing inclusion of virtual robotics teaching in teaching processes. Namely, industrial robotics is the driving force behind the modern economy, but industrial robots are extremely expensive and thus inaccessible to most educational institutions. In order for students to be ready for the labor market, programming and simulation of industrial robotic lines can be easily realized through virtual simulators of industrial robots [9, 10].

The paper presents an overview of programming environments and virtual robot simulators used in the teaching process at the University of Mostar in recent years. The analysis was done from the perspective of students and professors.

2 Overview of Tools for Programming and Virtual Simulation of Robots

2.1 mBlock

mBlock is a STEAM programming software tool designed for programming for kids. It is developed based on Scratch 3.0 and Arduino code. It supports block-based and text-based programming languages. mBlock also provides software programming services, software design services and maintenance of computer software services in the education of programming for those who want to promote their programming abilities [11]. With *mBlock*, children can not only create games and animations by dragging blocks or using Python code, but can also code robots or boards to do anything they can imagine. *mBlock* exposes children to cutting-edge technologies, allowing children to create projects with technologies like AI and IoT. Moreover, in the *mBlock* Community, children are able to share projects and learn from the like-minded. Scratch is a programming tool developed by MIT and is credited as the most globally influential programming language for children. Based on Scratch 3.0 an Arduino code, mBlock is versatile and user-friendly enough to offer you whatever Scratch can give. And it's quite easy to pick up because you can code simply by dragging and dropping blocks. Figure 1 shows the *mBlock* programing environment.

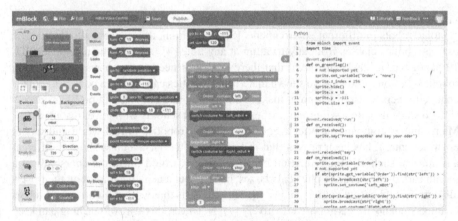

Fig. 1. *mBlock* programing environment [12]

With *mBlock*, users can easily switch to Python with one-click. After students grasp how to program with blocks, they can effortlessly move on to Python. *mBlock* allows users to program robots to do anything they can imagine. By showing the outcomes of coding in the physical world. Also, *mBlock* brings diversity into classrooms because it has the power that enables educators and students to turn different ideas into reality. *mBlock* integrates Microsoft cognitive services and Google deep learning into one tool. With these features, children can program to add more capabilities to mBlock, like age guessing or playing rock-paper-scissors games. We just hope to make it easier for children to master the fundamentals of AI. *mBlock* comes with the cloud service that is designed for IoT teaching. By working with robots or electronic modules, it is possible to take advantage of the feature to create fun projects, like Weather Report, Autonomous Plant Watering Robot and Smart Lighting. For students, the best way to learn about IoT is to see how it works in real life.

2.2 Arduino

Arduino is an open-source electronics platform based on easy-to-use hardware and software. Arduino boards are able to read inputs - light on a sensor, a finger on a button, or a Twitter message - and turn it into an output - activating a motor, turning on an LED, publishing something online. It is possible to give a command to the board what to do by sending a set of instructions to the microcontroller on the board. To do so it is possible to use the *Arduino* programming language (based on Wiring), and the *Arduino* Software (IDE), based on Processing [13]. Over the years *Arduino* has been the brain of thousands of projects, from everyday objects to complex scientific instruments. A worldwide community of makers - students, hobbyists, artists, programmers, and professionals - has gathered around this open-source platform. Their contributions have added up to an incredible amount of accessible knowledge that can be of great help to novices and experts alike. Figure 2 shows an *Arduino* simulator environment.

Arduino was born at the Ivrea Interaction Design Institute as an easy tool for fast prototyping, aimed at students without a background in electronics and programming.

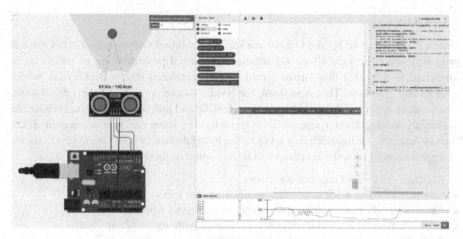

Fig. 2. *Arduino* simulator environment [14]

As soon as it reached a wider community, the *Arduino* board started changing to adapt to new needs and challenges, differentiating its offer from simple 8-bit boards to products for IoT applications, wearable, 3D printing, and embedded environments. The *Arduino* development platform supports a variety of *Arduino* controller boards. The *Arduino* UNO, for instance, is an *Arduino* board. This small computer can be programmed using the *Arduino* IDE [15].

An *Arduino* offers many different options and can be used in multiple applications.

The software the *Arduino* uses is open source, and can run in Windows, Mac, Linux, and other systems. Education version is for middle school, high school, and university educators who want to deliver relevant, fun, and creative STEAM lessons that enable all students to thrive *Arduino* Education's open-source approach and cross-curriculum content are essential tools that develop and empower students as they progress through their STEAM education. PRO version is designed to enable businesses to quickly and securely connect remote sensors to business logic within one simple IoT application development platform, transferring the productivity and creativity that makers enjoy with Arduino into the business world. Some of use *Arduino* in real life are Smart Homes, Industries and Medical. With *Arduino* boards it is possible to control the home activities with the control systems such as motion sensors, outlet control, temperature sensors, blower control, garage door control, air flow control, sprinkler control and bill of materials. Due to the easy programming environment, signal types, and easy adaptation in new set up, *Arduino* is used in many industries. *Arduino* boards are low cost, and flexible alternatives to the usual industrial devices for adding remote control and monitoring functionality to small legacy industrial systems. *Arduino* is used for designing many medical equipment's such as customizable Breathalyzer, little automatic slipper foot massager, Open-source EEG/ECG/EMG, Thermometer, Wi-Fi Body Scale with *Arduino* Board etc. [16].

2.3 Nvidia Isaac

Nvidia Isaac is part of Nvidia Omniverse software solution with bunch of other related programs which provide all-in-one solution for virtual programming of robots. It is important to note that this virtual world can be translated into real everyday world without any problems. That is to thank for Nvidia's development of programs in great detail, which replicate real world in a very scientific and precise way. Nvidia Omniverse is a hugely developed enterprise platform and is used by some very prominent companies such as Amazon, for their delivery services via flying drones. Nvidia Omniverse consists of a great number of software components, and some of them are:

- *Nucleus* – Core for Omniverse network,
- *Connectors* – For work with other applications for robotic development,
- *Extensions* – For extending capabilities of Omniverse Apps,
- *USD* – Universal Scene Description, developed with support from Pixar,
- *Audio2Face* – Lip syncing based on audio file,
- *Kaolin* – 3D accelerated deep learning app,
- *Machinima* – 3D cinematic viewer, for making cartoons/movies,
- *Isaac Sim* – Simulation tool for Nvidia Apps, *XR* – Virtual reality support, for entering created virtual worlds,

and many other programs related to optimization or specific need of the developer of the program [17].

For robotics and their use cases most important is Nvidia Isaac, it is a development tool for simulation of robotic systems which can be imported from some kind of CAD program. Most of existing robots are already imported into Nvidia's library and ready to be worked with. Nvidia Isaac Sim is a scalable robotics simulation application and synthetic data-generation tool that powers photorealistic, physically accurate virtual environments. This gives you a better, faster way to develop, test, and manage AI-based robots. With Isaac Sim, developers and researchers around the world can train and optimize AI robots for a wide variety of tasks. It also provides people simulation, collaboration robots safety analysis, lidar equipment simulation, backwards compatibility with Isaac ROS. Figure 3 shows Nvidia Isaac Sim simulation environment. Some key benefits over other simulation tools are:

- *Realistic simulation* – GPU enabled simulation using Nvidia PhysX 5;
- *Modular Architecture* – extension of capabilities is possible if needed;
- *Seamless connectivity and interoperability* – provided by Nvidia Connectors.

Nvidia Isaac Sim can be connected to Omniverse cloud for more powerful and more detailed simulation [19]. Currently is in beta, and available free of charge. For elementary school education, *Nvidia Isaac Sim* is a very powerful tool, maybe too powerful, in spite of using Python as its programming language, it's complex structure and vast capabilities are maybe more suited for older students. High schools and colleges are more suited use case for this type of tool. Its features are meant to be used by somewhat more of an advanced user, or at least a little bit older user. Although software is really intuitively made and logically drawn out, that cannot be taken from Nvidia's developers, it really is one complex piece of software which requires a little bit of background knowledge of robotics and robotic systems.

Fig. 3. *Nvidia Isaac Sim* simulation environment [18]

2.4   Gazebo

Gazebo is an open-source simulation tool brought by company called Open Robotics. It is available on Linux and Mac systems, with limited support for Windows machines as of March, 2023. *Gazebo* makes open-source software as its main goal, and Linux support make it logical on that front. Every component of Gazebo software solution for simulation is based on some kind of open-source code [20]. Software is mostly plugin based. For example, physics engine can be imported as a plugin, you can even develop your own physics engine, and if it's compatible with *Gazebo* software, it will work without a hitch [21]. Also, rendering engine is available as a plugin, and same principles apply here [22]. It is important to note that *Gazebo* provides rendering and physics engines of their own, for various versions of platforms, versions of software or even type of work you are trying to simulate on their tools.

Gazebo brings a fresh approach to simulation with a complete toolbox of development libraries and cloud services to make simulation easy. So, it is possible to iterate fast on new physical designs in realistic environments with high fidelity sensors streams, to test control strategies in safety, and to take advantage of simulation in continuous integration tests. *Gazebo* software developers are proud of modularity of their software solution, because its program can be run in various modes, there is a server mode, and GUI mode, which only connects to a server. Development of a simulation environment starts with creating a world. *Gazebo* provides default world with some simple shapes in it, but as it is open-source based, it can be customized in any way desirable [24]. To specify content of simulation, SDF format is used. SDF is an XML format that describes objects and environments for robot simulators, visualization, and control. Originally developed as part of the *Gazebo* robot simulator, SDF format was designed with scientific robot applications in mind [25]. With *Gazebo* installation package, many SDF models and world come pre-included, and because of open-source nature of the software solution, they can be modified and used completely free of charge. Main programming language is C++, which takes a bit of a learning curve to master, but for simple commands it's fairly easy to learn.. Figure 4 shows *Gazebo* virtual environment.

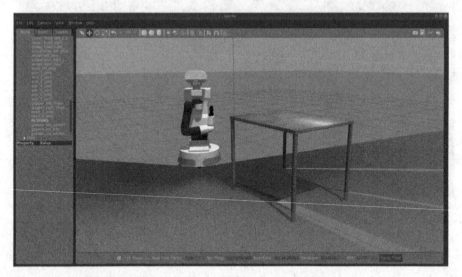

Fig. 4. Gazebo virtual environment [23]

Looking from an education standpoint, Open Robotics' software solution *Gazebo* is fairly available platform for learning and developing virtual worlds and robot simulations. One of the drawbacks is limited Windows support, and based on school's policy, it can either break it or make it for some particular school. If entire school is Windows-based, then this tool provides limited capabilities and is better off. But if school has Linux machines, this tool is an excellent choice, provided that the elementary schools have a teacher fairly comfortable with C++ programming language, which can be a minor setback in some situations, not necessarily for high schools and colleges. *Gazebo's* main strength is it's open-source nature and that is a point that cannot be taken from them. Unlike many other simulation software, *Gazebo* provides all of their tools and functions for free, and has built a community over the years, which cements its position as one of the best tools for robot development and simulation.

2.5 RoboDK

RoboDK is an enterprise software solution for simulation of industrial robots. It is a very powerful tool with vast capabilities, even more when taken into consideration that developers took only one type of robots and developed it as best as they could. This software solution possibly provides the most accurate simulation for industrial robots from all available software solutions out there, and allows you to get the most out of your robot [26]. At launch, the *RoboDK* library supported 200 robots from more than 20 robot manufacturers. RoboDK has grown quickly and is now used by companies of all sizes from startups to the world's largest corporations.

Some of the key benefits are that no programming skills are required because interface of *RoboDK* is laid out intuitively and provides needed functions already; offline programming of robots, which makes for faster set up of the robot at the factory; and its extensive library of over 600 robot arms. *RoboDK* software solution also supports porting of CAD models, turning them into robots and making motion model from them [27]. As an enterprise solution, huge number of robotic arms manufacturers is needed for collaboration, and *RoboDK* is partner with some of the world's best manufacturers, such as Kuka, Fanuc, Yaskawa, Staubli, Techman Robot, Nachi, ABB, Denso, Mecademic, Doosan, Mitsubishi, Universal Robots, Kawasaki, Aubo Robotics, Adept, Epson, Estun Robotics, Dobot, Hanwha, Han's Robot, Huibo, OTC, Comau, GSK, and many less-known brands. List is extensive, but that is the norm if enterprise software solution is at play [28]. Figure 5 shows *RoboDK* offline simulation software.

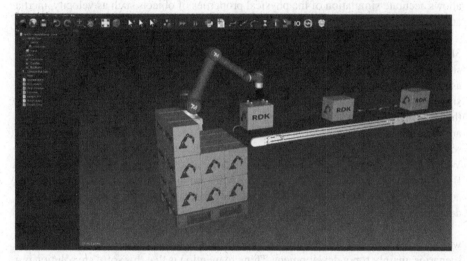

Fig. 5. *RoboDK* offline simulation software [30]

In February 2022, company introduced lightweight web version of its software, with education in mind. It is offered for free and includes some of the most common and widely used functions for robot manipulation and control [29]. RoboDK is available on various platforms, Windows 32-bit and 64-bit versions, Linux, Mac, even Android and iOS. There is also support for Raspberry Pi, which is a common development tool for young robotic enthusiasts [29]. For education purposes, use of Python as programming language, and intuitive interface, which writes commands as you click on buttons and tell robot what to do, make for one very appealing solution. Although simple as it can be, this is still an enterprise solution and has lots and lots of buttons, which could confuse elementary school students. Provided that the school has resources at hand and has a focus on industrial robots, main software is highly recommended for high schools and colleges. On the other hand, web version is perfectly suitable for elementary schools and even for high schools, as it provides enterprise leading technology for free.

2.6 SimSpark

SimSpark is a little bit lesser-known software solution, and information about it is really scarce. It is a generic physics simulation system for various multiagent simulations, supports developing physical simulations for AI and robotics research with an open-source application framework. *SimSpark* is commonly used in academic research and education. Simulations are created using Ruby and text-based RSG files. Different agents can participate in one simulation, connecting to *SimSpark* using UDP or TCP networks [31]. Multiagent stand for multiple simulators or agents running on one server, connected via network. Server provides physics simulation and virtual playground for agents to connect to it and to interact with each other. These worlds can be factory's manufacturing lane, complex polygon or even a football field. *SimSpark* uses the Open Dynamics Engine (ODE) for detecting collisions and for simulating rigid body dynamics. ODE allows accurate simulation of the physical properties of objects such as velocity, inertia and friction [32].

Very interesting fact is that *SimSpark* is the simulation engine for the RoboCup 3D Soccer Simulation League. In this simulation two teams play soccer with rules similar to regular soccer. The robots use simulated cameras and other sensors such as accelerometers, gyro meters and touch and audio sensors. Software agents process signals from these sensors (also known as perceptors) and generate control signals for the 22 hinges within each robot's body in order to achieve whatever forms of motion are required to win a game of soccer. The original soccer robot model was known as soccerbot, but since 2008 it has been replaced with a Nao robot inspired model [33]. With its code freely available to anyone with a wish to use it, it is available for everyone. But with much time allocated to RoboCup, software lost ground as other technologies advanced and is today mostly used for playing virtual soccer in Japan. Even official documents state that the software is a little bit dated [35].

Last commit on GitLab was in 2022, with minor updates, and last major overhaul was in 2019 [36]. From an educational standpoint, this software could be used in various scenarios, mainly robot development. Thing to mention is that this software solution is a little bit outdated and is not updated frequently. It would certainly be nice for elementary students to learn about robots as they play soccer against their school mates, but extremely

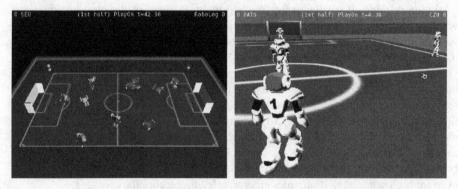

Fig. 6. Simulation of a robot soccer match in *SimSpark* [34]

limited documentation, tutorials and general availability of those resources make for one very steep learning curve, and huge motivation to use exactly this software. Multiagent support is one of the key benefits of this software solution, and unless it is absolutely needed for some particular educational application, there are objectively better, more modern and more regularly updated and supported software solutions out there. Figure 6 shows a simulation of a robot soccer match in SimSpark.

2.7 Robot Virtual Worlds

Robot Virtual Worlds, developed by Robomatter, is a virtual environment that enables students to learn how to program with or without a physical robot [37]. It uses a virtual VEX EDR or VEX IQ robot with sensors and motors in 3D environments which can be programmed with ROBOTC, the same language as physical robots. Also, it uses an in-built Level Builder which allows everyone to create, share and play levels [38]. This program also comes with a model importer, a measuring kit and a built-in achievements system for students which they get for completing challenges on different levels and it can be tracked to see which are progressing.

Robomatter's goal was to create a virtual 3D environment in which students can do everything with a robot as if it was in a classroom. *Robot Virtual Worlds* is mostly used so students can learn RobotC programming language because the robot programmed in this 3D environment will behave the same as a robot if they programmed it in real life. *Robot Virtual Worlds* environments are available in competition, fantasy or classroom environments. The environments are designed to provide new programmers with an interesting and fun programming environment. They usually include collectible objects and additional starting points making it ideal for teaching introductory programming concepts like path planning, encoder-based movements and sensor-controlled movement.

2.8 Webots

Webots is a professional mobile robot simulation software package. It offers a rapid prototyping environment, that allows the user to create 3D virtual worlds with physics properties such as mass, joints, friction coefficients, and many more [39]. The user can add simple passive objects or active objects called mobile robots which all have different locomotion schemes. They are also equipped with a number of sensors and actuator devices, such as distance sensors, drive wheels, cameras, motors, touch sensors, emitters, receivers. *Webots* allows users to launch a simulated NAO robot moving in a virtual world [40]. It offers a safe place test behaviors before playing them on a real robot. These are some of projects that have relied on *Webots*: Mobile robot prototyping, Robot locomotion research, Multi-agent research, Adaptive behavior research, Teaching robotics and Robot contests.

Webots contains a User Interface that is composed of four principal windows: the 3D window that display and allows interaction with the 3D simulation, the Scene tree which is a hierarchical representation of the current world, the Text editor that allows source code editing, and the Console that displays both compilation and controller outputs [41]. Figure 7 shows *Webots* robot simulator environment.

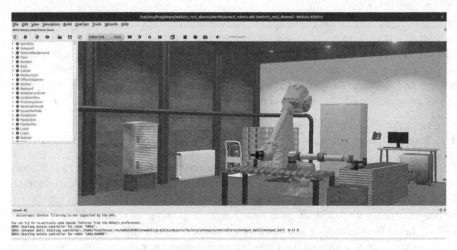

Fig. 7. *Webots* robot simulator environment [42]

2.9 OpenRAVE

OpenRAVE provides an environment for testing, developing, and deploying motion planning algorithms in real-world robotics applications. The main focus is on simulation and analysis of kinematic and geometric information related to motion planning. *OpenRAVE*'s stand-alone nature allows is to be easily integrated into existing robotics systems. It provides many command line tools to work with robots and planners, and the run-time core is small enough to be used inside controllers and bigger frameworks. An important target application is industrial robotics automation [43]. *OpenRAVE's* architecture is divided into four main components [44]:

- Core Layer that is composed of a set of Base Interface Classes
- Plugins Layer where plugins offer implementations of the Base Interface Classes
- Scripting Layer provides environments for Python and Octave/MATLAB
- Robot Database Layer implements a planning knowledge-base and simple interfaces

The plugin architecture allows users to easily write custom controllers or extend functionality, and any planning algorithm, robot control, or sensing-based subsystem can be distributed and dynamically loaded ad run-time [45]. Users of *OpenRAVE* can concentrate on the development of planning and scripting aspects of a problem without having to explicitly manage the details of robot kinematics and dynamics, collision detection, world updates, and robot control.

2.10 CoppeliaSim

The robotics simulator *CoppeliaSim*, with integrated development environment, is based on a distributed control architecture: each object/model can be individually controlled via an embedded script, a plugin, a ROS node, a remote API client, or a custom solution. This makes *CoppeliaSim* very versatile and ideal for multi-robot applications. Controllers

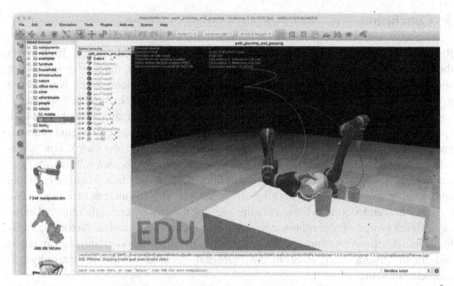

Fig. 8. *CoppeliaSim* virtual environment [47]

can be written in C/C++, Python, Java, Lua, MATLAB or Octave [46]. Figure 8 shows *CoppeliaSim* virtual environment.

CoppeliaSim is used for fast algorithm development, factory automation simulations, fast prototyping and verification, robotics related education, remote monitoring, safety double-checking as digital twin, and much more. It contains vision sensors with built-in image processing which is fully extendable, 3 physics engines: ODE, Bullet & Vortex, building block concept which combines basic objects and links various functionality via embedded scripts [48]. It can also visually compare several simulations runs, simulate dynamic particles, contains a model browser with highly portable modes with drag-and-drop functionality, and can simulate robots in different environments like land, water or in the air. *CoppeliaSim* offers powerful functions enabled by *CoppeliaSim* itself, enabled via plugins, add-ons, additional routines, or via extension modules. Following gives an overview of *CoppeliaSim's* main functions [49]: Geometric calculations, Kinematics, Dynamics, Data visualization/output, Data manipulation/transformation, Messaging/interfaces/connectivity, Paths/trajectories, Path planning, Synthetic vision, Custom user interfaces, Import/Export, Commands/settings and Miscellaneous. By default, *CoppeliaSim* executes a simulation by running one simulation step after another automatically. There are however many situations where it is important to be able to manually trigger each simulation step, to inspect each simulation step individually, or in order to synchronize *CoppeliaSim* with an external application. In those situations, a stepped or a synchronous mode is used.

3 Conclusion

Robotics has proven to be an ideal framework for teaching STEM subjects. Robotics in the classroom has proven to be a very good practice. However, the new generation of students is very connected to the technology of virtual environments, and it is necessary to create new curricula and teaching methods with which they can approach such technologies. Each of the presented virtual environments and robot simulators has its own specifics and can be used in different levels of education. By using virtual environments and robotic simulators, students can be taught to understand how robots work, how robots interact with the environment in which they operate, how to program robots using different programming languages and programming methods, and how to virtually model and simulate robots and their working environments. The advantages of using virtual environments and robotic simulators in the teaching process are certainly reflected in the rapid development of algorithms, consistent simulations of complete factory automation, rapid development of prototypes, programming in different programming languages and graphic programming environments, creation of virtual worlds with real physical characteristics, etc.

Robot simulators, as part of the robotics curriculum, allow students to become virtually involved in the development and programming of robots. In addition, simulators are a very useful tool that can simultaneously save resources and improve the educational process. All previously presented environments cover a very wide range of application areas, they use different methods and ways of programming, and are intended for different levels of education, and making some logical comparison between them is very complex. For this reason, this paper is focused on presenting the possibility of applying these tools as excellent solutions for teaching robotics within STEM educational programs.

References

1. Crnokić, B., Rezić, S.: Robots as an important factor in development of science and new technologies. In: 1th Internacionalna konferencija "NOVE TEHNOLOGIJE" razvoj i primjena "NT-2014", vol. 1, no. 1, pp. 123–133 (2014). http://www.robotika.ba/dokumenti/NT-2014.pdf
2. Crnokic, B., Grubisic, M., Volaric, T.: Different applications of mobile robots in education. Int. J. Integr. Technol. Educ. (IJITE) 6(3), 15–28 (2017). https://doi.org/10.5121/ijite.2017.6302
3. Stein, G., Lédeczi, A.: Enabling collaborative distance robotics education for novice programmers (2021)
4. Tselegkaridis, S., Sapounidis, T.: Simulators in educational robotics: a review. Educ. Sci. 11(1), 11 (2021). https://doi.org/10.3390/educsci11010011
5. Stein, G., Jean, D., Brady, C., Lédeczi, Á.: Browser-based simulation for novice-friendly classroom robotics. Front. Comput. Sci. 4, 167 (2023). https://doi.org/10.3389/FCOMP.2022.1031572
6. Choi, H., et al.: On the use of simulation in robotics: Opportunities, challenges, and suggestions for moving forward. Proc. Natl. Acad. Sci. USA 118, e1907856118 (2020). https://doi.org/10.1073/pnas.1907856118

7. Liu, A., Newsom, J., Schunn, C., Shoop, R.: Students learn programming faster through robotic simulation. Tech Dir. **72**(8), 16–19 (2013). https://www.cmu.edu/roboticsacademy/PDFs/Research/LearnProgrammingFasterThroughSimulation.pdf
8. López-Nicolás, G., Romeo, A., Guerrero, J.J.: Simulation tools for active learning in robot control and programming. In: 20th EAEEIE Annual Conference, EAEEIE 2009 - Formal Proceedings (2009). https://doi.org/10.1109/EAEEIE.2009.5335490
9. Lin, G., Chen, Y.: Application of virtual simulation in practical teaching of industrial robot specialty. In: Proceedings of the 2022 3rd International Conference on Artificial Intelligence and Education (IC-ICAIE 2022), pp. 1507–1511. Atlantis Press (2023). https://doi.org/10.2991/978-94-6463-040-4_225
10. Wang, Z.: Design of virtual simulation teaching platform for mechanical manufacturing. In: SSER 2018, vol. 238, pp. 198–201 (2018). https://doi.org/10.2991/sser-18.2018.41
11. Mblock. https://www.mblock.cc/introduction-to-product/. Accessed 13 Mar 2023
12. mBlock 3 vs mBlock 5 - Makeblock Education. https://education.makeblock.com/help/mblock-block-based-mblock-3-vs-mblock-5/. Accessed 23 Mar 2023
13. Arduino. https://www.arduino.cc/en/Guide/Introduction/. Accessed 13 Mar 2023
14. The Best Arduino Simulators of 2023 (Online & Offline) | All3DP. https://all3dp.com/2/best-arduino-simulators-online-offline/. 23 Mar 2023
15. Fischer Technik. https://www.fischertechnik.de/en/teaching/arduino-microbit-u-co/arduino
16. Role of Arduino in Real World Applications. https://www.ijstr.org/final-print/jan2020/Role-Of-Arduino-In-Real-World-Applications-.pdf. Accessed 13 Mar 2023
17. Carnegie Mellon Robotics Academy. https://www.cmu.edu/roboticsacademylast. Accessed 14 Mar 2023
18. NVIDIA Isaac Sim on Omniverse Now Available in Open Beta | NVIDIA Technical Blog. https://developer.nvidia.com/blog/nvidia-isaac-sim-on-omniverse-now-available-in-open-beta/. Accessed 23 Mar 2023
19. Nvidia Omniverse documentation. https://docs.omniverse.nvidia.com/. Accessed 7 Mar 2023
20. Isaac Sim. https://developer.nvidia.com/isaac-sim. Accessed 7 Mar 2023
21. Gazebo documentation. https://gazebosim.org/docs. Accessed 9 Mar 2023
22. Gazebo physics library. https://gazebosim.org/libs/physics. Accessed 9 Mar 2023
23. How to Move a Gazebo Model from Terminal – VarHowto. https://varhowto.com/how-to-move-a-gazebo-model-from-command-line-ros/. Accessed 23 Mar 2023
24. Gazebo rendering library. https://gazebosim.org/libs/rendering. Accessed 9 Mar 2023
25. SDF simulation format. http://sdformat.org/. Accessed 9 Mar 2023
26. RoboDK simulation. https://robodk.com/simulation. Accessed 9 Mar 2023
27. RoboDK documentation. https://robodk.com/doc/en/. Accessed 9 Mar 2023
28. RoboDK supported robots list. https://robodk.com/supported-robots. Accessed 9 Mar 2023
29. RoboDK for Web. https://robodk.com/blog/robodk-web/. Accessed 10 Mar 2023
30. RoboDK Simulation and Offline Programming Software for TM | Techman Robot. https://www.tm-robot.com/en/product/robodk-simulation-and-offline-programming-software-for-tm/. Accessed 23 Mar 2023
31. SimSpark SourceForge page. https://simspark.sourceforge.net/. Accessed 10 Mar 2023
32. SimSpark Wikipedia page. https://en.wikipedia.org/wiki/SimSpark. Accessed 10 Mar 2023
33. Boedecker, J., Asada, M.: SimSpark – concepts and application in the RoboCup 3D soccer simulation league. Autonomous Robots, Osaka University, November 2008. https://www.semanticscholar.org/paper/SimSpark-%E2%80%93-Concepts-and-Application-in-the-RoboCup-Boedecker-Asada/872b60cbbf89bda70488d3089958140740a60a14
34. SimSpark – Concepts and Application in the RoboCup 3 D Soccer Simulation League Semantic Scholar. https://www.semanticscholar.org/paper/SimSpark-%E2%80%93-Concepts-and-Application-in-the-RoboCup-BoedeckerAsada/872b60cbbf89bda70488d30899958140740a60a14/. Accessed 23 Mar 2023

35. SimSpark GitLab page. https://gitlab.com/robocup-sim/SimSpark. Accessed 10 Mar 2023
36. Robot Virtual Worlds. https://www.generationrobots.com/en/401609-robot-virtual-worlds-40-for-lego-minstorms-1-user-perpetual-license.html. Accessed 10 Mar 2023
37. Robot Virtual Worlds official YouTube video. https://www.youtube.com/watch?v=Wj13Zv RWjeE. Accessed 10 Mar 2023
38. User's guide to Palm Island. https://docplayer.net/30629987-A-user-s-guide-for-the-palm-island-robot-virtual-world-palm-island-robot-to-the-rescue-robot-virtual-world.html. Accessed 12 Mar 2023
39. Introduction to Webots, https://cyberbotics.com/doc/guide/introduction-to-webots. Accessed 10 Mar 2023
40. Webots Aldebaran documentation. http://doc.aldebaran.com/2-1/software/webots/webots_index.html. Accessed 10 Mar 2023
41. Webots User Interface. https://cyberbotics.com/doc/guide/the-user-interface. Accessed 10 Mar 2023
42. How to Install and Demo the Webots Robot Simulator for ROS 2 – Automatic Addison. https://automaticaddison.com/how-to-install-and-demo-the-webots-robot-simulator-for-ros-2/. Accessed 23 Mar 2023
43. OpenRAVE documentation. http://openrave.org/docs/latest_stable/. Accessed 10 Mar 2023
44. OpenRAVE architecture. http://openrave.org/docs/latest_stable/architecture/#architecture. Accessed 10 Mar 2023
45. OpenRAVE overview. http://openrave.org/docs/latest_stable/overview/#overview. Accessed 10 Mar 2023
46. CoppeliaSim. https://www.coppeliarobotics.com/. Accessed 12 Mar 2023
47. Getting Started with the CoppeliaSim Simulator - Northwestern Mechatronics Wiki. http://hades.mech.northwestern.edu/index.php/Getting_Started_with_the_CoppeliaSim_Simulator/. Accessed 23 Mar 2023
48. CoppeliaSim official overview video. https://www.youtube.com/watch?v=gBYqOBdIcaY. Accessed 12 Mar 2023
49. CoppeliaSim User Manual. https://www.coppeliarobotics.com/helpFiles/. Accessed 12 Mar 2023

Evaluating LightGBM Classifier for Knowledge Tracing on EdNet Dataset

Marija Habijan(✉) and Irena Galić

Faculty of Electrical Engineering, Computer Science and Information
Technology Osijek, 31000 Osijek, Croatia
`marija.habijan@ferit.hr`

Abstract. Knowledge tracing is critical in educational data mining to accurately predict student performance and knowledge in future interactions. In this study, we utilized the EdNet dataset to implement different classifiers and evaluate their performance in knowledge tracing. We found that the LightGBM classifier outperformed other classifiers, achieving the highest accuracy of 0.723 on the test set. Furthermore, we applied three ensemble methods, including boosting, bagging, and stacking, to investigate if they could further improve the performance of the LightGBM classifier. Our experimental results showed that the stacking method provided the most significant improvement, while the bagging and boosting methods did not yield significant improvements. These findings suggest that the LightGBM classifier, combined with the boosting method, can be an effective approach for knowledge tracing and have potential practical applications in education.

Keywords: Artifical Intelligence · Education · Interactive Educational Systems · Knowledge Tracing · LightGBM · Personalized Education

1 Introduction

Teaching is a crucial activity for facilitating the transfer of knowledge. It is widely acknowledged that one critical aspect of effective teaching is the ability of human educators to monitor the progress of their student's learning. This ability allows teachers to adjust their instructional approach, pace, and materials to optimize the growth of each student's knowledge. With the emergence of online education platforms [16], intelligent tutoring systems [14], and educational games [10], traditional education systems have been complemented or even replaced in some cases over the past three decades. The COVID-19 pandemic has further accelerated the digital transformation of education, forcing teachers and students worldwide to rapidly adapt to online learning modes to mitigate the disruption caused by the pandemic. However, while growing demand for computer-based teaching technologies, technology-enhanced instruction has also brought new challenges. One such challenge is effectively tracking students' learning progress through online interactions with instructional materials, commonly called the Knowledge Tracing (KT) problem. KT is an essential aspect of modern educational systems that aims to observe, represent, and quantify a

D. Vasić and M. Kundid Vasić (Eds.): MoStart 2023, CCIS 1827, pp. 33–44, 2023.
https://doi.org/10.1007/978-3-031-36833-2_3

student's knowledge state, such as their mastery level of the skills underlying the instructional materials, aiming to improve their learning processes and outcomes. It involves tracking the progress of individual students in real-time to identify their strengths and weaknesses, adapt learning materials to their needs, and provide personalized feedback and support [1].

KT can help educators create a personalized learning environment catering to students' needs. It allows teachers to identify knowledge gaps, evaluate the effectiveness of instructional materials, and tailor teaching strategies to match the learning pace of each student. This approach can motivate students by providing instant feedback on their progress, promoting self-reflection and self-regulation, and enhancing engagement with the learning materials. Moreover, KT is an effective tool for predicting student performance, improving instructional outcomes, and enhancing the educational experience. By analyzing student performance data, KT can identify the underlying cognitive processes and learning strategies students use, which can inform the development of more effective instructional techniques. It can also help to identify students who may require additional support or remediation, enabling educators to intervene before problems escalate.

The concept of KT has gained significant attention from researchers and educators due to its potential to revolutionize traditional classroom teaching [11], and it can be achieved through various methods, including machine learning algorithms, data mining techniques, and educational analytic tools [5,13]. In this work, we will utilize the EdNet dataset to implement various classifiers to evaluate their performance in knowledge tracing. Specifically, we will investigate the performance of the LightGBM classifier, which has shown promising results in previous studies. We will also apply three ensemble methods, boosting, bagging, and stacking, to enhance the performance of the LightGBM classifier. We aim to identify the most effective approach for knowledge tracing using the LightGBM classifier and explore its practical applications in education.

1.1 Related Research

As online education platforms continue to evolve, the task of KT has become increasingly important in providing personalized education [2]. Various deep learning techniques, such as Deep Knowledge Tracing (DKT), have been employed to model a student's knowledge state in a summarized hidden vector using Recurrent Neural Networks (RNNs) [13,18]. On the other hand, a dynamic key-value memory network (DKVMN) utilizes Memory Augmented Neural Network to perform knowledge tracing [15,19]. The DKVMN method uses two matrices called key and value to learn the relationship between the exercises and the knowledge component and the student's knowledge level. In contrast, the parameters of the DKT model cannot be easily understood. The DKVMN method is more understandable because it explicitly maintains a representation matrix for the knowledge component and the student's knowledge level [8].

Traditional methods for knowledge tracing have been outperformed by methods based on Recurrent Neural Networks (RNN), but these methods struggle with sparse data, which is common in real-world situations where students interact with few knowledge concepts [6]. To address this issue, transformers [17], initially designed for language understanding, have been proven to outperform other approaches. For example, Pandey et al. [12] proposed a new approach to knowledge tracing, which is the task of modeling a student's mastery of knowledge concepts as they engage in a sequence of learning activities. They developed a method that identifies the relevant knowledge concepts from a student's past activities and predicts their mastery based on these concepts. This method, called Self Attentive Knowledge Tracing (SAKT), uses a self-attention-based approach to identify the relevance between knowledge concepts. On the other hand, Zhang et al. [20] propose a Sequential Self-Attentive model for Knowledge Tracing (SSAKT). SSAKT leverages question information based on Multidimensional Item Response Theory (MIRT) to capture the relations between questions and skills. The model utilizes a self-attention layer to capture the relations between questions further. Notably, unlike traditional self-attention networks, the self-attention layer in SSAKT incorporates Long Short-Term Memory networks (LSTM) for positional encoding. Additionally, a context module is designed to capture contextual information. Experimental results on four real-world datasets demonstrate that SSAKT outperforms existing Knowledge Tracing (KT) models. Furthermore, a case study is conducted to illustrate the model's effectiveness in capturing the relations between questions and skills. The findings suggest that SSAKT presents a promising approach for advancing the field of Knowledge Tracing. In addition, a new model called Separated Self-Attentive Neural Knowledge Tracing (SAINT) [3], which is based on the Transformer architecture, has been developed for knowledge tracing. The SAINT model uses an encoder-decoder structure, where the exercise and response embedding sequences are inputted separately into the encoder and decoder. The encoder applies self-attention layers to the sequence of exercise embeddings, while the decoder alternates between applying self-attention layers and encoder-decoder attention layers to the sequence of response embeddings. By separating the input, the authors were able to stack multiple attention layers, resulting in improved AUC. Another study by Lee et al. [9] proposes a neural pedagogical agent that can update user models in real time for predicting user response correctness, which is crucial for mobile education applications where users are frequently added and educational material is often static.

2   Methodology

Light Gradient Boosting Machine (LightGBM) [7] is a tree-based model that uses the gradient boosting algorithm, which works by iterative improving an ensemble of weak decision trees. LightGBM uses verdict trees that are utilized to map a function, such as the one from the input space X to the gradient space G. A training set with s-dimensional vectors x_1, x_2, and x_n is assumed to be available in the space X. In each iteration of gradient boosting, all negative gradients of a loss function with respect to the output model are represented as g_1, g_2, up to g_n. The decision tree partitions each node based on the most informative feature, which maximizes the information gain. This type of model measures data improvement by computing the variance after partitioning, which can be represented by the following formula:

$$Y = tree0(\mathbf{X}) - lr \cdot tree1(\mathbf{X}) - lr \cdot tree2(\mathbf{X}) - lr \cdot tree3(\mathbf{X}) \tag{1}$$

Suppose there is a training dataset, O, on a fixed node of a decision tree. The variance gain for dividing measure j at a point d for that node can be defined as:

$$V_{j|O}(d) = \frac{1}{n_O} \left(\frac{\left(\sum_{\{x_i \in O : x_{ij} \le d\}} g_i \right)^2}{n_{l|O}^j(d)} + \frac{\left(\sum_{\{x_i \in O : x_{ij} > d\}} g_i \right)^2}{n_{r|O}^j(d)} \right) \tag{2}$$

where $n_O = \sum I [x_i \in O]$, $n_{l|O}^j(d) = \sum I [x_i \in O : x_{ij} \le d]$ and $n_{r|O}^j(d) = \sum I [x_i \in O : x_{ij} > d]$. The decision tree algorithm selects the optimal splitting point, d_j, for feature j by finding the value that maximizes the variance gain, $V_j(d)$. The algorithm then calculates the largest gain, $V_j(d_j)$, for that feature. The data is subsequently divided into left and right child nodes based on feature j at the selected splitting point, d_j.

LightGBM utilizes a technique called Gradient-based One-Side Sampling (GOSS), which improves the training speed without sacrificing accuracy by selecting only a subset of training samples with significant gradients. GOSS selects instances with large gradients, while random sampling is performed on instances with small gradients. The training dataset is represented as O for each decision tree node, and the variance gain or dividing measure at a node's point d is denoted as j and can be expressed mathematically as:

$$\tilde{V}_j(d) = \frac{1}{n} \left(\frac{\left(\sum_{x_i \in A_l} g_i + \frac{1-a}{b} \sum_{x_i \in B_l} g_i \right)^2}{n_l^j(d)} + \frac{\left(\sum_{x_i \in A_r} g_i + \frac{1-a}{b} \sum_{x_i \in B_r} g_i \right)^2}{n_r^j(d)} \right),$$
$$\tag{3}$$

Another important feature of LightGBM is that it can handle categorical features by converting them into numerical values based on their frequency, reducing the need for pre-processing. One key aspect of LightGBM that sets it apart from other gradient-boosting frameworks is its use of a histogram-based approach to split numerical features. Rather than sorting the feature values before splitting them, LightGBM bins the values into discrete histograms and computes the split points based on the histogram statistics. This reduces the memory footprint and computation time required for finding the optimal split point, especially for high-dimensional datasets. Overall, LightGBM's efficiency, scalability, and ability to handle categorical features and use of histogram-based splitting make it a powerful tool for various machine learning tasks, including classification.

2.1 Ensemble Methods

Ensemble techniques refer to the methods that employ multiple learning algorithms or models to generate an optimal predictive model. The model derived from these techniques exhibits improved performance compared to the base learners when taken alone. The ensemble techniques used in this work are bagging, boosting, and stacking, as shown in Fig. 1.

Boosting combines multiple weak classifiers to create a strong classifier. The basic idea behind boosting is to sequentially train weak learners on the same data, with each subsequent learner being trained to improve upon the errors made by the previous learners. This allows the ensemble to converge towards a strong classifier that can make accurate predictions on the data. On the other hand, bagging involves training multiple instances of the same base model on different subsets of the data. These models are then combined to create an ensemble that can make predictions based on a majority vote or averaging of the predictions made by the individual models. The main goal of bagging is to reduce the variance in the ensemble by ensuring that each model is trained on a slightly different subset of the data. Stacking is an ensemble method that involves combining the outputs of multiple base models with training a meta-model that can make final predictions. In stacking, the predictions made by the individual models are used as input features to train a meta-model. This meta-model can be a simple linear model or a more complex neural network and is trained to make final predictions based on the outputs of the individual models. In LightGBM, these ensemble methods can be used to improve the accuracy and generalization of the model.

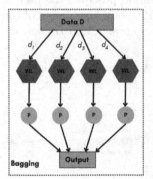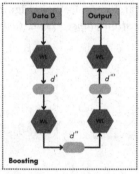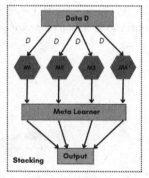

Fig. 1. Different types of ensemble methods: bagging, boosting and stacking. In this context, a weak learner is represented as WL, while d_1, d_2, d_3, and d_4 are random samples taken from the dataset D. The updated training data sets, denoted as d', $d"$, and $d"'$, are created based on the results from the previous weak learner.

3 Experiments and Results

In order to provide a comprehensive understanding of our approach and results, we begin this section by describing the EdNet dataset that was used in our experiments. We then provide detailed information regarding the implementation and training of our classification models and an analysis of the experimental results.

3.1 Dataset Description

The EdNet dataset [4] comprises 131,441,538 interactions from 784,309 students who have used Santa since 2017. The service, available on mobile devices and as a web application, is designed to equip students with the necessary skills to excel in the TOEIC Listening and Reading Test. The average number of interactions per student is 441.20. Santa offers 13,169 problems and 1,021 lectures, each labeled with 293 unique skills, which have been accessed 95,294,926 and 601,805 times, respectively. This is the largest publicly available education dataset in terms of the number of students, interactions, and interaction categories.

The dataset consists of four continuous features: *timestamp*, which measures the time between user interaction and the first event from that user, *prior question elapsed time*, which represents the average time a user took to solve each question in the previous bundle, *content id*, an ID code for the user interaction, and *task container id*, an ID code for the batch of questions or lectures. Additionally, there are three categorical features: *answered correctly*, which indicates whether the user responded correctly (1 for correct, 0 for incorrect, −1 for no answer, i.e., watching lectures), *user answer*, which represents the user's answer to the question (0, 1, 2, or 3, and −1 for no answer, i.e., watching lectures), and *content type*, which is either 0 if the event was a question posed to the user or 1 if the event was the user watching a lecture. Figure 2 shows histograms of the continuous features *prior question elapsed time*, *task container*, and *content id*.

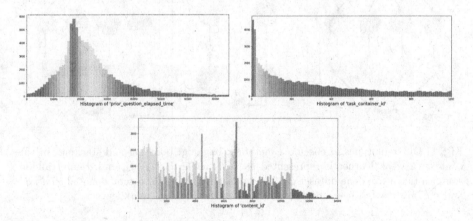

Fig. 2. Histograms of the continuous features.

3.2 Implementation Details

To preprocess the data, the *user answer* column was dropped, rows with missing values were removed, and the remaining missing values were imputed using mode and mean imputation techniques. The PyCaret library was then used to set up and train several classification models, including logistic regression, Gradient Boosting, Ridge, Ada Boost, Linear Discriminant Analysis, Random Forest, Extra Trees, Logistic Regression, Naive Bayes, K-Neighbors, Decision Tree, Support Vector Machine with Linear Kernel, and LightGBM. In addition, ensemble models were created using bagging and boosting techniques, and a stacked model was also trained to improve performance. The hyperparameters of the LightGBM model were optimized using Bayesian optimization through the scikit-optimize library. The final ensemble model was created using a stack of multiple LightGBM models, with one model being optimized using the standard tuning and the other model using Bayesian optimization. The model was trained using 10-fold cross-validation, and the area under the receiver operating characteristic curve (AUC-ROC) was used as the evaluation metric.

3.3 Results Analysis

This section presents the evaluation results of various classification algorithms for knowledge tracing on the EdNet dataset. In this subsection, we compare the performance of different algorithms using several evaluation metrics such as accuracy, the area under the curve (AUC), recall, precision, F1 score, Kappa, and Matthews correlation coefficient (MCC). The goal is to identify this dataset's most efficient algorithm for knowledge tracing. It is worth noting that higher accuracy, AUC, recall, precision, F1 score, Kappa, and MCC indicate better classification model performance. Therefore, our results show that the classification model performed better when these metrics had higher values. These findings highlight the importance of using multiple evaluation metrics to assess classification models' performance comprehensively. Table 1 provides an overview of the results obtained by different classification algorithms for knowledge tracing on the EdNet dataset.

The results show that the Gradient Boosting Classifier obtained the highest accuracy (0.7070) among all the classifiers. The Ridge Classifier, on the other hand, achieved an accuracy of 0.6973 but had a zero AUC value. The Ada Boost Classifier and the Random Forest Classifier scored reasonably well, with an accuracy of 0.6952 and 0.6901, respectively. In contrast, the Extra Trees Classifier obtained an accuracy of 0.6750, slightly lower than the others. The Logistic Regression and Naive Bayes classifiers had the same accuracy of 0.6748 but performed poorly regarding the recall, precision, F1 score, Kappa, and MCC. The K Neighbors Classifier and Decision Tree Classifier also had low accuracy of 0.6401 and 0.6340, respectively. The SVM with a linear kernel had the lowest accuracy of 0.5348. LightGBM showed promising results with an accuracy of 0.7156, higher than most other algorithms. The LightGBM (tuned) algorithm, which was further optimized, achieved an accuracy of 0.7203 and an AUC of

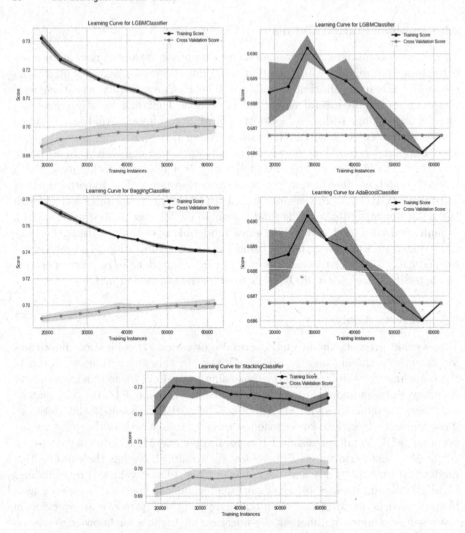

Fig. 3. Learning curves for the LightGBM classifier trained on the dataset.

0.7026, the highest values among all the classifiers. The LightGBM (ensemble) algorithm also performed well, with an accuracy of 0.7177 and an AUC of 0.6965. The LightGBM (Boosting) algorithm had a relatively lower accuracy of 0.6934 and an AUC of 0.5444 compared to the other LightGBM models. Finally, the LightGBM (Stacked) algorithm had an accuracy of 0.7198 and an AUC of 0.7040, among the best results obtained by all the algorithms. Figure 3 shows confusion matrices for different LightGBM methods.

The fact that the Logistic Regression and Naive Bayes classifiers have a Kappa and MCC value of 0 suggests that these classifiers are not performing better than random. Kappa and MCC are metrics that consider the agreement

Table 1. Comparison of the performance of different classifiers on a given dataset based on several evaluation metrics. The evaluation metrics used are accuracy (Acc.), the area under the ROC curve (AUC), recall (Rec.), precision (Prec.), F1 score (F1), Cohen's kappa coefficient (Kappa), and Matthews correlation coefficient (MCC). The table shows the values of these metrics obtained for each classifier. Higher values for Acc., AUC, Rec., Prec., F1, Kappa, and MCC indicate better performance.

Model	Acc.	AUC	Rec.	Prec.	F1	Kappa	MCC
Gradient Boosting Classifier	0.7070	0.6689	0.6924	0.6891	0.6253	0.1768	0.2597
Ridge Classifier	0.6973	0.0000	0.6909	0.6558	0.6254	0.1674	0.2227
Ada Boost Classifier	0.6952	0.6326	0.6915	0.6537	0.6261	0.1678	0.2201
Linear Discriminant Analysis	0.6926	0.6059	0.6347	0.6480	0.6210	0.1550	0.2053
Random Forest Classifier	0.6901	0.6609	0.7150	0.6584	0.6605	0.2264	0.2409
Extra Trees Classifier	0.6750	0.6387	0.7102	0.6451	0.6514	0.2061	0.2145
Logistic Regression	0.6748	0.5346	0.3333	0.4554	0.5438	0.0000	0.0000
Naive Bayes	0.6748	0.5337	0.3333	0.4554	0.5438	0.0000	0.0000
K Neighbors Classifier	0.6401	0.5900	0.3736	0.6048	0.6163	0.1172	0.1211
Decision Tree Classifier	0.6340	0.5905	0.7134	0.6370	0.6355	0.1933	0.1933
SVM - Linear Kernel	0.5348	0.0000	0.3466	0.4643	0.4429	0.0446	0.0696
LightGBM	0.7156	0.6903	0.7010	0.7121	0.6398	0.2058	0.2928
LightGBM (tuned)	0.7203	0.7026	0.7095	0.7131	0.6546	0.2318	0.3067
LightGBM (Bagging)	0.7177	0.6965	0.7054	0.7106	0.6477	0.2190	0.2982
LightGBM (Boosting)	0.6934	0.5444	0.6667	0.4825	0.5684	0.0910	0.2399
LightGBM (Stacked)	0.7198	0.7040	0.7142	0.7036	0.6626	0.2436	0.3032

between predicted and true labels beyond what is expected by chance. A Kappa or MCC score of 0 means that the agreement between the predicted and true labels is no better than what would be expected by random chance. There could be several reasons why these classifiers are not performing well. One possibility is that the underlying assumptions of the classifiers do not hold for the data at hand. Logistic Regression assumes a linear relationship between the input features and the target variable, while Naive Bayes assumes that the input features are independent. If these assumptions do not hold, then the classifiers may not be able to capture the complex relationships between the input features and the target variable. Given that, the Logistic Regression and Naive Bayes classifiers may not be well-suited for the particular dataset (Fig. 4).

The difference in performance among the classifiers can be attributed to the underlying algorithms' ability to capture complex patterns in the data, handle data sparsity, and perform feature selection. For instance, LightGBM algorithms performed well because they are gradient-boosting algorithms that handle sparse data well and perform feature selection. In contrast, Naive Bayes and Logistic Regression classifiers are simpler algorithms that may not capture the complex relationships between features. SVM with a linear kernel had the lowest accuracy because it could not capture the non-linear relationships between features. Overall, the LightGBM classifiers show promising results for this classification

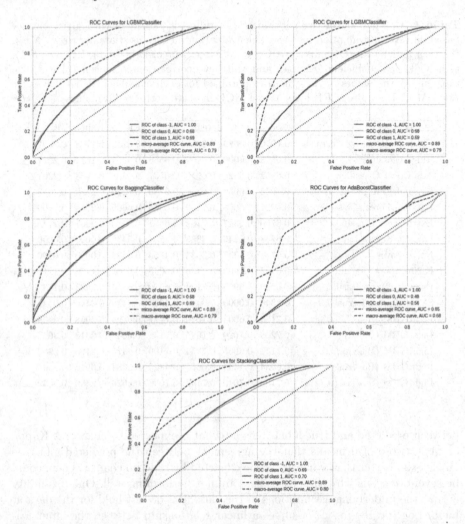

Fig. 4. Receiver Operating Characteristic (ROC) curves of different LightGBM classifiers. The ROC curves show the trade-off between the true positive rate (sensitivity) and false positive rate (1-specificity) for different classification thresholds. The area under the curve (AUC) is a measure of the classifier's overall performance, with values closer to 1 indicating better discrimination between the positive and negative classes. The LightGBM classifiers evaluated in this study include: LightGBM, tuned LightGBM, boosted LightGBM, bagging LightGBM, and stacking LightGBM. The AUC values for each classifier are reported in Table 1.

problem, with LightGBM (tuned) achieving the best overall performance. Therefore, it can be considered as the efficient algorithm for knowledge tracing on the EdNet dataset.

4   Conclusion

This study employed the EdNet dataset to implement various classifiers to assess their performance in knowledge tracing. The LightGBM classifier outperformed other classifiers with an accuracy of 0.7203 on the test set. To improve the performance of the LightGBM classifier, three ensemble methods were applied, including boosting, bagging, and stacking. Experimental results demonstrated that the stacking method yielded the most significant improvement, while the bagging and boosting methods did not produce significant improvements. These findings indicate that combining the LightGBM classifier with the stacking method can be an effective approach for knowledge tracing and have practical applications in education.

In conclusion, this study highlights the potential of using the LightGBM classifier with ensemble methods for knowledge tracing on the EdNet dataset. The results suggest that these methods can achieve high accuracy and AUC scores and can assist in identifying students who may be struggling early on. Future research can build upon these findings by exploring the impact of different features and using deep learning techniques to improve the model's accuracy. Despite the potential benefits of Knowledge Tracing, challenges still need to be addressed in its implementation. These include issues related to data privacy, ethical concerns, and the need for effective communication and collaboration between educators, students, and stakeholders. However, as the field of education continues to evolve, the potential benefits of Knowledge Tracing will likely continue to drive research and development in this area.

References

1. Abdelrahman, G., Wang, Q.: Knowledge tracing with sequential key-value memory networks, pp. 175–184, July 2019. https://doi.org/10.1145/3331184.3331195
2. Abdelrahman, G.M., Wang, Q., Nunes, B.P.: Knowledge tracing: a survey. ACM Comput. Surv. **55**, 1–37 (2022)
3. Choi, Y., et al.: Towards an appropriate query, key, and value computation for knowledge tracing. In: Proceedings of the Seventh ACM Conference on Learning @ Scale (2020)
4. Choi, Y., et al.: EdNet: a large-scale hierarchical dataset in education. In: Artificial Intelligence in Education, pp. 69–73 (2019)
5. Corbett, A.T., Anderson, J.R.: Knowledge tracing: modeling the acquisition of procedural knowledge. User Model. User-Adap. Inter. **4**, 253–278 (2005)
6. Kang, W.C., McAuley, J.: Self-attentive sequential recommendation. In: 2018 IEEE International Conference on Data Mining (ICDM), pp. 197–206 (2018)
7. Ke, G., et al.: LightGBM: a highly efficient gradient boosting decision tree. In: NIPS (2017)
8. Khajah, M.M., Lindsey, R.V., Mozer, M.C.: How deep is knowledge tracing? ArXiv abs/1604.02416 (2016)
9. Lee, Y., et al.: Creating a neural pedagogical agent by jointly learning to review and assess. ArXiv abs/1906.10910 (2019)

10. Long, Y., Aleven, V.: Educational game and intelligent tutoring system: a classroom study and comparative design analysis. ACM Trans. Comput.-Human Interact. **24**, 1–27 (2017). https://doi.org/10.1145/3057889
11. Lyu, L., Wang, Z., Yun, H., Yang, Z., Li, Y.: Deep knowledge tracing based on spatial and temporal representation learning for learning performance prediction. Appl. Sci. (2022)
12. Pandey, S., Karypis, G.: A self attentive model for knowledge tracing. ArXiv abs/1907.06837 (2019)
13. Piech, C., et al.: Deep knowledge tracing. In: NIPS (2015)
14. Psotka, J., Massey, L., Mutter, S.A.: Intelligent tutoring systems: lessons learned (1988)
15. Santoro, A., Bartunov, S., Botvinick, M.M., Wierstra, D., Lillicrap, T.P.: One-shot learning with memory-augmented neural networks. ArXiv abs/1605.06065 (2016)
16. Vardi, M.Y.: Will MOOCs destroy academia? Commun. ACM **55**, 5–5 (2012)
17. Vaswani, A., et al.: Attention is all you need. ArXiv abs/1706.03762 (2017)
18. Yeung, C.K., Yeung, D.Y.: Addressing two problems in deep knowledge tracing via prediction-consistent regularization. In: Proceedings of the Fifth Annual ACM Conference on Learning at Scale (2018)
19. Zhang, J., Shi, X., King, I., Yeung, D.Y.: Dynamic key-value memory networks for knowledge tracing. In: Proceedings of the 26th International Conference on World Wide Web (2016)
20. Zhang, X., Zhang, J., Lin, N., Yang, X.: Sequential self-attentive model for knowledge tracing. In: International Conference on Artificial Neural Networks (2021)

POS-Only Tagging Using RNN for Croatian Language

Josipa Juričić and Branko Žitko(✉)

Faculty of Science, University of Split, Rudera Boškovića 33, 21000 Split, Croatia
bzitko@pmfst.hr

Abstract. Part-of-speech (POS) tagging is one of the fundamental tasks in the field of natural language processing. This paper gives an overview of methods used for POS tagging and explores the research done so far, with a focus on POS tagging of the Croatian language. The latest techniques of POS tagging come from the field of deep learning. Commonly used deep learning models are various types of artificial neural networks, such as RNN, LSTM and BiLSTM models. In order to determine the efficiency of using different neural networks for POS tagging, RNN and LSTM models were implemented. The models were trained and evaluated on the hr500k dataset (reference corpus of Croatian texts). The results showed the overfitting problems of RNN models which is why the highest accuracy models achieved on the test dataset was 78.57%. The result indicated the need to also research MSD tagging of Croatian language given its morphologically complex structure.

Keywords: Natural Language Processing · Part-of-speech Tagging · POS · Neural Networks · RNN · LSTM

1 Introduction

Natural language processing (NLP) is a field of artificial intelligence. It uses computer techniques for the purpose of learning, understanding and generating human language. Early approaches in NLP researching focused on automating the analysis of the linguistic structure of languages and developing technologies such as machine translation, speech recognition, and speech synthesis [17]. Today researchers are refining and using such tools in real-world applications, creating text-to-speech tools, searching for health or financial information on social media or identifying feelings and emotions toward products and services in marketing [17].

Part-of-speech tagging (POS) is one of the fundamental tasks in natural language processing. This process assigns a tag to each word which indicates a part of speech that word belongs to. Tags are assigned with respect to the meaning of the word and its connection to the adjacent words in the sentence. Part-of-speech tagger receives as an input a series of words and a tagged dataset (or corpus) from which it learns how to recognize different types of words. POS tagging does not solve a particular problem in natural language processing, but it is a prerequisite for many other processes. This task

D. Vasić and M. Kundid Vasić (Eds.): MoStart 2023, CCIS 1827, pp. 45–62, 2023.
https://doi.org/10.1007/978-3-031-36833-2_4

is necessary before tasks such as sentiment analysis, text translation, grammar checking, speech recognition and many others. If POS tagging is poorly performed, it negatively affects all tasks that follow it, and for this reason many authors state the importance of finding a model that will most successfully solve this task. POS tagging also helps to create language models used in speech synthesis systems or in speech recognition systems where knowledge of part-of-speech tags allows for the creation of more natural pronunciation in speech synthesis systems and greater accuracy in speech recognition systems [20].

The following chapters show an overview of methods in natural language processing that are commonly used in part-of-speech tagging. It also shows the need to use neural networks and deep learning methods for such tasks. Given that most articles and research on the application of neural networks in POS tagging refer to the English language, the idea to research the POS tagging of Croatian language turned out to be interesting. For this reason, a review of the literature based on POS tagging of the Croatian language was explored to determine the achievements made so far for this topic. In the end, models of two architectures of deep neural networks (RNN and LSTM) were implemented and the accuracies of these models for POS tagging compared in order to determine which approach is the most successful one.

2 Related Work

There are several methods of POS tagging: rule-based, transformation-based and stochastic methods. Rule-based POS taggers assign a POS tag to a word based on manually created or learned language rules, while stochastic taggers determine the POS tag in the given the context based on probabilities calculated from the annotated corpus [18]. A combination of stochastic methods and rule-based methods is known as transformation-based POS tagging which automates the process of calculating probability of applied rules.

The oldest known POS tagging method is a system that used a rule-based approach, where a set of written rules and contextual information about the word were applied to assign tags to words [23], in which case the rules are handwritten, learned, or both [12]. In 1992, Eric Brill presented a POS tagger based on rules or, as he called them, transformations [29]. For his POS tagging system to work, he needed a corpus of words with properly tagged types of words from which to draw information. With the obtained information and the defined rules, the system was trained to conclude which is the most probable POS tag of the word. All that was needed, in addition to a corpus of POS tagged words, was a set of template rules that the model could use to design new tagging features. Brill's POS tagger can also be defined as a transformation-based tagger that learns by finding and minimizing errors [29]. Acedański [1] presented Brill's POS tagger that was adapted for morphologically rich languages, specifically for Polish language. The author stated significant improvements compared to previous works as his tagger achieved an accuracy of 92.44% for Polish language [1]. This improvement was achieved by upgrading the original Brill tagger with transformation templates that take prefixes and suffixes into account and by introducing parallel execution [1]. Li, Mao and Wang [41] proposed a new approach in improving the accuracy of rule-based POS taggers.

The authors stated that the results of their approach yielded even better results than methods such as a two-way neural network that previous research considers one of the best approaches [41].

Hidden Markov model (HMM) is a widely used method of stochastic POS tagging. Given a sequence (such as words, letters or sentences) HMM calculates the probability distribution over a series of tags and predicts the best sequence of tags [20]. HMM is based on the Markov chain model that describes the sequence of potential events [21]. In the HMM model, the Markov chain is hidden, but we can conclude about its properties through the given observed states. In case of the POS tagging, this means that the observed states are words and hidden states are tags. The POS tag of a word can be inferred by observing the previous hidden state i.e. tag.

However, HMM models have been shown to need a considerable number of augmentations to achieve high accuracy [20]. Farizki Wicaksono and Purwarianti [15] combined several ways to improve the accuracy of POS tagging using the HMM method. According to the results, their methods achieved model accuracy of 96.50% for a corpus that had more than 15 000 words [15]. Qiao, Bian, Xu and Tao [33] proposed a new extension of the HMM model they called the diverse HMM model. Results confirmed the effectiveness of proposed model in relation to the "regular" HMM model [33]. Ananda, Hanifmuti and Alfina [8] used a hybrid model that was a combination of HMM model and rule-based tagging which made a 2.03% increase in model accuracy. Another method based on the probability of a particular tag sequence is a Conditional Random Field (CRF) method. Chiche and Yitagesu [11] compared the performances of various algorithms and the results showed that the CRF POS tagger has outperformed the others (among which was also HMM) with the highest accuracy of 94.08%.

The latest techniques of POS tagging come from the field of deep learning. Commonly used deep learning sequential models are various types of artificial neural networks, such as RNN, LSTM and BiLSTM models.

2.1 POS Tagging Using Neural Networks

An artificial neural network is a series of algorithms that seek to recognize fundamental relationships in a dataset through a process that mimics the way the human brain works. A neuron in an artificial neural network is a mathematical function that collects and classifies information according to a specific architecture [18].

A single-layer perceptron is considered a simple model of an artificial neural network which performs the task of binary classification. Single-layer perceptron contains four main parameters: inputs, weights, net sum and activation function (see Fig. 1). An input layer is a layer where each input is represented by a numerical value (x_1, x_2,... x_n). Each input has its corresponding weight. Weights (w_1, w_2,... w_n) are values which represent the importance of each input. Function that sums the products of each input with its corresponding weight is called the net sum. The result of the net sum function is compared to a defined threshold using an activation function which determines one of two possible outputs (binary classification). Simply put, a perceptron is the place where computation occurs. It combines input data with a set of weights, which either amplify or dampen that input, thereby attaching significance to the inputs given the task the algorithm is trying to learn. Inputs and weights are added up, and then that sum passes through the activation function to determine whether and to what extent this signal should further progress through the network to influence the end outcome [30].

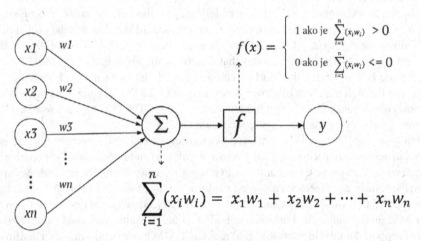

$$f(x) = \begin{cases} 1 \text{ ako je } \sum_{i=1}^{n} (x_i w_i) > 0 \\ 0 \text{ ako je } \sum_{i=1}^{n} (x_i w_i) <= 0 \end{cases}$$

$$\sum_{i=1}^{n} (x_i w_i) = x_1 w_1 + x_2 w_2 + \cdots + x_n w_n$$

Fig. 1. Single-layer perceptron

A multilayer perceptron is a neural network consisting of three parts: an input layer, one or more hidden layers, and an output layer [11]. For the given input data, the neural network provides classifications or output signals to which input data can be mapped to. Hidden layers fine-tune the input weights until the network error limit is minimal. Learning takes place when the weights are adjusted so that the grid can generate accurate outputs [14].

Deep learning is the name used for complex neural networks, i.e., artificial neural networks with three or more layers. The depth of the neural network is determined by the number of layers through which the data must pass in a multi-stage process of pattern recognition. In deep learning networks, each layer of nodes is trained on a special set of features based on the output of the previous layer [30].

The middle layer of the classical (Feed-Forward) neural network can consist of multiple hidden layers, each with its own activation functions and weights. The recurrent neural network (RNN) will standardize different activation functions, weights and biases so that each hidden layer has the same parameters (see Fig. 2) [34]. Then, instead of creating more hidden layers, they will create one and pass over it as many times as necessary [34]. The recurrent neural network, simply put, works on the principle of saving the output of a certain layer and returning it back to the input to predict the output of the next step. When making a decision in the RNN model, the current input and what has been learned from the previous input are taken into account, which is stored in the RNN memory [22]. Internal memory allows RNN models to be very precise in predicting what is coming next and are therefore often used to predict sequential data such as speech, text, financial data and the like. RNN networks represent an improvement of classical methods in natural language processing [16].

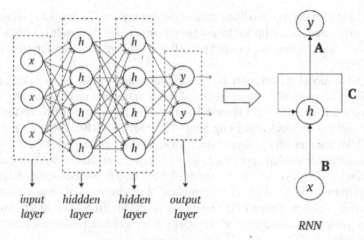

input   *hiddden*   *hidden*   *output*
layer   *layer*   *layer*   *layer*

RNN

Fig. 2. Feed Forward NN → RNN

Marques and Lopes [27] explored the need of large amounts of manually labeled texts to train RNN models and proposed a model of a neural network capable of overcoming this problem. Different neural network models apply to the problem of learning word type parameters from a very small Portuguese training corpus model. The results obtained indicate an accuracy improvement rate above 97% for the training corps with approximately 15,000 words [27].

Dinarelli and Tellier [13] studied different architectures of recurrent neural networks for sequence tagging. They state that in the research on recurrent neural networks mainly two architectures were used: Elman's RNN and Jordan's RNN. The difference between the two models lies in the feedback within the RNN model. In Elman's model, the connection is a loop in a hidden layer, and Jordan's RNN has a feedback link between the output and hidden layers. Dinarelli and Tellier proposed two new RNN models that surpass Elman's and Jordan's accuracies [13].

Recurrent neural networks suffer from the problem of gradient disappearance. Simply put, a gradient measures how much the output changes if a small change is made to the input, and the problem arises when the gradient decreases so much as it returns to previous steps that its value becomes extremely small which does not contribute to learning in a significant manner [32]. An improvement over RNN is the LSTM that solves the issue of gradient disappearance. Long Short-Term Memory (LSTM) is a special type of feedback neural network that has the ability to remember data over a longer period of time. LSTM contains three doors: input, forget and output doors. The forget door decides which information should be discarded or retained in such a way that information from the previous hidden state and information from the current input passes through the sigmoid function [32]. The sigmoid function returns values that occur between 0 and 1: the closer the value is to zero means that it should be forgotten, and the closer it is to the unit means that it is important and should be retained [32]. To update the state of the cell, there is an input door, while the output door decides what should be the next hidden state. First, the previous hidden state and the current input to the sigmoid function are passed on, and then the new modified state of the cell is passed to the tanh function [32]. Then the tanh output is multiplied by a sigmoid output, and the result is a hidden state. The new cell state (Ct) and the new hidden cell state (ht) are then transferred to the next time step [32].

The LSTM model records only past states, but in some cases, such as tagging data series, it is useful to know both previous and future states at a given time. The solution to this problem is a special LSTM model architecture consisting of two LSTM layers, which we call the Bidirectional Long Short-Term Memory (BiLSTM) [26]. In short, BiLSTM adds another LSTM layer, which changes the direction of information flow. Previous features are singled out by the first LSTM layer, and future features are captured by the second LSTM layer in which a series of input data flows backwards. Eventually, the outputs from both LSTM layers are combined in several ways, such as average, sum, multiplication or concatenation [37]. Compared to LSTM, BiLSTM is much slower and requires more time when training, which is why it is recommended to use it only in the necessary situations [37].

Lorincz, Nutu and Stan [24] investigated the tagging of Romanian texts and proposed an LSTM model in combination with a fully connected output layer for predicting POS tags. According to the results, their LSTM model achieved the highest accuracy of 99.18% [24]. The authors concluded that their proposed method is language independent because no linguistic knowledge was applied in the input features of the model [24]. Balwant [9] investigated the classification of fake news on social media. The proposed architecture included a combination of BiLSTM model and the convolutional neural network (CNN). The results showed that the resulting hybrid architecture significantly improves the effectiveness of fake news detection [9]. Kumar [22] also combined the BiLSTM and CNN model in sentiment analysis. According to the results of the proposed model, the accuracy increased (98.6%) and the execution time was reduced compared to traditional methods [22]. AlKhwiter and Al-Twairesh [7] compared POS tagging results using the BiLSTM model with the results of applying the CRF method. The results of their research for POS tagging of Arabic showed an accuracy for the BiLSTM model of 96.5%, leading the way over the CRF method [7].

2.2 POS Tagging of the Croatian Language

The Croatian language is considered to be a morphologically very rich language, which poses a greater challenge for computer word processing than for word processing of languages such as English. In Croatian language, words are divided into two categories: 1. Changeable words (nouns, pronouns, adjectives, numbers and verbs), 2. Immutable words (adverbs, prepositions, conjunctions, particles and interjection) [38].

The universal set of tags for word types (universal part-of-speech tags, UPOS), which are common to many languages, consists of the following tags: ADJ (adjective), INTJ (interjection), PUNCT (punctuation), ADP (adposition), NOUN (noun), SCONJ (coordinating conjunction), ADV (adverb), NUM (number), SYM (symbol), AUX (auxiliary verb), PART (particle), VERB (verb), CCONJ (coordinating conjunction), PRON (pronoun), X (other), DET (determinant), PROPN (proper noun).

MSD (morphosyntactic descriptors) stands for morphosyntactic tags often used in tagging highly inflectional languages such as South Slavic languages (Slovenian, Croatian, Serbian, etc.) [25, 28]. These tags contain additional features such as grammatical categories of gender, number and case. MSD tags used in POS tagging of the Croatian language are in accordance with the MULTEXT-East dataset [2]. The use of the MSD tags greatly increases the total number of tags so corpora can be up to ten times greater than the 50–100 tags commonly used for English language [20].

In natural language processing the POS tagging of English language is already a well-researched topic and different models have been built with the precision up to 98% [11]. In the case of highly inflectional and morphologically complex languages evaluated models achieve lower accuracies and precisions [1].

Agić and Tadić [2] applied stochastic methods, using TnT tagger, for morphosyntactic tagging of Croatian texts. The TnT tagger reached the human error level, achieving the highest accuracy of 98.63% [2]. According to the results, their tagger correctly tagged more than 98% of test sets on average, and most MSD errors appeared on the types with the highest number of possible tags per word while errors for POS tagging were almost insignificant [2].

Agić, Dovedan and Tadić [4] explored several methods of combining HMM model outputs for POS or MSD tagging with inflectional lexicon for the Croatian language in order to improve the accuracy of tagging Croatian texts. Their model (which they called CPT), when combined with a lemmatizer based on the Croatian morphological lexicon, in such a way that the lemmatizer gives morphological features to the tagger when it encounters unknown words, surpassed TnT tagger for the given test cases [4]. However, they omitted POS results from testing because both TnT and CPT were able to achieve accuracy over 95% without additional modules so they focused on improving the accuracy of MSD tagging [4]. They compared the results with previous research [2] and stated that although CPT showed better results than TnT taggers in tagging unknown words, it still dealt with fewer unknowns in the test cases [4]. In their later work [5] these authors presented CroTag - stochastic POS/MSD tagger used to improve the tagging of Croatian texts. The authors explained the need to combine it with a large lexicon of the Croatian language in order to create a hybrid system for more accurate tagging of the Croatian texts [5]. Their results showed that CroTag functions at a high level in terms of tagging using the HMM model [5].

Agić, Dovedan and Tadić [6] presented the results of their experimentation with a model that used a combination of five POS taggers, where their individual outputs were combined using tagger voting rules. Three taggers used were based on the HMM model (CroTag, HunPoS and TnT), the fourth was based on the SVM (support vector machines) method (SVMTool), and the fifth used a decision tree method (TreeTager) [6]. The results showed that the tagger voting idea of a combination of multiple taggers outperformed individual taggers in most test cases [6]. However, the differences between the individual taggers and the combined tagger have been shown not to be statistically significant which should be taken into account in future studies [6].

Peradin and Šnajder [31] implemented a constraint grammar (CG) that used context-dependent manually created rules to disambiguate the possible grammatical readings of words in running text. The authors described the development of a morphological tagger for the Croatian language, which used a morphological analyzer based on the reflective lexicon and the MULTEXT-East corpus [31]. Their grammar consisted of 290 rules organized into cleanup and mapping, disambiguation rules and heuristic rules. Their method resulted in a precision of 96.1% for POS tagging and 88.2% for MSD tagging [31].

Hladek, Staš and Juhar [19] proposed a classifier based on the Hidden Markov Model, used to solve the problem of POS tagging of Slavic languages, such as Slovak, Czech or Polish. Similar to Croatian, these languages are morphologically rich and have a large vocabulary. Experiments have shown that the combination of several sources of information, such as suffix-based probabilities of observations, crossing probabilities of simplified labels, and morphological vocabulary for morphological analysis, bring important improvements in tagging accuracy [19].

Agić, Ljubešić and Merkler [3] explored the statistical models for MSD tagging which they applied in lemmatization and MSD tagging of Croatian and Serbian texts. The models compared were HunPoS, CST, PurePoS, SVMTool and TreeTagger [3]. The tools with the best performance proved to be CST lemmatizer and HunPos tagger [3]. In the evaluation of these models, the accuracy of 87.72% for MSD and the accuracy of 97.13% for POS tagging of the Croatian language were achieved [3].

Meftah, Semmar, Sadat and Raaijmakers [28] described the morphosyntax tagging of Twitter posts using CEA List DeepLIMA, a tool that is a multilingual text analysis platform based on deep learning. Their approach focused on morphosyntax tagging of Twitter posts in three South Slavic languages: Slovenian, Croatian and Serbian. The authors proposed the use of neural network models and portable learning models due to the lack of tagged datasets for this problem [28]. The proposed neural network architecture was another form of bidirectional neural network - BiGRU (bidirectional Gated Recurrent Unit). According to the results, POS tagging without the application of portable learning gave (for Slovenian language) an accuracy of 89.55%, and with the application of portable learning 91.71% [28].

Ljubešić and Dobrovoljc [25] compared improvements in the transition from traditional approaches of POS tagging to neural methods for South Slavic languages (Slovenian, Croatian and Serbian). In their research, they used reldi-tagger (a tagger that uses a CRF algorithm) for the traditional approach, and stanfordnlp (a state-of-the-art tool in neural morphosyntax analysis). The results showed significant differences between reldi-tagger and stanfordnlp tool [25]. The results showed that some of the most common errors for reldi-tagger were significantly reduced by the Stanfordnlp tool [25].

Ulčar and Robnik-Sikonja [36] trained two trilingual BERT-like models, one of which was for Croatian, Slovenian, and English language, called CroSloEngual BERT. BERT (Bidirectional Encoder Representations from Transformers) was designed to help computers better understand ambiguity of words using word context [36]. The proposed model showed significant improvements for POS tagging, compared to multilingual BERT model [36].

Ljubešić and Lauc [39] presented an evaluation of their newly developed BERTić model for the tasks of MSD tagging, named entity recognition and sequence classification tasks. On the task of MSD tagging, BERTić model outperformed other models, but it was attributed to the larger amount of data presented to the BERTić model [39].

3 Experimental Setup

This section details the experimental setup used to implement the POS tagger for the Croatian language using RNN models. The experiments were conducted using Keras, a deep learning application programming interface (API), which runs on top of the TensorFlow, machine learning platform. The goal was to implement and compare different RNN models for the task of POS tagging texts in Croatian language.

In order to train and test the models, it was essential to obtain a corpus of properly tagged Croatian sentences. The publicly available corpus that was chosen was the Hr500k corpus. The Hr500k corpus is a reference corpus of Croatian texts containing a total of 900 documents divided into 24,794 sentences containing 506,457 words. The entire corpus is tagged with UPOS and MSD (MULTEXT-East) tags. Analysis of the corpus showed that the training set contains 20 159 sentences with a total of 415 328 tagged words, which are tagged with 17 UPOS tags (see Table 1). Furthermore, the test set has 2 672 sentences with 51 364 tagged words, also tagged with 17 UPOS.

Table 1. POS tags in train and test sets (%)

	train set (%)	test set (%)		train set (%)	test set (%)
NOUN	22.53	21.10			
PUNCT	12.08	13.13	DET	4.20	3.83
ADJ	11.06	11.04	PRON	3.86	3.98
VERB	9.70	9.50	SCONJ	2.87	2.96
ADP	8.94	8.84	PART	1.77	1.89
AUX	6.23	6.39	NUM	1.51	1.66
ADV	5.20	5.13	X	1.02	1.25
PROPN	4.56	4.70	INTJ	0.06	0.10
CCONJ	4.39	4.44	SYM	0.04	0.07

The neural network expects numerical data as an input, which is why there was a need for a numerical representation of the input text. For this reason, the first necessary step was to convert a sequence of words of the annotated corpus into a series of integers. For example, the sentence from the corpus ['Volim', 'pjevati', '.'], with its corresponding tags ['VERB', 'VERB', 'PUNCT'], gets converted into [472, 6540, 2], with its corresponding tags set as [2, 4].

In order for neural network to work efficiently it is necessary for input data to be of equal or similar shape (in this case equal lengths). So, the next step was to define equal lengths of all sentences in the corpus because it contained sentences of different lengths. On average, sentences in the corpus have about 20 words, while the longest sentence has 255 words and the shortest has only one word. In order to set all sentences to an equal length, it was necessary to either extend short sentences or shorten long sentences to a fixed length. Sentence length of 50 words was selected as a fixed sentence length. After this step, the example sentence ['Volim', 'pjevati', '.'], gets converted into [0, 0, 0, 0, 0, 0, 0, 0, 0, 0, 0, 0, 0, 0, 0, 0, 0, 0, 0, 0, 0, 0, 0, 0, 0, 0, 0, 0, 0, 0, 0, 0, 0, 0, 0, 0, 0, 0, 0, 0, 0, 0, 0, 472, 6540, 2], with its corresponding tags [0, 0, 0, 0, 0, 0, 0, 0, 0, 0, 0, 0, 0, 0, 0, 0, 0, 0, 0, 0, 0, 0, 0, 0, 0, 0, 0, 0, 0, 0, 0, 0, 0, 0, 0, 0, 0, 0, 0, 0, 0, 0, 0, 0, 4, 4, 2].

Word embeddings is a type of numerical representation of words that allows words of similar meanings to have a similar numerical representation where individual words are represented as vectors of real values in a predefined vector space [10]. Each word is mapped to one vector, and vector values are learned in a way reminiscent of a neural network. Therefore, the technique is often placed in the field of deep learning [10]. The standard for developing pre-trained word embeddings has become a Word2vec model. Word2vec is a natural language processing technique that uses the Continuous Bag of Words (CBOW) or Skip-gram shallow neural network to create a Word2vec model that understands the connections between words in a given text [35]. The result of learning is the so-called embedding matrix, which contains vector representations of words. For morphologically rich languages, it is possible to improve these representations with embeddings for character n-grams, representing words as the average of these embeddings [40]. That is what the FastText model does as an extension to Word2vec model. However, the weights needed for the next steps were calculated using Word2vec model, not FastText. For further research, the use of FastText could also be explored.

For training it was necessary to divide the training set into two parts: the training set and the validation set. A training set is a set for which weights are calculated and a set from which the model learns. A validation set is a set used to evaluate models during training and adjust model parameters.

3.1 Training

When a neural network starts training and learning from the given input data, the weights, unless otherwise defined, are randomly initialized. Given that weights are an important part of the neural network and that they decide on the importance of input data, this kind of a start would not give good results. However, during training, these weights change, prediction error is reduced with each epoch, and in the end, the network produces high accuracy results. In short, training is carried out by randomly setting the weights to some starting values and using these weights to predict a certain number of tags. This prediction is compared with the correct tag and uses the loss function to find a way to reduce the predication error. After the prediction error is reduced, the weights are reset, a certain number of tags are re-predicted, they are compared with the correct tags, a way to reduce the error is found, and so on again.

Considering different initial weights that the neural network can use during training, three RNN models have been implemented. They all have the architecture as shown in Fig. 3, but differ in the method of setting the initial weights of the model. RNN1 is a model with arbitrarily initialized weights that are not updated during training, RNN2 is a model with arbitrarily initialized weights that are updated during training and RNN3 is a model with weights generated by the Word2vec model, which are updated during training. Using the same architecture LSTM networks were also implemented, and the only difference is in replacing the RNN layer with the LSTM layer. Given the different initial weights, there are also three LSTM models. LSTM1 is a model with arbitrarily initialized weights that are updated during training and LSTM2 is a model with weights generated by the Word2vec model (which are updated during training). BiLSTM is a two-way LSTM model with weights generated by the Word2vec model (which are updated during training).

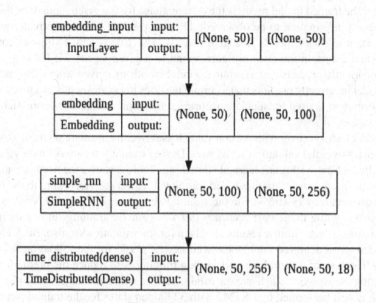

Fig. 3. RNN architecture.

Each of the implemented architectures is a simple neural network model that has an embedding layer, RNN layer and a dense layer (see Fig. 3). Embedding layer is a vectorization layer which transforms the words of input sentences into a dimension 100 vector. The RNN layer receives the output of the previous layer, i.e. a list of sentences of shape 50 × 100. After the data passes through this layer, the output is of shape 50 × n (n is the number of hidden states of the layer). Dense layer is a fully connected layer that selects the appropriate POS tag, and serves as the output layer of the model where the data is of shape 50 × 18: each sentence consists of 50 words, and each word is represented by a vector whose length corresponds to the total number of UPOS tags.

Hyperparameter tuning was done by changing the batch size, the number of hidden states and the number of epochs. For experimentation purposes, all the models were trained with 16, 32 and 256 hidden states. The number of epochs chosen for training was 10 and the batch size was 32. The loss function used was categorical crossentropy (computes the crossentropy loss between the labels and predictions), the optimizer used was Adam (stochastic gradient descent method) and the activation function was softmax (assigns probabilities to each class). In order to make the models perform better, two regularization methods were tried, L1 and L2. However, the models showed slightly better accuracies for L2 method, which was finally used in training of all models.

4 Evaluation

To evaluate how well the trained models have learned to predict the POS tags for the given text, implemented models can be compared during training (with respect to the validation set), and after training (by comparing the predictions of the model with the exact tags from the test dataset). The metrics that are observed during training are accuracy and loss. After the trained model predicts the different tags for the given input data, there are four types of information to be observed: TP (true positive - model correctly predicts that a certain tag corresponds to a given word), TN (true negative - model correctly predicts that a certain tag does not correspond to a given word), FP (false positive - model incorrectly predicts that a certain tag corresponds to a given word), false negative (FN - model incorrectly predicts that a certain tag does not corresponds to a given word). This information is used to calculate accuracy, precision, recall and f-score metrics on the test dataset.

Training history, along with accuracy and losses over the training set, provides those same metrics over the validation set as well. During training, the model uses validation set to validate how well it has learned something. Table 2 shows the accuracy and loss values of the models for training set and for the validation set. According to the results, the highest accuracy (99.96%) for the training set is achieved by BiLSTM with 32 hidden states, while the lowest accuracy (99.47%) for the training set has the RNN3 with 16 hidden states. Similar results are given for the validation set also. BiLSTM with 256 hidden states achieved the highest accuracy (97.49%) for the validation set during training. The task of a neural network during training is to reduce the prediction error by updating the weights to achieve the minimum loss which is measured by loss value. This task is best performed by LSTM2 with 32 hidden states for the training set and by BiLSTM with 256 hidden states for the validation set (see Table 2).

Trained models are further used to generate predictions of POS tags on the test set. Accuracy and precision were calculated for each of the implemented neural network architectures on the test set (see Table 3). The model with the highest percentage of accurately assigned POS tags proved to be the RNN1 model with 32 hidden states (a simple RNN model with randomly initialized weights that are not changed during training), with an accuracy of 78.57%. The lowest accuracy achieved the RNN2 model with 32 hidden states model (model with arbitrarily defined weights that are updated during training) with an accuracy of 76.38%. It can be observed that the differences between accuracies of the given models are almost insignificant; all accuracies are around 76% or 78%.

To summarize, BiLSTM model achieved the highest accuracy during the training, both on training set (99.96%) and validation set (97.49%). But, on the test set the highest accuracy (78.57%) was achieved by the RNN1 model with 32 hidden states. Furthermore, prediction accuracies for both of these models can be checked individually for each of the UPOS tags. This is done to find out what are the most often made mistakes by both of these models. It can be observed that the BiLSTM model made the greatest number of mistakes by predicting tags NUM (numbers), X (other or unknown words) and PROPN (proper nouns) (see Table 4). When tagging sentences from test set, BiLSTM model makes the most mistakes tagging words as nouns instead of an adjective (2376 mistakes), as verbs instead of nouns (1801 mistakes) or nouns instead of adjectives (1659 mistakes) (see

Table 2. Accuracy and loss values for training set and validation set

	accuracy	loss	val_accuracy	val_loss
RNN2(16)	0.9976	0.0679	0.9652	0.1555
RNN2(32)	0.9992	0.0213	0.9671	0.2050
RNN2(256)	0.9985	0.0586	0.9673	0.1257
RNN3(16)	0.9947	0.0789	0.9663	0.1351
RNN3(32)	0.9984	0.0300	0.9669	0.1797
RNN3(256)	0.9968	0.0588	0.9676	0.1158
LSTM1(16)	0.9976	0.0852	0.9657	0.1438
LSTM1(32)	0.9958	0.1133	0.9674	0.1233
LSTM1(256)	0.9976	0.0741	0.9671	0.1252
LSTM2(16)	0.9959	0.0864	0.9665	0.1389
LSTM2(32)	0.9991	0.0277	0.9677	0.1814
LSTM2(256)	0.9977	0.0597	0.9693	0.1113
BLSTM(16)	0.9959	0.1094	0.9718	0.1156
BLSTM(32)	0.9996	0.0449	0.9721	0.1265
BLSTM(256)	0.9993	0.0503	0.9749	0.0959

Table 3. Accuracy, precision and recall for test set

	accuracy	precision	recall		accuracy	precision	recall
RNN1(16)	0.7823	0.2799	0.2919	LSTM1(16)	0.7657	0.2933	0.2936
RNN1(32)	0.7857	0.3022	0.2987	LSTM1(32)	0.7666	0.2969	0.2975
RNN1(256)	0.7818	0.2968	0.2940	LSTM1(256)	0.7662	0.2967	0.2976
RNN2(16)	0.7647	0.2928	0.2925	LSTM2(16)	0.7669	0.2981	0.2987
RNN2(32)	0.7638	0.2922	0.2895	LSTM2(32)	0.7660	0.2978	0.2957
RNN2(256)	0.7667	0.2987	0.2991	LSTM2(256)	0.7668	0.2974	0.2969
RNN3(16)	0.7662	0.2958	0.2953	BLSTM(16)	0.7670	0.2985	0.2979
RNN3(32)	0.7656	0.2929	0.2926	BLSTM(32)	0.7671	0.2953	0.2951
RNN3(256)	0.7664	0.2972	0.2965	BLSTM(256)	0.7678	0.2995	0.2985

Table 4). The most common mistakes of RNN1 model are tagging words as nouns instead of adjectives (4006 mistakes), verbs (2889 mistakes), propositions (1782 mistakes) or determinants (907 mistakes) (see Table 5).

The further analysis showed that 230 sentences, out of 2672 sentences of test dataset, had 50% correctly predicted tags per sentence, 145 sentences had around 33% correctly tagged words and 120 sentences had 40% correctly tagged words (see Table 6). Only 17

Table 4. Most common mistakes of BiLSTM model

correct tag	ADJ	VERB	NOUN	NOUN	PROPN	PRON	VERB
predicted	NOUN	NOUN	ADJ	VERB	NOUN	DET	ADJ
number of mistakes	2376	1801	1659	1640	986	864	863

Table 5. Most common mistakes of RNN1 model with 32 hidden states

correct tag	ADJ	VERB	PROPN	ADV	DET	PRON	NOUN
predicted	NOUN	NOUN	NOUN	NOUN	NOUN	DET	VERB
number of mistakes	4006	2889	1782	1152	907	828	743

Table 6. Correctly tagged words per sentence of RNN1 model

Correctly tagged words per sentence (%)	Number of sentences
50	230
33.33	145
40	120
…	…
86.67	1
88.89	1
100	17

sentences in the test dataset had all tags correctly predicted. So, out of 2672 sentences, 2655 sentences had at least one wrongly tagged word. It gives the per-sentence accuracy of 0.6% for RNN1 model on test dataset. For BiLSTM model, per-sentence accuracy of 0.45% was achieved. The results showed that the greatest number of sentences, 188 out of 2672, had 50% correctly predicted tags and only 12 sentences had all correctly predicted tags (Table 7). Focusing on sentence length (see Table 8), the sentences of lengths 40–50, the longest sentences in dataset, on average had 37.52% correctly predicted tags. Sentences that had less than 10 words on average had 32.52% correctly predicted tags. On average, the longer sentences had greater number of correctly predicted tags then the sentences with fewer words (Table 8).

Table 7. Correctly tagged words per sentence of BiLSTM model

Correctly tagged words per sentence (%)	Number of sentences
50	188
33.33	175
40	124
...	...
85.71	1
87.50	1
100	12

Table 8. Correctly predicted tags per sentence length

Number of words in a sentence	Correctly predicted tags (%)
50	35.76
49	38.01
48	34.03
...	...
3	31.11
2	32.14
1	31.58

5 Conclusion

This paper gives an overview of methods used for POS tagging and the application of neural networks for such a task. The workings of RNN neural network models are described and their application in POS tagging is presented through an overview of available research. Various RNN architectures are implemented to obtain models that would learn to annotate Croatian texts with UPOS tags. Simple RNN model with 32 hidden states achieved the highest accuracy of 78.57%.

The Croatian language is considered morphologically very rich language, which proved to be more challenging for computerized natural language processing than analytical languages, such as English. With this in mind, standard POS tags are not enough to describe and asses its complex structure which is why most research focuses on MSD tagging [25, 28]. For this reason, there is a need for further research and a thorough comparison of different neural network architectures for both POS and MSD tagging of the Croatian language. As proposed by several other authors [22, 25, 26] it is a good idea to combine RNN models with other POS methods which should yield even better accuracies for the POS tagging of Croatian language.

References

1. Acedański, S.: A morphosyntactic brill tagger for inflectional languages. In: Loftsson, H., Rögnvaldsson, E., Helgadóttir, S. (eds.) NLP 2010. LNCS (LNAI), vol. 6233, pp. 3–14. Springer, Heidelberg (2010). https://doi.org/10.1007/978-3-642-14770-8_3
2. Agić, Ž., Tadić, M.: Evaluating morphosyntactic tagging of Croatian texts. In: Proceedings of the 5th International Conference on Language Resources and Evaluation Genova: ELRA (2006)
3. Agić, Ž., Ljubešić, N., Merkler, D.: Lemmatization and morphosyntactic tagging of Croatian and Serbian. In: Proceedings of the 4th Biennial International Workshop on Balto-Slavic Natural Language Processing, pp. 48–57. Association for Computational Linguistics, Sofia (2013)
4. Agić, Ž., Tadić, M., Dovedan, Z.: Combining part-of-speech tagger and inflectional lexicon for Croatian. In: Erjavec, T., Žganec Gros, J. (eds.) Proceedings of the 6th Language Technologies Conference, pp. 116–121. Institute Jožef Stefan, Ljubljana (2008)
5. Agić, Ž., Tadić, M., Dovedan, Z.: Improving part-of-speech tagging accuracy for croatian by morphological analysis. In: Informatica, Ljubljana, Slovenia, pp. 445–451 (2008)
6. Agić, Ž., Tadić, M., Dovedan, Z.: Tagger voting improves morphosyntactic tagging accuracy on Croatian texts. In: Lužar-Stiffler, V., Jarec, I., Bekić, Z. (eds.) Proceedings of the 32nd International Conference on Information Technology Interfaces. SRCE University Computer Centre, pp. 61–66. University of Zagreb, Croatia (2010)
7. Alkhwiter, W., Al-Twairesh, N.: Part-of-speech tagging for Arabic tweets using CRF and Bi-LSTM. Comput. Speech Lang. (65) (2021)
8. Ananda, M.R., Hanifmuti, M.Y., Alfina, I.: A hybrid of rule-based and hmm-based part-of-speech tagger for Indonesian. In: International Conference on Asian Language Processing, Singapore, Singapore, pp. 280–285 (2021)
9. Balwant, M.K.: Bidirectional LSTM basedOn POS tags and CNN architecture for fake news detection. In: 10th International Conference on Computing, Communication and Networking Technologies (ICCCNT), Kanpur, India, pp. 1–6 (2019)
10. Machine Learning Mastery. https://machinelearningmastery.com/what-are-word-embeddings. Accessed 10 Sept 2022
11. Chiche, A., Yitagesu, B.: Part of speech tagging: a systematic review of deep learning and machine learning approaches. J. Big Data 9(1), 1–25 (2022). https://doi.org/10.1186/s40537-022-00561-y
12. DEVOPEDIA, Part-of-Speech Tagging. https://devopedia.org/part-of-speech-tagging. Accessed 05 Sept 2022
13. Dinarelli, M., Tellier, I.: New recurrent neural network variants for sequence labeling. In: Gelbukh, A. (eds) Computational Linguistics and Intelligent Text Processing. CICLing, Lecture Notes in Computer Science, vol 9623. Springer, Cham (2016)
14. ELEMENTS OF AI. https://course.elementsofai.com. Accessed 09 Sept 2022
15. Farizki Wicaksono A., Purwarianti, A.: HMM based part-of-speech tagger for bahasa Indonesia. In: Proceedings of the 4th International MALINDO (Malaysian-Indonesian Language) Workshop (2010)
16. Hasan, F.M.: Comparison of Different POS Tagging Techniques for Some South Asian Languages. BRAC University, Thesis (2006)
17. Hirschberg, J., Manning, C.D.: Advances in natural language processing. In: Science, vol. 349, pp. 261–266 (2015)
18. INVESTOPEDIA. https://www.investopedia.com/terms/n/neuralnetwork.asp. Accessed 09 Sept 2022

19. Juhár, J., Staš, J., Hladek, D.: Dagger: the slovak morphological classifier. In: Proceedings ELMAR-2012, Zadar, Croatia (2012)
20. Jurafsky, D., Martin, J.H.: Speech and Language Processing, 2nd edn. Prentice Hall, Upper Saddlr River (2008)
21. Kumar, A.: Hidden Markov Models Explained with Examples, In: Data Analytics, https://vitalflux.com/hidden-markov-models-concepts-explained-with-examples/, last accessed 2022/09/06
22. Kumar, N.K.S., Malarvizhi, N.: Bi-directional LSTM-CNN combined method for sentiment analysis in part of speech tagging (PoS). In: International Journal of Speech Technologies, vol. 23, pp. 373–380 (2020)
23. Kumawat, D., Jain, V.: POS tagging approaches: a comparison. Int. J. Comput. Appl. **118**, 32–38 (2015)
24. Lorincz, B., Nutu, M., Stan, A.: Romanian Part of Speech Tagging using LSTM Networks, In: IEEE 15th International Conference on Intelligent Computer Communication and Processing, pp. 223–228. (2019)
25. Ljubešić, N., Dobrovoljc, K.: What does neural bring? analysing improvements in morphosyntactic annotation and lemmatisation of Slovenian, Croatian and Serbian. In: Proceedings of the 7th Workshop on Balto-Slavic Natural Language Processing, pp. 29–34 (2019)
26. Maimaiti, M., Wumaier, A., Abiderexiti, K., Yibulayin, T.: Bidirectional long short-term memory network with a conditional random field layer for uyghur part-of-speech tagging. Information **8**, 157 (2017)
27. Marques, N., Lopes, G.: A Neural Network Approach to Part-of-Speech Tagging (2008). https://www.researchgate.net/publication/250806272_A_Neural_Network_A pproach_to_Part-of-Speech_Tagging
28. Meftah, S., Semmar, N., Sadat, F., Raaijmakers, S.: Using neural transfer learning for morphosyntactic tagging of south-slavic languages tweets. In: Proceedings of the Fifth Workshop on NLP for Similar Languages, Varieties and Dialects, pp. 235–243. (2018)
29. Megyesi, B.: Brill's rule-based PoS tagger. Thesis. University of Stockholm, Sweden (2001)
30. PATHMIND. A Beginner's Guide to Neural Networks and Deep Learning. http://wiki.pat hmind.com/neural-network. Accessed 06 Sept 2022
31. Peradin, H., Šnajder, J.: Towards a constraint grammar based morphological tagger for Croatian. In: International Conference on Text, Speech and Dialogue, pp. 174–182 (2012)
32. Phi, M.: Illustrated Guide to LSTM's and GRU's: A step by step explanation, Medium. https://towardsdatascience.com/illustrated-guide-to-lstms-and-gru-s-a-step-by-step-explanation-44e9eb85bf21. Accessed 09 Sept 2022
33. Qiao, M., Bian, W., Xu, R.Y., Tao, D.: Diversified hidden markov models for sequential labeling. In: IEEE 32nd International Conference on Data Engineering, pp. 1512–1513 (2016)
34. SIMPLILEARN. Recurrent Neural Network (RNN) Tutorial: Types and Examples. https://www.simplilearn.com/tutorials/deep-learning-tutorial/rnn. Accessed 06 Sept 2022
35. Svoboda, L., Beliga, S.: Evaluation of Croatian word embeddings. In: Proceedings of the Eleventh International Conference on Language Resources and Evaluation, pp. 1512–1518 (2018)
36. Ulčar, M., Robnik-Sikonja, M.: FinEst BERT and CroSloEngual BERT: less is more in multilingual models. In: International Conference on Text, Speech, and Dialogue, pp. 104–111 (2020)
37. Zvornicanin, E.: Differences Between Bidirectional and Unidirectional LSTM. Baeldung on Computer Science. https://www.baeldung.com/cs/bidirectional-vs-unidirectional-lstm. Accessed 10 Sept 2022
38. Živković-Mandić, J. Gramatika hrvatskoga jezika. Oktatási Hivatal (2021)
39. Ljubešić, N., Lauc, D.: BERTić -- The Transformer Language Model for Bosnian, Croatian, Montenegrin and Serbian. ArXiv (2021)

40. Krithika V.: Introduction to fasttext embeddings and its implication. In: Analytics Vidhya (2023). https://www.analyticsvidhya.com/blog/2023/01/introduction-to-fasttext-embeddings-and-its-implication/
41. Li, H., Mao, H., Wang, J.: Part-of-speech tagging with rule-based data preprocessing and transformer. Electronics **11**, 56 (2021)

Web Scraping Fire Incidents and Assessment of Fire Impact - A Case Study of Split and Dalmatia County Fires

Selena Knežić Buhovac[1]([✉]), Ljiljana Šerić[2], Antonia Ivanda[2],
and Damir Krstinić[2]

[1] Faculty of Mechanical Engineering, Computing and Electrical Engineering,
University of Mostar, Mostar, Bosnia and Herzegovina
`selena.knezic@fsre.sum.ba`
[2] Faculty of Electrical Engineering, Mechanical Engineering and Naval Architecture,
University of Split, Split, Republic of Croatia
`{ljiljana,Antonia.Senta.00,damir.krstinic}@fesb.hr`

Abstract. This paper presents a framework for initiating a fire incidents database using web scraping and impact assessment techniques. The methodology used for correct space, time, and impact association is described. The dataset used in this study was collected from media reports published daily by the Croatian Fire Association during a specific period. Each incident in the collected data was assigned an estimated time of occurrence and evaluated for its impact level. The study includes a comparison of the obtained results with the official reports of fire impact. In this context, impact refers to the extent of damage caused by the fire incident.

Keywords: Web scraping · regular expressions · text mining

1 Introduction

1.1 Motivation

The motivation for this paper was to construct a comprehensive dataset on fire incidents. It is necessary to gather information on all relevant aspects of each fire, including its location, date and time of occurrence, cause, severity, and any damage or loss caused. By analyzing this dataset, it is possible to identify patterns in the spatial and temporal distribution of fires, enabling us to determine the areas and times that are most susceptible to fire outbreaks, and the factors that contribute to their frequency and intensity. This information can then be utilized to formulate effective fire prevention and management strategies and to develop emergency response plans that are more efficient. Ultimately, the aim is to minimize the impact of fires on people, property, and the environment, and to foster greater safety and resilience in communities that are affected by this hazard.

D. Vasić and M. Kundid Vasić (Eds.): MoStart 2023, CCIS 1827, pp. 63–76, 2023.
https://doi.org/10.1007/978-3-031-36833-2_5

1.2   Related Work

Web scraping, which is also referred to as web extraction or harvesting, involves the process of extracting information from the World Wide Web (WWW) and storing it in a file system or database for future use or analysis [1]. The main objective of web scraping is to gather data from websites and convert it into a structured format, such as spreadsheets, databases, or comma-separated values (CSV) files, that is easily interpretable and usable for analysis or other purposes [2]. There are several web scraping methods and they are described and compared in paper [3]. The listed methods are regular expressions or Regex. Regex is a pattern consisting of specific characters and symbols that define a set of words or characters across multiple alphabets [4]. Next listed is HTML DOM. The HTML Document Object Model (HTML DOM) is a widely accepted standard used to manipulate HTML elements by accessing, modifying, adding, or removing them from a web page [5]. XPath is also a web scraping method. It's a fundamental component of the XSLT standard (Stylesheet Language Transformation), and it allows for the traversal of elements and attributes within XML (eXtensible Markup Language) documents [6].

Official and user-generated content published on the web and social media are a useful tools for emergency assessment [7] and public opinion mining. Web scrapping coupled with sentiment analysis and opinion mining techniques have been used for assessment of public opinion about COVID-19 [8], enforced measures [9], governmental decisions [10], war [11], climate change [12] and emergency responses. Infectious diseases [13], wildfires [14], earthquakes [15] are emergency events where social involvement is expected and online texts can be used as a sensor [16] for impact assessment. Emotions towards specific emergency events can be assessed using various techniques, such as keywords and Sentiment lexicon model [17], statistical approaches like TF-IDF, LDA (Latent Dirichlet Allocation) or LSA (LDA) [18] or deep learning techniques [19]. However, the credibility of such user-generated content is not verified, and lots of efforts are invested in the assurance of the quality and credibility of such data [20]. Official reports and structured text mining has been extensively used in medical data examination [21]. Assessment of drought effects including fires [22], classification techniques of narratives about the accident has been reviewed in [23].

Wildfires are a significant threat to ecosystems, wildlife, and human life. Understanding the factors that contribute to the occurrence and severity of wildfires is crucial for effective prevention and management. However, obtaining and analyzing data on past fire events can be challenging due to the unstructured nature of the available information.

Text mining techniques provide a means of extracting structured data from unstructured sources such as official reports. By leveraging these techniques, we can construct a dataset that facilitates the analysis of fire event data on a larger scale. This structured data can be used to identify trends and patterns in fire occurrence, assess the effectiveness of mitigation measures, and make informed decisions about future prevention strategies.

Moreover, the proposed measure of wildfire impact can provide a standardized method of evaluating the severity and consequences of a fire event. By comparing this measure to real-world impact, it can help researchers and policymakers to better understand the efficacy of prevention and mitigation efforts and make more informed decisions about future prevention strategies.

Overall, the use of text mining techniques to construct structured datasets and measure wildfire impact represents a valuable approach to understanding and managing the threat of wildfires. By harnessing the power of machine learning we can better analyze and interpret the data on fire occurrence and impacts, and take more effective steps to prevent and mitigate the devastating effects of these natural disasters.

2   Materials and Methods

2.1   Study Area

Croatia is one of the countries at a high risk of forest fires, particularly during the summer season. Seven coastal counties, including the Adriatic islands, face a constant threat of high to very high fire risks, mainly because of densely-packed conifer forests [24]. The Split-Dalmatia County (SD County) is the largest of the 21 counties in Croatia, with a size of 14106.40 km^2 [25] and is the focus of this paper. It is located in the central part of the Adriatic coast, and its location is shown in Fig. 1. SD County is known for its beautiful coastline and islands, historical cities, and cultural heritage. The probability of fires occurring and spreading is significantly increased due the warm and arid summers, strong dry winds, and Mediterranean terrain and vegetation [26]. SD County is a beautiful and unique region with a rich history and culture, but it is also facing significant challenges related to climate change and other environmental issues. In general, wildfires in Split-Dalmatia County have become more frequent and severe in recent years due to a combination of factors, including climate change, land-use practices, and human activity. These fires can be especially challenging to fight due to the region's rugged terrain, dry vegetation, and strong winds, which can cause flames to spread rapidly and unpredictably.

To combat these fires, firefighting agencies in Split-Dalmatia County and throughout Croatia have developed sophisticated systems for detection, response, and prevention. These systems include ground crews, aerial assets, and specialized equipment such as bulldozers and water bombers. They also rely on close coordination and communication among agencies at the local, regional, and national levels.

2.2   Data Source

In this paper, we used data about fire incidents in the study area from a period of two years (2021 and 2022) from two different sources. Text from The Croatian Fire Association (CFA) media reports and intervention management records from Fire Intervention Management System (FIMS).

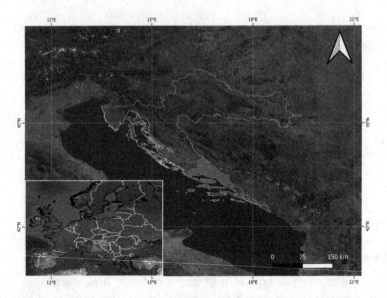

Fig. 1. Geographic location of Split Dalmatia County in the Republic of Croatia in the context of Europe

The Croatian Fire Association (CFA) Media Reports: The CFA is the primary government agency accountable for fire suppression and regularly publishes official reports regarding significant fire interventions throughout Croatia [27]. These reports are in the format of short concise texts that contains crucial information about recent events. Usually, the text contains the date, time, and describes the type of fire, number of firefighters, fire vehicles, aerial vehicles, and other essential details related to the incident. The majority of posts are recognized in a structured manner, following a template that ensures consistency across all reports. An example of a post translation in English would be:

> *"On February 2 at 4:51 p.m., ŽVOC Šibenik received a report about a fire in an open space in the area of Zablaće. It was a fire of grass, low vegetation, and maquis on an area of 4 ha. 28 firefighters with 10 fire engines from IVP Šibenik, JVP Šibenik and Vodice, DVD Šibenik, Zablača and Brodarica-Krapanj took part in the firefighting intervention."*

From the post content it can be easily derived that:

- Date of fire: February 2nd
- Report time: 4:51 PM
- The fire occurred in a location: Šibenik-Knin County
- The near location: Zablaće
- Type of incident: Fire of grass, low vegetation, and maquis
- The burned area: 4 ha
- Number of firefighters involved: 28
- Number of vehicles: 10

By utilizing this source and applying automatic extraction of data from text, we were able to compile a comprehensive dataset of fire incidents, which enabled us to conduct a detailed analysis of the spatial and temporal distribution of fires in Croatia. The data provided by the CFA is highly reliable, making it a valuable resource for researchers and policymakers alike.

However, the textual format makes it unusable for analysis of trends, states, and fire impact assessment. Extraction of quantitative description from pure text gives us material for visualization and assessment of fire-related events in the area. The insights gained from the analysis of the quantified dataset can be used to develop more effective fire prevention and management strategies, reducing the impact of wildfires on people, property, and the environment. Since the CFA posts are available online on official CFA web page [27] we were able to implement a web scrapping software that will collect the texts, extract description of each post and store the collection of texts in a dataset.

Fire Intervention Management System (FIMS): The data from the FIMS [28] was analyzed as the second source of information. This system provides official records of all firefighting interventions. In this work we used only records of wildfires and their corresponding interventions. The FIMS is updated on a daily basis within the Republic of Croatia. The data used in this study include date, location of the wildfire, and details such as the number of firefighters, firefighting trucks, and aircrafts engaged, and the size of the burned area. This dataset is fully structured and formatted as a table of intervention records, where each row represents an intervention, and columns are associated with information about the intervention. In our work, we used the intervention records as ground truth data describing the situation and impact of fire in the study area. Furthermore, we proposed an equation for calculating quantitative measure of fire impact on a daily basis. This measure was used as a ground truth description of a day's fire impact in the study area.

The FIMS database is an official database with restricted access. The database content used in this research was received on request from the County Firefighting Association of Split and Dalmatia County.

2.3   Data Mining

The data from the CFA dataset were written in the form of posts, and we needed to preprocess them so that they could be further analyzed and compared with the FIMS data. Using data mining we came to further results. Data mining is a fundamental step in the process of uncovering knowledge, which seeks to identify stimulating and potentially valuable insights from large sets of data [29]. As first step of data mining, keywords were obtained to calculate the fire impact. It will be mentioned detailed in Sect. 2.4 about Impact assessment. Moreover, we narrowed our focus to wildfires that occurred exclusively in Split-Dalmatia County during the two years period, from January 1st, 2021 to January 1st, 2023. To obtain the necessary data for our research, we utilized regular expressions to extract the numerical values from the CFA's posts. Regular expressions, also known as Regexes, offer a powerful tool for searching and identifying text based on patterns rather than precise matches, thus providing an abstraction of keyword search [30]. Regexes are often used in data mining as a tool for pattern recognition and data extraction. Posts describe the size of burned area and the number of firefighters, vehicles, and aircrafts engaged in fire extinguishing. Numerical values representing this information were extracted. One additional parameter used to measure the severity of a wildfire is the number of words used to describe it in CFA posts. The assumption is that the more words are used, the larger and more complex the fire was, and the more resources were required to contain and extinguish it. As a general rule, one media report post was published per day. On some days there were no posts at all regarding fire interventions in the study area. However, on days when there were multiple interventions on fires with high impacts, more than one post was published. For such situations, we aggregated the impact of all posts regarding the study for a day and summed all numerical values extracted from texts.

The dataset with quantitative descriptions of posts is depicted in Table 1. The table only shows the first few rows of the dataset.

Statistical description of the obtained dataset is shown in Table 2.

To extract the relevant data from FIMS, we applied a straightforward filter based on the dates of January 1st, 2021 to January 1st, 2023, and limited our search to records related to wildfires in Split-Dalmatia County. Other methods were not necessary as FIMS is a database that only includes numerical values such as the number of firefighters, vehicles involved, and the burned area, along with the date and duration of each intervention.

Table 1. from media report posts

	Date	Burned Area (Ha)	Number of vehicles	Number of firefighters	Number of air forces	Total number of words
0	2021-01-03	10.00	2	3	0	621
1	2021-01-04	10.00	0	0	0	193
2	2021-01-06	0.00	17	70	0	550
3	2021-01-17	0.00	6	16	0	345
4	2021-01-21	15.00	20	80	0	472
5	2021-01-22	0.00	20	80	0	400
6	2021-02-16	3.00	10	38	0	377
...	...	...	...	...	...	...

Table 2. Statistical description of dataset extracted from media report posts

	Burned Area (Ha)	Number of vehicles	Number of firefighters	Number of air forces	Total number of words
count	97	97	97	97	97
mean	35.31	13.37	32.21	26.57	409.98
std	171.78	43.65	58.19	209.24	147.65
min	0	0	0	0	111
25%	0	0	0	0	322
50%	5	3	16	0	379
75%	14	13	47	1	484
max	1643	417	445	2023	975

For gaining better results normalization was applied to collected data in dataframes. Normalization refers to the method of modifying attribute data in order to achieve a desired and predefined range, which can potentially enhance the efficiency of data mining [31].

2.4 Impact Assessment

In the scope of this paper, we define the impact of fire as a measure describing how rough the fire situation was on the day in the study area. There are several features that can describe the fire impact, such as burned area, number of interventions, total duration of interventions, number of firefighters/vehicles/aircrafts involved in interventions, but each one of them is insufficient by itself. Thus we define our cumulative measure of fire impact that will be used for impact assessment based on available data. We assume that FIMS system holds accurate and precise information about intervention and thus we use FIMS based impact assessment as truth and accurate fire impact. This impact assessment is based on a simple calculation that takes into account a cumulative number of participants in all fire interventions on a specific day, and duration of interventions. As a part of this paper, we examined the possibility to make an impact assessment from pure text. Keywords and numerical values extracted from the text, such as burned areas, the number of firefighters, vehicles, and firefighters, were utilized to predict how big/severe the fire situation in the observed area actually was. We propose a measure of situation severity in the observed study area that is based on actual intervention data from FIMS.

For FIMS data, the impact was defined and calculated with the equation:

$$i = num\_firefig + num\_ve + d \qquad (2.1)$$

where

i is the impact,
$num\_firefig$ is the number of firefighters who participated in extinguishing the wildfire,
num_ve is the number of fire trucks who participated in extinguishing the wildfire, and
d is duration of intervention

2.5 Simple Moving Average (SMA)

A Simple Moving Average (SMA) is a widely used method of computing the average of the previous n data points in a time series dataset. The calculation involves equally weighting each data point, with no specific weighting factors applied.

$$SMA = \frac{P_M + P_{M-1} + ... + P_{M-(n-1)}}{n} \qquad (2.2)$$

where

P_M refers to the value of a data point at a specific time step, namely time M, n refers to the number of data points that are used in a calculation. It indicates the sample size of the data being analyzed.

When calculating successive values, a new data point is included in the formula's summation, and the oldest data point is removed [32]. This process is known as a rolling calculation or rolling window, where the calculation is performed on a fixed window of the most recent n data points. As new data points become available, the window shifts forward in time and the oldest data point is dropped from the calculation. This allows for a dynamic calculation that can capture trends and changes in the data over time. This method was applied to time series of assessed fire impact after normalization. In this way, we smoothed the time series of impact values which resulted with a more robust time series and more observable seasonality, trends, and extremes. The time series of assessed fire impact for the two years period in the study area is shown in Fig. 2. We can clearly see the early spring and late summer periods as periods with higher fire impact.

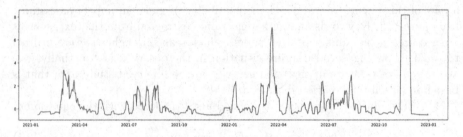

Fig. 2. Impact of fire in Split and Dalmatia County for each day for two years period

The objective of this research was to assess the fire impact directly from openly available data - the media reports- by automatically transforming the textual description into the numerical assessment of fire impact value based on features extracted from the text. However, the relationship between extracted features and the assessed fire impact is not straightforward. Thus we used additional transformation of values and searched for the non-linear relationship that would be able to predict the fire impact from future media reports without insight into fire intervention database data.

2.6   Horizontal Data Augmentation

To enhance the algorithm's performance, we aimed to optimize the dataset by augmenting it since the original dataset was limited to only 100 samples. However, gathering additional data was difficult, so we decided to use *feature augmentation* or *horizontal augmentation*. This approach involves synthetically increasing the number of features in the dataset. To achieve this, we applied four distinct transformations (logarithmic (2.3), square (2.4), square root (2.5), and reciprocal (2.6)) to each feature value F_i, including variables such as *hectares, vehicles, firefighters, aircrafts, and word count*, present in the dataset [33]. Using this method, we were able to expand the dataset horizontally, which resulted in more diverse and comprehensive data being available to feed into the algorithm.

$$valueLog = \log_{10}(F_i) \qquad (2.3)$$

$$valueSquare = F_i^2 \qquad (2.4)$$

$$valueRoot = \sqrt{F_i} \qquad (2.5)$$

$$valueRec = \frac{1}{F_i} \qquad (2.6)$$

2.7   Multiple Linear Regression Model

Multiple linear regression (MLR) is a commonly used statistical technique for modeling the relationship between a dependent variable (y) and two or more independent variables (x_i) referred to as explanatory variables, with the goal of predicting the value of the dependent variable [34]. In this study, the dependent variable is impact, which gives a certain weight to an individual post based on keywords related to the severity of a fire that occurred at a certain time. The equation [35] of a multiple linear regression model can be represented as (2.7):

$$y = \beta_0 + \beta_1 x_1 + \ldots + \beta_n x_n \qquad (2.7)$$

where:

y is the dependent variable or in our study impact,

β_0 is the intercept or bias which is only a constant number,

β_i are the regression coefficients represent the change in the dependent variable associated with a one-unit change in the corresponding explanatory variable, and

$x_{i(i=1,2,\ldots,n)}$ are the independent variables or features in our study, referred to as *hectares, vehicles, firefighters, aircrafts, and word count*.

3   Results

Two datasets were obtained as described in Sect. 2.2. Our objective is to predict the daily fire impact calculated on FIMS dataset from features extracted from CFA dataset. In order to achieve it we used multiple linear regression as described in the previous section. The dependent variable for prediction was the impact value after applying Eq. (2.7) on FIMS dataset, scaling, and moving average-based smoothing. The independent variables were variables extracted from the text and augmented using Eqs. (2.3),(2.4),(2.5), and (2.6). We merged the two obtained datasets using the date as the key value for merging. This means that the values extracted and accumulated for texts describing the fires on a date were associated with the value of fire impact after scaling and smoothing for the same date.

We implemented multiple linear regression algorithms based on sklearn library for Python programming language. The training of the MLR parameters was performed on the whole dataset since the amount of data was not sufficient for an efficient test train split. For the trained predictor we calculated the following evaluation metrics:

- R^2 score: The coefficient of determination, also known as R^2, is a statistical measure that quantifies how well a regression model fits the data by indicating the proportion of the variance in the dependent variable that can be explained by the independent variable(s). This measure can be calculated by dividing the explained variance by the total variance in the dependent variable, resulting in a value between 0 and 1, where a value of 1 indicates a perfect fit of the model to the data [36].
- MAE (Mean Absolute Error): statistical metric commonly used to evaluate the performance of a regression model. It measures the average of the squared differences between the predicted and actual values of the dependent variable across all data points [37].
- MSE (Mean Squared Error): a straightforward metric that is used to evaluate the accuracy of a regression model. It is calculated by taking the sum of the absolute differences between the predicted and actual values of the dependent variable, and then dividing that sum by the total number of data points [38].
- RMSE (Root Mean Squared Error): commonly used metric for evaluating the accuracy of a regression model. The calculation of RMSE involves three simple steps. First, the calculation of the total square error, which is the sum of the squared differences between the predicted and actual values of the dependent variable across all data points. This means that the larger errors have a greater impact on the total square error than the smaller errors, as they contribute more to the sum in proportion to their squared values. The next step is to divide the total square error by the number of data points to obtain the mean square error (MSE). This metric provides a measure of the average squared error of the model. Finally, taking the square root of the MSE to obtain the RMSE. This metric provides a measure of the average magnitude of the errors of the model, which is easier to interpret than the squared values of the MSE [38].

Evaluation results obtained for linear regression applied on the merged dataset are shown in Table 3.

Merging two datasets on dates resulted in a smaller dataset of only 100 rows. This may indicate that the datasets do not have a large overlap in their date ranges or that there are missing values that could not be filled through merging. In any case, a small dataset can limit the ability to perform linear regression analysis and may result in less reliable or less generalizable results. In further work extending the range of dates in CFA posts could be a useful step to obtain a larger dataset and potentially improve the results of the analysis.

Table 3. Results of linear regression, prediction of impact on FIMS data

Measure	Value
SCORE:	0.3769
MAE:	1.4629
MSE:	4.4016
RMSE:	2.0980

Finally we compared the time-series of predicted and assessed value of fire impact for the dates we had the media reports available. The time series plot is shown in Fig. 3. We can see that even though the exact values of fire impact were not predicted precisely, higher fire impact periods are correctly predicted only based on texts from the media reports.

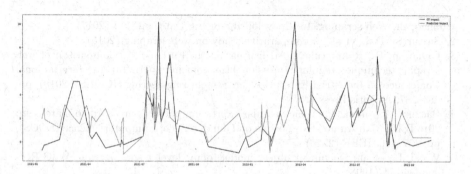

Fig. 3. Plot for impact and predicted impact

4   Conclusions

In this paper, we described, demonstrated, and evaluated a methodology for the assessment of fire impact for a period or date solely based on media report texts. The proposed methodology is based on structured information extracted from texts using regular expression and training an algorithm for impact prediction. In order to achieve this we defied the quantification for assessment of fire impact based on the official fire intervention database and the cumulative value of intervention efforts employed. The resulting model predicts the fire impact with a similar dynamic as the impact calculated on the official data, but the precision of prediction is not accurate. It is likely that the model needs to be improved in order to accurately predict the impact for FIMS based on the data available. This could involve using additional features or adjusting the model parameters to better fit the data. In addition, performance could be improved by training the model on a larger data set, which could be achieved by extending the observed time period over which the training data is taken. Further analysis and experimentation may be necessary to identify the best approach for improving the model's performance. In addition to the factors already considered in this research, it may be important to include the time lapse between when a fire occurs and when posts about the fire are made. This is because CFA posts may not be updated in real-time during an actual fire, and there could be a delay before relevant information is shared. However, the presented model can be used as a tool for assessment of fire impact dynamic in a season or for comparison of fire impact for longer period of time since it can be fully automated and does not require human engagement.

Acknowledgment. The authors would like to express their gratitude to the Split-Dalmatia County Firefighting Association for their contributions to this paper.

References

1. Zhao, B.: Web scraping. In: Encyclopedia of Big Data, pp. 1–3 (2017)
2. Sirisuriya, D.S., et al.: A comparative study on web scraping (2015)
3. Gunawan, R., Rahmatulloh, A., Darmawan, I., Firdaus, F.: Comparison of web scraping techniques: regular expression, html dom and xpath. In: 2018 International Conference on Industrial Enterprise and System Engineering (ICoIESE 2018), pp. 283–287. Atlantis Press (2019)
4. Backurs, A., Indyk, P.: Which regular expression patterns are hard to match? In: 2016 IEEE 57th Annual Symposium on Foundations of Computer Science (FOCS), pp. 457–466. IEEE (2016)
5. Wood, L., et al.: Document object model (dom) level 1 specification. W3C Recommend. **1** (1998)
6. Clark, J., DeRose, S., et al.: Xml path language (xpath) (1999)
7. Xuanhua, X., Yin, X., Chen, X.: A large-group emergency risk decision method based on data mining of public attribute preferences. Knowl.-Based Syst. **163**, 495–509 (2019)
8. Singh, M., Jakhar, A.K., Pandey, S.: Sentiment analysis on the impact of coronavirus in social life using the bert model. Soc. Netw. Anal. Min. **11**(1), 33 (2021)
9. Es-Sabery, F., et al.: A mapreduce opinion mining for covid-19-related tweets classification using enhanced id3 decision tree classifier. IEEE Access **9**, 58706–58739 (2021)
10. Stylios, G., et al.: Public opinion mining for governmental decisions. Electron. J. e-Gov. **8**(2), 202–213 (2010)
11. Chen, B., et al.: Public opinion dynamics in cyberspace on Russia-Ukraine war: a case analysis with Chinese weibo. IEEE Trans. Comput. Soc. Syst. **9**(3), 948–958 (2022)
12. Li, Z.: Chinese public perception of climate change on social media: an investigation based on data mining and text analysis. J. Environ. Public Health **2022** (2022)
13. García-Díaz, J.A., et al.: Opinion mining for measuring the social perception of infectious diseases. an infodemiology approach. In: Valencia-García, R., Alcaraz-Mármol, G., Del Cioppo-Morstadt, J., Vera-Lucio, N., Bucaram-Leverone, M. (eds.) CITI 2018. CCIS, vol. 883, pp. 229–239. Springer, Cham (2018). https://doi.org/10.1007/978-3-030-00940-3_17

14. Verma, S., et al.: Natural language processing to the rescue? extracting "situational awareness" tweets during mass emergency. In Proceedings of the International AAAI Conference on Web and Social Media, vol. 5, pp. 385–392 (2011)
15. Zheng, Z., Shi, H.Z., Zhou, Y.C., Lu, X.Z., Lin, J.R.: Earthquake impact analysis based on text mining and social media analytics. arXiv preprint arXiv:2212.06765 (2022)
16. Shi, K., Peng, X., Lu, H., Zhu, Y., Niu, Z.: Application of social sensors in natural disasters emergency management: a review. IEEE Trans. Comput. Social Syst. (2022)
17. Bernabé-Moreno, J., Tejeda-Lorente, A., Porcel, C., Fujita, H., Herrera-Viedma, E.: Quantifying the emotional impact of events on locations with social media. Knowl.-Based Syst. **146**, 44–57 (2018)
18. Cao, J., Xuanhua, X., Yin, X., Pan, B.: A risky large group emergency decision-making method based on topic sentiment analysis. Expert Syst. Appl. **195**, 116527 (2022)
19. Zhang, L., Wang, S., Liu, B.: Deep learning for sentiment analysis: a survey. Wiley Interdisc. Rev. Data Mining Knowl. Disc. **8**(4), e1253 (2018)
20. Xia, X., Yang, X., Wu, C., Li, S., Bao, L.: Information credibility on twitter in emergency situation. In: Chau, M., Wang, G.A., Yue, W.T., Chen, H. (eds.) PAISI 2012. LNCS, vol. 7299, pp. 45–59. Springer, Heidelberg (2012). https://doi.org/10.1007/978-3-642-30428-6_4
21. Lucini, F.R., et al.: Text mining approach to predict hospital admissions using early medical records from the emergency department. Int. J. Med. Inf. **100**, 1–8 (2017)
22. de Brito, M.M., Kuhlicke, C., Marx, A.: Near-real-time drought impact assessment: a text mining approach on the 2018/19 drought in Germany. Environ. Res. Lett. **15**(10), 1040a9 (2020)
23. Goh, Y.M., Ubeynarayana, C.U.: Construction accident narrative classification: an evaluation of text mining techniques. Accid. Anal. Prevent. **108**, 122–130 (2017)
24. Stipaničev, D., Vuko, T., Krstinić, D., Štula, M., Bodrožić, L.: Forest fire protection by advanced video detection system-croatian experiences. In: Third TIEMS Workshop-Improvement of Disaster Management System, Trogir (2006)
25. SD County: Regional Characteristics of Split-Dalmatia County. https://www.dalmacija.hr/zupanija/informacije. Accessed 21 Feb 2023
26. Šerić, L., Ivanda, A., Bugarić, M., Braović, M.: Semantic conceptual framework for environmental monitoring and surveillance-a case study on forest fire video monitoring and surveillance. Electronics **11**(2), 275 (2022)
27. Official page: CFD. https://hvz.gov.hr////
28. FIMS intervention management system. https://hvz.gov.hr/istaknute-teme/informatizacija/sustav-upravljanje-vatrogasnim-intervencijama/101
29. Nguyen, G., et al.: Machine learning and deep learning frameworks and libraries for large-scale data mining: a survey. Artif. Intell. Rev. **52**, 77–124 (2019)
30. Chapman, C., Stolee, K.T.: Exploring regular expression usage and context in python. In: Proceedings of the 25th International Symposium on Software Testing and Analysis, pp. 282–293 (2016)
31. Agarwal, S.: Data mining: data mining concepts and techniques. In: 2013 International Conference on Machine Intelligence and Research Advancement, pp. 203–207. IEEE (2013)
32. Hansun, S.: A new approach of moving average method in time series analysis. In: 2013 Conference on New Media Studies (CoNMedia), pp. 1–4. IEEE (2013)

33. Ivanda, A., Šerić, L., Bugarić, M., Braović, M.: Mapping chlorophyll-a concentrations in the Kaštela bay and brač channel using ridge regression and sentinel-2 satellite images. Electronics **10**(23), 3004 (2021)
34. Jobson, J.D.: Multiple Linear Regression, pp. 219–398. Springer, New York (1991)
35. Kim, S.W., Jung, D., Choung, Y.J.: Development of a multiple linear regression model for meteorological drought index estimation based on landsat satellite imagery. Water **12**(12) (2020)
36. Mansouri, E., Feizi, F., Jafarirad, A., Arian, M.: Remote-sensing data processing with the multivariate regression analysis method for iron mineral resource potential mapping: a case study in the Sarvian area, central Iran. Solid Earth **9**, 373–384 (2018)
37. Kavitha, S., Varuna, S., Ramya, R.: A comparative analysis on linear regression and support vector regression. In: 2016 Online International Conference on Green Engineering and Technologies (IC-GET), pp. 1–5. IEEE (2016)
38. Willmott, C.J., Matsuura, K.: Advantages of the mean absolute error (MAE) over the root mean square error (RMSE) in assessing average model performance. Clim. Res. **30**(1), 79–82 (2005)

Bichronous Online Learning During the COVID-19 Pandemic – A Case Study on Teaching the Teachers

Matea Markić Vučić[1]([✉]), Suzana Tomaš[2], Angelina Gašpar[3], and Slavomir Stankov[4]

[1] SPARK School, Mostar, Bosnia and Herzegovina
mateamarkic@gmail.com
[2] Faculty of Humanities and Social Sciences, University of Split, Split, Croatia
[3] Catholic Faculty of Theology, University of Split, Split, Croatia
[4] Faculty of Science, University of Split, Split, Croatia

Abstract. Researchers have put much effort into developing effective online teaching and learning methods to support the pursuit of education during the COVID-19 pandemic. This research aims to provide insight into experiences gained from the bichronous online learning course Teaching the Teachers, intended to improve teachers' knowledge and skills in using information and communication technology. A group of 44 primary and secondary school teachers from Bosnia and Herzegovina was involved in the research, conducted in May and June 2020. The online course was available through Moodle system and the digital flashcard system Memory. The teachers that used the Memory outperformed those that learned on Moodle. A novel corpus-based approach to the online discussion forum proved to be an effective tool in assessing the teachers' use of topic-related terminology. We measured the correlation between formative and summative assessments.

Keywords: Teaching to Teachers · Bichronous Online Learning · Moodle · Digital Flashcards Technology · Formative Assessment

1 Introduction

Skills requirements are evolving rapidly due to technological changes affecting many professions, including teaching. To prepare students for a more self-determined life and increase their likelihood of success and contentment in education, teachers must keep pace with advanced information communication technology-based teaching and learning methods. Also, they have to adjust to individual students' abilities, learning styles, and background knowledge. As a result, they try to use learning management systems, communication, or other tools to create or access educational content. Although designing an online course can be time-consuming and laborious, it offers various teaching, learning, and assessment approaches.

Martin and Oyarzun [1] classify online courses as asynchronous online learning, synchronous online learning, MOOC (Massive Open Online Courses), Blended/Hybrid,

D. Vasić and M. Kundid Vasić (Eds.): MoStart 2023, CCIS 1827, pp. 77–90, 2023.
https://doi.org/10.1007/978-3-031-36833-2_6

Blended Synchronous, and Multi-modal models. Much research has been done on the blending of online and face-to-face learning, but bichronous online learning has not been sufficiently discussed. A recent study by Florence et al. [2] defines bichronous online learning as "the blending of both asynchronous and synchronous online learning, where students can participate in anytime, anywhere learning during the asynchronous parts of the course, but then participate in real-time activities for the synchronous sessions. The amount of the online learning blend varies by the course and the activities included in the course." Studies on the blending of synchronous elements during the asynchronous courses show that such a model improves student learning outcomes, retention, and engagement [3, 4]. De Villa and Manalo [5] explore the pre-implementation of distance learning in the new normal.

To quickly adjust to pandemic-driven shifts in education, teachers familiarize themselves with different online learning platforms, attend webinar sessions, watch video tutorials, etc. Scherer et al. [6] examine teacher profiles as the key to determining their readiness for online teaching and learning in higher education. Zylfiu and Rasimi [7] deal with teacher opinions regarding the challenges and advantages of online learning. Rice and Deschaine [8] problematize the current online teacher education landscape and make recommendations for practices that prepare and support online teachers.

Unlike the studies [9] and [10] that examine students' views on the benefits of online education, this research focuses on teachers' experiences in the online learning environment. Schools in Bosnia and Hercegovina use Moodle only to enrich in-class teaching. The reasons are manifold: the lack of teacher education programs, institutional support, funding and incentives for e-course design and delivery, teachers' negative self-perceptions of digital competences and reluctance to use educational technologies. However, the Covid-19 pandemic forced an adjustment to virtual learning and motivated us to offer the free bichronous online learning course *E-learning: Teaching the Teachers*. It was designed for primary and secondary school teachers to facilitate their transition to online teaching and to examine the efficiency of the bichronous online learning strategy.

The Moodle learning management system is used in the research since it provides the framework for all aspects of the e-learning process, including data mining and learning analytics. According to Xu and Inganson [11] flashcards are a useful tool for learning. They are frequently used for memorizing new words when learning language. When combined with spaced repetition, they can produce long-term knowledge retention. Digital flashcards may facilitate students' technical vocabulary learning efforts [12]. The Memory system (memory.com) is a comprehensive free online self-study tool designed for teachers and students. Students use it for self-testing and to improve their self-regulated learning. The system uses artificial intelligence techniques to generate and deliver questions. Memory incorporates various inputs such as hesitation time, the number of backspace hits, flashcard flips, average typing speed, and other variables to automatically calculate the teacher's performance and to know the best time for repeating questions and setting due dates for practicing at the correct time intervals. Formative assessments are commonly said to be for learning because teachers use the results to modify and improve teaching techniques during an instructional period. Summative assessments are said to be of learning because they evaluate academic achievement after an instructional period. "When the cook tastes the soup, that is formative assessment.

When the customer tastes the soup, that is a summative assessment", defined by Black and William [13]. Summative assessment that uses evidence from learning activities not only enables the full range of goals to be assessed but encourages, indeed requires, the practice of formative assessment [14]. Rutkowski [15] evaluated the correlation between formative tests and final exam results claiming there was an "indisputable correlation between student engagement in taking formative quizzes and the final result". The case [16] illustrates that formative and summative assessment are interlinked and interdependent: it is not the tools that differentiate summative from formative assessment but rather the way that information and judgments generated by applying the tools are used.

Kelle [17] argues that all research methods have specific limitations and strengths and proposes to combine qualitative and quantitative ones to compensate for their mutual and overlapping weaknesses. This paper examines the efficiency of bichronous online learning, employing mixed assessment methods and educational technologies, specifically digital flashcard technology. The following research questions guided the flow of research:

1. Is bichronous online learning an effective transition strategy?
2. Is there a correlation between formative and summative assessment?
3. Does the Memory system enhance learning?
4. Can the corpus-based approach to discussion forums reveal the teachers' use of topic-related terminology?

The contributions of this paper can be summarized as follows:

- Adequately balanced bichronous online learning can be an effective transition strategy.
- To the best of our knowledge, this is the first study that employs a novel corpus-based approach to forum analysis.
- The Memory system enhances learning.

2 Materials and Methods

We used a hybrid method design. Qualitative methods included the corpus-based analysis of the discussion forum and the analysis of closed-ended questions from the online survey. Quantitative methods included formative and summative assessments for monitoring and assessing teachers' learning and open-ended questions from the online survey.

2.1 Participants

A group of 44 teachers (32 primary and 12 secondary teachers) from seven cities in Bosnia and Hercegovina participated in the study. The group consisted of 36 female and 8 male teachers of different subjects such as informatics (10), foreign or native languages (9), teacher education (8), pedagogy (4), mathematics (2), religious education (2), biology (2), psychology (1), physical training (1), technical culture (1), history (1), music (1), physics (1), philosophy (1). The SPARK School Association, Mostar (www.spark.ba), organized the free bichronous online course in May and June 2020.

We collected data using the discussion forum, summative and formative tests, Moodle learning analytics and an online survey. The participation of teachers was voluntary, and their online survey responses were anonymous.

2.2 Instruments

The discussion forum enabled the teacher interaction in discussing the following topics: (1) the advantages and disadvantages of e-learning, (2) the role of teachers in the 21st century (3) explaining Moodle by using an analogy with modular Lego bricks. Each teacher had to post at least one discussion (not less than 250 words) and respond to peer discussion at least twice. We assessed their engagement according to the frequency of watching videos, discussion participation (posts and responses), and linguistic analysis of discussion content. Moodle test included embedded answer (cloze) questions such as multiple-choice, matching, numerical, and true-false question types. The online survey included 31 questions referring to the course structure and content (20 questions), participating teachers (10 questions) and course instructors (1 question). There were 20 close-ended questions and 11 open-ended questions. They answered closed-ended questions by selecting one of the offered statements on a 5-point scale ranging from complete disagreement (1) to complete agreement (5).

2.3 Tentative Bichronous Online Learning Course

The course consists of synchronous online learning (4 online classes via Google Meet) and asynchronous online learning (discussion forum, online learning and testing, online survey), as shown in Table 1. We informed teachers about learning outcomes, instructional modalities, assignments, modes of interaction with peers and instructors, and revision lessons in *online classes*. The *online discussion forum* enabled interaction among teachers, an opportunity to examine whether such interaction can result in a better understanding of a given topic and an insight into teachers' engagement in watching and discussing the following videos: eLearning intro[1]; Teaching in the 21st century[2], and Moodle explained with LEGO[3]. *Learning activities* in Phases 1 and 2 included fifteen Moodle lessons and six flashcard Memory lessons. On the basis of the final test results, we divided teachers into two groups of 12 in Phase 2. One group used Memory flashcards (Memory group) and another Moodle (Moodle group). *Formative and summative assessments* in both Phases included three or two formative tests and a final test on Moodle (Table 1).

---

[1] https://www.youtube.com/watch?v=TrrzTSp60RI.

[2] https://www.youtube.com/watch?v=OTIBDR4Dn2g.

[3] https://www.youtube.com/watch?v=C-p2KqU7QD4.

Table 1. Bichronous online learning course structure.

Timeline	Activities	Learning content
May 6, 2020	Online class – Google Meet	E-learning – a new educational paradigm E-learning and e-learning systems environment
May 7–17, 2020	Teachers' discussion forum	Videos: eLearning intro video Teaching in the 21st Century Moodle explained with Lego
May 20, 2020	Online class – Google Meet	Revision lesson
May 20–June 1, 2020	Online learning, teaching and testing (Phase 1: E-learning - basic concepts)	Learning & Teaching (Moodle) E-learning (L1); E-learning system (L2); The term e-learning (L3); The eight dimensions of the e-learning framework (L4) Formative Test 1 – 20 questions (Moodle) Short answers 8; multiple-choice 9; matching 1; numerical 1; true-false 1 Learning & Teaching (Moodle) Structure and components of the e-learning system (L5) E-learning system configuration and e-learning objects (L6) Formative Test 2 – 15 questions (Moodle) Short answers 5; multiple choice 4; matching 5; true-false 1 Learning & Teaching (Memory) Hybrid learning (L7) Formative Test 3 – 15 questions (Moodle) short answers 6; multiple choice 2; matching 6; numerical 1 Final Test – 30 questions (Moodle) short answers 11; multiple choice 11; matching 8
June 3, 2020	Online class – Google Meet	Revision lesson

(continued)

Table 1. (*continued*)

Timeline	Activities	Learning content
June 4–18, 2020	Online learning, teaching and testing (Phase 2: Moodle about Moodle)	Learning & Teaching (Moodle) Moodle system basics (L1); Moodle system interface (L2) Teachers and their roles in the Moodle system (L3) Resources and activities (L4) Formative Test 1 – 15 questions (Moodle) short answers 5; multiple choice 7; matching 3 Learning & Teaching (group 1 – Memory; group 2 - Moodle) Lesson (L5); Assignment (L6); Quiz (7); Forum (L8); Glossary (L9) Formative Test 2 – 16 questions (Moodle) short answers 5; multiple choice 7; matching 4; Final Test – 31 questions (Moodle) short answers 10; multiple choice 14; matching 7
June 22, 2020	Online class – Google Meet	Revision lesson Teachers' feedback on the course quality
June 24, 2020	Online survey	Teachers' evaluation of the online course

2.4 Data Analyses

The correlation between formative tests and final tests was measured by using Pearson's correlation coefficient. The Odum Institute and data from the U.S. Department of Education [18] that the recommended evaluation points of 0.3 and 0.7 refer to the weak, moderate, and strong correlations. We can use a predictive value of the correlation coefficient to predict future teachers' performance and feedback. A t-test measured whether there was a significant difference between the two groups in Quiz results. A new corpus-based approach to the online discussion forum assessed teachers' usage of topic-related terminology. To the best of our knowledge, the suggested approach is unique. Domain-specific vocabulary helped overcome cultural and linguistic misunderstandings and facilitated communication. We used descriptive statistics to analyze the responses to closed-ended questions in the online survey.

3   Results

The results were presented according to the course phases, including the discussion forum, formative and summative assessments, teaching, and knowledge assessment.

3.1   Discussion Forum Activities

Out of 44 teachers, 33 watched the videos at least once, whereas 11 teachers dropped out. The videos were watched more than once by 10 teachers. 25 (75.75%) teachers created a discussion, 24 (72.72%) a post, and 16 (48.48%) partially completed the task. However, only 8 teachers (24.24%) fully completed the task (Table 2). The discussion forum allowed teachers to share and update knowledge about the topic of discussion. A corpus-based approach was applied to examine whether teachers used topic-related terminology to improve their understanding of course materials. We used an online text analysis tool (Sketch Engine) to generate a small Forum-corpus (5,827w) in the Croatian language, consisting of the written communication of the best eight teachers who fully completed the task. The Forum-corpus was contrasted to the general language reference corpus, the Croatian Web (hrWaC 2.2. RFTagger), for keywords (multi-words) extraction that reflected the topic of the focus corpus.

Table 2. Teachers' task completion scores.

	Watching videos	N
Task 1	Videos watched at least once	33
	Videos watched more than once	10
	Discussion and posts	
Task 2	Discussion created	25
	Post created	24
	Discussion created $>= 1$ and post created $>= 2$	16
	Did not participate	21
	Discussion watched	36
	Fully completed task	8
	The discussion was not related to the task	12

Table 3 shows ten top-ranking multi-words selected from the automatically generated list of keywords. Teachers also used synonyms for terms in the Bosnian, Croatian, and Serbian languages. The concordance lists (terms occurring in their context) indicated that teachers used topic-related terminology while discussing specific topics. Since the linguistic landscape in B&H is diverse due to different languages and language varieties, the corpus-based analysis showed that teachers' discussions did not lose focus. Teachers could articulate and defend their positions, and make arguments and counter-arguments.

Table 3. Ten top-ranking multi-words expressions occurring in their context.

	Multi-word expression	Learning content
1	online nastava (nastava na daljinu, elektronska nastava) *online teaching*	teacher's competencies and skills, life-long learning, the need to combine online and traditional instruction, play-based learning, disadvantages of online teaching
2	tradicionalna nastava (nastava u učionici, standardna nastava) *traditional instruction*	peer-to-peer learning, knowing and understanding each other, teachers' fear of technology
3	prednosti e-učenja *advantages of e-learning*	learning triangle, self-paced learning and comfort
4	nedostatak e-učenja *disadvantages of e-learning*	computer literacy, self-motivation, social isolation, lack of face-to-face communication, time-consuming, inadequate technical equipment, the absence of in-group humour
5	uloga učitelja *role of a teacher*	knowledge transfer, mentoring students, Bloom's taxonomy, creative and critical thinking
6	platforma Moodle *Moodle platform*	Lego cubes, knowledge and skill development, collaborative work, interactive learning, Moodle's multilingual capabilities, millions of users, visualization
7	procjena znanja *knowledge assessment*	new communication channels, quizzes, self-assessment, progress monitoring, immediate feedback to students
8	kombinacija tradicionalne i online nastave *combining traditional and online instruction*	hybrid learning, blended learning, best results
9	video zapis *educational video*	continual professional development, lifelong learning, benefits of educational video
10	nastava usmjerena na učenika *student-centred instruction*	student or teacher-centered instruction, communication and cooperation with students, the credibility of information and students' engagement

Using topic-related terminology, they could improve their critical-thinking abilities and peer-to-peer learning.

We also analyzed the dynamics of the discussion forum from 07–17 May. Figure 1 indicates the lack of teacher engagement in the initial and final parts of the discussion forum. On May 12, we used the hook effect asking them a thought-provoking question: 'Will online learning replace teachers?' to stimulate their discussion and involvement.

The hook effect resulted in the highest number of teachers engaged (n = 20) in discussions (607) recorded on May 13 (the day after the hook effect). The lack of teacher engagement is probably due to their inadequate English language proficiency (videos were in English), age (most of them have had long teaching experience), and reluctance for new technologies. Also, their teaching obligations significantly increased during the pandemic.

Teachers made 1503 logs to browse the forum and twice the smaller number of 880 logs to create discussions and posts. One teacher did not watch videos but discussed the topics and commented on posts. Three teachers expressed their critical views on the course curriculum in the discussion forum. One teacher reported the gap between theoretical learning and practical work. The remaining two teachers argued that there was a balance between theoretical and practical knowledge. Of 22 teachers who took at least one test, 17 did two formative tests and the final test. There was a moderate positive correlation between test 1 and the final test and a strong positive correlation between test 2 and the final test. As for the final tests, 15 teachers took both tests. Figure 2 presents the final results and teachers' final grades.

Moodle quizzes replaced traditional paper tests. The Moodle quiz analytics provided a more detailed analysis of answers and quiz results. Of 24 teachers, 16 took the quiz. We split them into two groups, each having eight teachers. The Memory group had an average score of 85%, and the Moodle group had a significantly lower score of 60.67%. The Quiz results measured by the t-test indicated a difference between the two groups since the t-value was 2.91465 and the p-value was .004624 ($p < .05$). The results showed that the Memory group achieved similar results in all formative and final tests. Table 4 shows an assessment timeline.

Table 4. Assessment timeline.

Topic	Test type		Quiz deadline	Attempts
E-learning 2020-05-20–2020-06-01	Phase 1	Formative Test 1	2020-05-27 11:59 PM	22
		Formative Test 2	2020-05-27 11:59 PM	19
		Formative Test 3	2020-05-29 11:59 PM	19
		Final test	2020-06-05 11:59 PM	20
Moodle about Moodle 2020-06-04–2020-06-17	Phase 2	Formative Test 1	2020-06-12 11:59 PM	18
		Formative Test 2	2020-06-18 11:59 PM	20
		Formative test 3	2020-07-05 11:59 PM	20

The correlation between activity type and quiz results supported the assertion that flashcards were a "collaborator" in learning. The Memory group achieved better results because they likely exercised the gap-fill question type within the Quiz activity (Fig. 2).

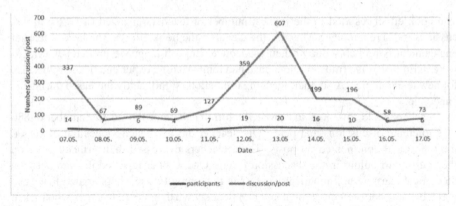

Fig. 1. Discussion forum dynamics.

3.2 Formative and Summative Assessment

In this research, formative and summative assessments aimed to improve the process of learning and identify teachers' difficulties. The main goal of formative assessments was to observe the teachers' progress and keep them engaged during the learning process. The objective of summative assessments was to achieve learning outcomes. Of 26 teachers who took at least one test, 12 did all formative tests and the final test. We calculated the correlation between three formative tests and the final test using Pearson's correlation coefficient. As shown in Table 5, there were moderate positive correlations between test 2 and the final test and test 3 and the final test. There was a weak positive correlation between test 1 and the final test (Table 6).

Table 5. Correlation between formative and final test – Phase 1.

	Test 1	Test 2	Test 3	Final test
Test 1	1			
Test 2	0.032419861	1		
Test 3	0.032419861	0.12525786	1	
Final test	0.046620821	0.417542138	0.68196011	1

Table 6. Correlation between formative and final test – Phase 2.

	Test 1	Test 2	Final test
Test 1	1		
Test 2	0.032419861	1	
Final test	0.046620821	0.417542138	0.68196011

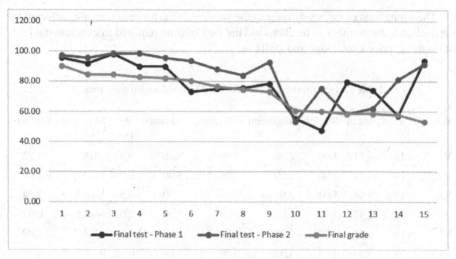

Fig. 2. Final test results and final grades.

3.3 Online Survey

The purpose of the online survey was teachers' feedback on their satisfaction and perceived learning outcomes. At the end of the course, teachers completed the online survey reporting their positive and negative experiences. A total of 19 teachers responded to 11 closed-ended questions) and 6 open-ended questions. As shown in Table 7, the mean values of variables, ranging from 3,37 to 4,68, indicated that teachers agreed with all statements. The lowest scores referred to the teachers' self-perceived knowledge acquisition (V10) and English language proficiency (V11). The availability of instructors (V3) via e-mail or online discussion had the highest score.

As for the analysis of the 6 open-ended questions, most teachers (12) reported they were satisfied with the online course structure, organization,. technical support, and instructors' expertise and availability. They also claimed that their engagement was affected by work overload, the time spent performing their regular duties at schools, the English language proficiency required for watching videos, the lack of in-person peer-to-peer interaction and the imbalance between theory and practice. Their suggestions for improvement included: (i) videos available in the native language; (ii) a more detailed description of online platforms; (iii) more practical work.

The high dropout of teachers was not surprising since the online course was free and voluntary. However, to get a clue about teachers' engagement, we calculated the sitting time for the 14 teachers, recorded by the Moodle, and it was 252.7 h (18.5 h on average). We also asked teachers to estimate their average daily time spent learning (39-day online course). Their self-estimated sitting time ranged from 0.25 to 1.5 h per day, making 438.75 h (31.34 h per teacher approximately). Ten teachers overestimated their time, three teachers underestimated it, and only one teacher realistically assessed it.

The limitations of this study refer to the validity of the presented results, affected by the decline in the number of teachers and the lack of time required to examine the level of teachers' prior knowledge and skills.

Table 7. Descriptive statistics for the 11 closed-ended questions.

Variable	Valid N	Mean	Median	Minimum	Maximum	Variance	Std. Dev	Skewness	Kurtosis
V1	19	4.11	4.00	2.00	2.00	5.00	0.81	−0.91	1.22
V2	19	4.11	4.00	3.00	3.00	5.00	0.74	−0.17	−1.00
V3	19	4.68	5.00	3.00	3.00	5.00	0.58	−1.77	2.54
V4	19	3.47	3.00	1.00	1.00	5.00	1.02	−0.45	0.67
V5	19	4.05	4.00	1.00	1.00	5.00	1.18	−1.25	1.09
V6	19	3.84	4.00	3.00	3.00	5.00	0.83	0.32	−1.49
V7	19	3.74	4.00	2.00	2.00	5.00	0.93	0.13	−1.10
V8	19	4.00	4.00	2.00	2.00	5.00	1.11	−0.55	−1.18
V9	19	4.11	4.00	2.00	2.00	5.00	0.94	−0.68	−0.47
V10	19	3.37	3.00	1.00	1.00	5.00	1.07	−0.23	0.09
V11	19	3.42	4.00	1.00	1.00	5.00	1.12	−0.97	0.67

Legend: V1 - the understanding of course objectives and assignments; V2 - the course content; V3 - the availability of the instructor via email or online discussion; V4 - the lack of in-person peer-to-peer interaction; V5 - course satisfaction; V6 - the relevance of assignments, quizzes and tests; V7 - the quality of quiz questions; V8 - the quality of multimedia; V9 - technical support; V10 - knowledge acquisition; V11 - the English language proficiency

4 Discussion and Conclusions

This paper highlighted the need for embracing e-learning and e-learning systems, either because of their proven benefits or global school closure prompted by the Covid-19 pandemic. Many teachers were struggling with educational technologies and imposed online teaching. We offered the bichronous online course to facilitate the shift from traditional to online teaching and learning. Despite significant dropout, most teachers followed the guidelines for a topic-centered online discussion and could easily use Moodle LMS, the forum tool, and the digital flashcard system Memory. A new corpus-based approach to the discussion forum showed that by using topic-related vocabulary teachers could improve their critical-thinking abilities and peer-to-peer knowledge exchange, despite their different languages or language varieties. The hook effect could provoke teacher engagement but only temporarily. The qualitative and quantitative data indicated a positive correlation between formative and summative assessments.

However, the formative assessments could not increase teacher motivation and engagement. The group that learned using the Memory system was more successful than the Moodle group. The spaced practice design could probably reduce teachers working memory loads, allowing them to optimize their learning and retention. The overall teacher satisfaction with the online course was positive. The methods and tools employed in this research proved to be efficient since four teachers could design and deliver online courses for primary and secondary school learners. Teachers became more aware that the integration of educational technologies can enhance their professional development and student opportunity to develop the skills needed in the 21st century (collaboration and teamwork, critical thinking, problem-solving, creativity, technology literacy, leadership, etc.) The multiple assessment modes aimed to promote independent and self-regulated learning.

Acknowledgements. This paper is a part of the work supported by the United States Office of Naval Research grant, N00014-20-1-2066 "Enhancing Adaptive Courseware based on Natural Language Processing".

References

1. Martin, F., Oyarzun, B.: Distance learning. In: Foundations of Learning and Instructional Design Technology. Edtech Books (2017). https://www.researchgate.net/publication/335798695_Distance_Learning. Accessed 11 Dec 2020
2. Florence, M., Polly, D., Ritzhaupt, A.: Bichronous Online Learning: Blending Asynchronous and Synchronous Online Learning|EDUCAUSE, 8 September 2020. https://er.educause.edu/articles/2020/9/bichronous-online-learning-blending-asynchronous-and-synchronous-online-learning. Accessed 11 Dec 2020
3. Badawi, N.: Undergraduate Student Attitudes Towards Synchronous Events in Online Instruction. Argosy University/Phoenix (2017)
4. Peterson, A.T., Beymer, P.N., Putnam, R.T.: Synchronous and asynchronous discussions: Effects on cooperation, belonging, and affect. Online Learn. J. **22**(4) (2018). https://doi.org/10.24059/olj.v22i4.1517
5. De Villa, J.A., Manalo, F.K.B.: Secondary teachers' preparation, challenges, and coping mechanism in the pre-implementation of distance learning in the new normal. IOER Int. Multidisciplinary Res. J. **2**(3), 144–154 (2020). https://doi.org/10.5281/zenodo.4072845
6. Scherer, R., Howard, S.K., Tondeur, J., Siddiq, F.: Profiling teachers' readiness for online teaching and learning in higher education: who's ready? Comput. Human Behav. **118**, 106675 (2021). https://doi.org/10.1016/j.chb.2020.106675
7. Zylfiu, B.G., Rasimi, A.: Challenges and advantages of online learning: the case of Kosovo by Dr. Bahtije Gerbeshi Zylfiu, Dr. Adhurim Rasimi : SSRN. Int. J. Manage. **11**(10), 1873–1880 (2020). https://papers.ssrn.com/sol3/papers.cfm?abstract_id=3743171. Accessed 29 Mar 2021
8. Rice, M.F., Deschaine, M.E.: Orienting toward teacher education for online environments for all students. Educ. Forum **84**(2), 114–125 (2020). https://doi.org/10.1080/00131725.2020.1702747
9. Rustempasic, D., Djapo, N.: The e-Learning in Bosnia and Herzegovina Classrooms|IEEE DataPort (2021). https://ieee-dataport.org/documents/e-learning-bosnia-and-herzegovina-classrooms. Accessed 29 Mar 2021
10. Miloshevska, L., Gajek, E., Dzanić, N.D., Hatipoğlu, Ç.: Emergency online learning during the first Covid-19 period: students' perspectives. Explor. Engl. Lang. Linguist. **8**(2), 110–143 (2020). https://doi.org/10.2478/EXELL-2021-0002

11. Xu, X., Ingason, A.K.: Developing flashcards for learning Icelandic. In: Proceedings of the 10th Workshop on Natural Language Processing for Computer Assisted Language Learning, pp. 55–61 (2021). www.malfong.is/files/mim_tagset_files_en.pdf. Accessed 16 Dec 2021

12. Yüksel, H.G., Mercanoğlu, H.G., Yılmaz, M.B.: Digital flashcards vs. wordlists for learning technical vocabulary (2020). https://doi.org/10.1080/09588221.2020.1854312

13. Black, P., Wiliam, D.: Assessment and classroom learning. Assess Educ. **5**(1), 7–74 (1998). https://doi.org/10.1080/0969595980050102

14. Dolin, J., Black, P., Harlen, W., Tiberghien, A.: Exploring relations between formative and summative assessment. In: Dolin, J., Evans, R. (eds.) Transforming Assessment. CSER, vol. 4, pp. 53–80. Springer, Cham (2018). https://doi.org/10.1007/978-3-319-63248-3_3

15. Rutkowski, J.: Evaluation of the correlation between formative tests and final exam results - theory of information approach. Int. J. Electron. Telecommun. **62**(1), 55–60 (2016). https://doi.org/10.1515/ELETEL-2016-0007

16. Houston, D., Thompson, J.N.: Blending formative and summative assessment in a capstone subject: 'it's not your tools, it's how you use them'. J. Univ. Teach. Learn. Pract. **14**(3) (2017). https://files.eric.ed.gov/fulltext/EJ1170183.pdf. Accessed 16 Dec 2021

17. Kelle, U.: Combining qualitative and quantitative methods in research practice: purposes and advantages. Qual. Res. Psychol. **3**(4), 293–311 (2006). https://doi.org/10.1177/147808870 6070839

18. The Odum Institute, Pearson's Correlation Coefficient and the Consolidated State Performance Report (2012–2013): High School Science Proficiency Across the U.S. States. SAGE Publications, Ltd., December 2015. https://doi.org/10.4135/9781473960596

Artificial Intelligence Fuzzy Logic Expert System for Prediction of Bevel Angle Quality Response in Plasma Jet Manufacturing Process

Ivan Peko[1]([✉]) [iD], Boris Crnokić[2] [iD], and Igor Planinić[2]

[1] Faculty of Science, University of Split, Split, Croatia
ivan.peko@fesb.hr
[2] Faculty of Mechanical Engineering, Computing and Electrical Engineering,
University of Mostar, Mostar, Bosnia and Herzegovina
boris.crnokic@sum.ba, igor.planinic@fsre.sum.ba

Abstract. This paper presents application of artificial intelligence (AI) fuzzy logic technique for creating expert system that will be able to predict bevel angle as quality response in plasma jet cutting process. Bevel angle is significant cut quality response in plasma nonconventional manufacturing process that appears due to instability and deflection of the plasma jet during cutting and penetration in workpiece. Initial point for development of AI fuzzy logic expert system is experimental work. In this paper experimentations were conducted on aluminum sheet 5083 thickness 8 mm by varying four process parameters gas pressure, cutting speed, arc current and cutting height. Due to complexity of manufacturing process a few constraints regarding parameters values combinations in experimental plan were identified. In order to define relations between input parameters and bevel angle response fuzzy logic AI technique was applied. Prediction accuracy of developed fuzzy logic model was checked by using mean absolute percentage error (MAPE) and coefficient of determination (R2) between experimental and predicted data. Also, response surface plots were created to visualize input parameters effects on the analyzed cut quality response. Presented fuzzy logic expert system enables better understanding and control of manufacturing process as well as it serves as basis for further and more detailed experimentations in this area.

Keywords: artificial intelligence · fuzzy logic expert system · plasma manufacturing · bevel angle · quality

1 Introduction

Plasma jet manufacturing process is very usually present in metal and shipbuilding industry especially in cutting and preparing metal sheets for welding procedure. In plasma jet cutting process it is very important to reach the best possible cut quality in order to minimize time and costs for further postprocessing techniques such as cut flattening, cleaning and grinding. In order to define optimal cutting conditions usually

© The Author(s), under exclusive license to Springer Nature Switzerland AG 2023
D. Vasić and M. Kundid Vasić (Eds.): MoStart 2023, CCIS 1827, pp. 91–103, 2023.
https://doi.org/10.1007/978-3-031-36833-2_7

try error approach of the machine operator as well as previous experience was applied. In this case it is desirable to have one artificial system that will be able to analyze influence of process parameters effects on the various cut quality responses such as: kerf width, bevel angle, surface roughness, dross appearance etc. Also, such system will be able to help deeply understand manufacturing process as well as to define optimal manufacturing regions. In these cases, artificial intelligence techniques such as fuzzy logic, artificial neural networks and machine learning serve as good mechanisms for modeling and prediction of manufacturing process responses. Their applications is even more appropriate in plasma jet manufacturing process that due to its complexity and noises contains lot of vague and imprecise informations. Until today, many authors applied various techniques and conducted comprehensive experimental investigations to analyze effects of the process parameters and to find out optimal conditions in plasma jet manufacturing process.

Kadirgama et al. [1] conducted experimental investigations on aluminium alloy 6061 to analyze influence of the arc current, standoff gap and gas pressure on the heat affected zone as process response. They used response surface method to discuss process parameters effects and partial swarm optimization algorithm for optimization of the heat affected zone. Hamid et al. [2] analyzed influence of arc current, feed rate, gas pressure and cutting distance on surface roughness and conicity responses in plasma jet cutting process of aluminium alloy 5083 thickness 10 mm. They applied grey relational analysis and analysis of variance (ANOVA) to define process parameters effects and optimal cutting conditions that lead to minimal surface roughness and conicity responses. Patel et al. [3] applied main effects plots to check plasma manufacturing process parameters effects on the material removal rate, top and bottom kerf width and bevel angle quality responses. Process parameters that were considered in experimentations on the aluminium 6082 thickness 5 mm are: arc current, standoff distance, gas pressure and cutting speed. ANOVA was used to discuss significance of each parameter and their interactions on the analyzed responses. Kumar das et al. [4] conducted experimental trials to investigate influence of the gas pressure, arc current and torch height on the material removal rate and surface roughness in plasma jet cutting process of steel EN31. They applied grey relational analysis and ANOVA to define process parameters contribution on cut quality responses as well as for multi objective optimization. Peko et al. [5] created regression models to define mathematical relations between input parameters such as cutting speed, arc current and cutting height and responses: kerf width, bevel angle, surface roughness, material removal rate. Experimentations were conducted on aluminium alloy 5083 thickness 3mm. In order to discuss significance of process parameters and their interactions on considered responses ANOVA was applied. Multi objective optimization was performed by Desirability analysis and optimal cutting area was visually presented. Peko et al. [6] generated AI fuzzy logic expert system for prediction of dross height in plasma jet cutting process of aluminium alloy 5083 thickness 3 mm. Input parameters in fuzzy logic model were cutting speed, arc current and cutting height. Prediction accuracy of developed fuzzy logic model was checked by comparison between experimental and predicted dross height data. Finally, 3D response surface plots were presented to visualize effects of process parameters on dross height response as well as to identify optimal manufacturing conditions. Peko et al. [7] generated artificial neural network (ANN) model to mathematically describe relations between input process parameters such as cutting speed, arc current and cutting height and kerf width response in plasma jet cutting process of aluminium plate 5083 thickness 3 mm. Experimental data served as basis for artificial neural network training procedure. Prediction accuracy of developed ANN model was checked by comparison between experimental and predicted data on data sets for validation and testing. In order to check influence of process parameters and their interactions on kerf width response 2D and 3D response plots were created. These plots were also applied for defining optimal cutting conditions that result with minimal kerf width values. Peko et al. [8] defined ANN model for prediction of surface roughness in plasma jet cutting process of aluminium alloy 5083 thickness 3 mm. They conducted experimental trials by varying two process parameters: cutting speed and arc current. Developed ANN model was checked by following mean squared error (MSE) in training process and correlation coefficient (R) between experimental and ANN predicted data. After validation of ANN model was proved 2D and 3D plots were generated to discuss process parameters effects and to determine process parameters values that lead to minimal surface roughness. Peko et al. [9] applied artificial intelligence fuzzy logic technique to model relations between input process parameters: gas pressure, cutting speed, arc current and cutting height and output response: dross height in plasma jet manufacturing process of aluminium alloy 5083 thickness 8 mm. Developed fuzzy logic model was checked by using mean absolute percentage error (MAPE) and coefficient of determination (R^2) as comparison measures between experimental and predicted data. Fuzzy expert system of dross height served as basis for further more detailed experimentations as well as for better understanding and control of plasma manufacturing process. Peko et al. [10] analyzed influence of gas pressure, cutting speed, arc current and cutting height on top and bottom kerf width responses in plasma jet manufacturing process of aluminium alloy 5083 thickness 8 mm. In order to mathematically describe relations between input parameters and output responses fuzzy logic technique was applied. Generated fuzzy logic model of top and bottom kerf width was validated by comparison between experimental and predicted data. MAPE and R^2 were applied as validation measures. Finally, 3D responses surface plots were defined to discuss parameters interactions effects on analyzed responses and to determine optimal parameters values that result with as narrow kerf as possible. Kerf widths fuzzy logic expert system serves as good foundation for more detailed experimentations that cover as wider experimental space as possible as well as basis for inclusion of other process responses in analysis.

In this paper authors applied artificial intelligence fuzzy logic technique to create expert system for prediction of bevel angle response depending on different process parameters values within covered experimental space. Process parameters that were analyzed are gas pressure, cutting speed, arc current and cutting height. Fuzzy logic expert system was developed based on data that were collected in experimental investigations on aluminium plate 5083 thickness 8 mm. Created AI fuzzy logic expert system will serve as base for further investigations as well as for better comprehension and control of plasma manufacturing process of aluminium alloy 5083.

2 Experimental Procedure

In this paper experimental trials were conducted on aluminium alloy 5083 thickness 8 mm. This alloy is very present in shipbuilding industry and various marine applications due to its good strength and corrosion resistance. FlameCut 2513 (Arpel Automation) was applied as CNC plasma manufacturing machine. Arc current source was LG 100 IGBT Inverter Air Plasma Cutting Machine. Compressed air was used as plasma gas. Compressed air was prepared, purified and dried in compressor SCK5 200 PLUS (ALUP Kompresoren Gmbh).

Experimental trials were conducted according to Taguchi L_{27} orthogonal array by varying gas pressure, cutting speed, arc current and cutting height on three levels. In all trials nozzle has constant outlet diameter 1.2 mm. Due to complexity of plasma jet manufacturing process and target to search as wide experimental space as possible there are several constraints regarding parameters values combinations at which plasma jet cutting is not possible. These constraints are shown in Fig. 1 with bold blue lines. Consequently, there are 9 experimental points that are not included into Taguchi L_{27} plan.

In all experimental trials parallel straight cuts length of 80 mm were made. Bevel angle α [°] was defined as follows:

$$\alpha[°] = \left| tan^{-1}\left(\frac{W_t - W_b}{2s} \right) \right| \tag{1}$$

where: s [mm] is sheet thickness, Wt [mm] and Wb [mm] are top and bottom kerf widths, Fig. 2. In Fig. 3 experimental cuts as well as bevel angle response were presented. Top and bottom kerf widths were measured using Universal Toolmaker's Microscope on three equally distanced places: in the middle of the cut and 15 mm on the left and right side along the cut length. Finally, mean value of top and bottom kerf width was calculated and following Eq. 1 bevel angle response was defined. Experimental plan and bevel angle results are presented in Table 1.

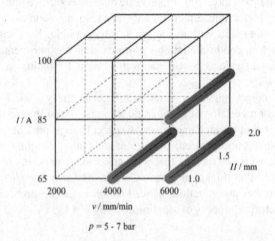

Fig. 1. Process constraints

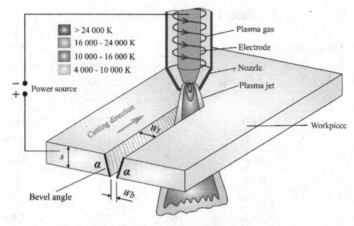

Fig. 2. Experimental setup and bevel angle response

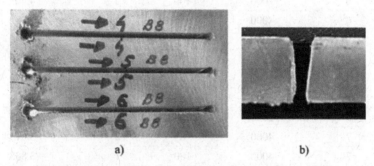

Fig. 3. a) Few experimental trials, b) bevel angle at trial number 9

3 Fuzzy Logic Modelling

Fuzzy logic is artificial intelligence technique that is very useful to model processes and systems where uncertain and vague informations are usual. Very often noises and complexities in process or system that should be modeled result with incomplete and ambiguous data. Due to that application of traditional mathematical modeling and optimization procedures is not possible. In these cases, AI fuzzy logic technique represents good tool to develop functional relations between inputs and outputs and build artificial reasoning system that would be able to predict data and simulate future states of analyzed problem. In this paper, AI fuzzy logic technique was applied to develop artificial expert system that will predict bevel angle response depending on various process parameters values and represent base for further experimental investigations.

In order to develop artificial expert system and perform outputs prediction fuzzy logic system applies few modules: fuzzification module, fuzzy inference module and defuzzification module. Fuzzification module converts inputs and outputs real data into fuzzy values using different membership functions. Membership functions can be: Gaussian, triangular, trapezoidal etc. These functions add to each value of inputs and outputs

Table 1. Experimental results

Exp. No.	Process parameters				Response
	Gas pressure p/bar	Cutting speed v/mm/min	Arc current I/A	Cutting height H/mm	Bevel angle α/°
1	5	2000	65	1	3.780
2	5	2000	85	1.5	4.033
3	5	2000	100	2	3.576
4	5	4000	85	2	4.328
5	5	4000	100	1	3.608
6	5	6000	100	1.5	4.286
7	6	2000	65	1	4.400
8	6	2000	85	1.5	4.261
9	6	2000	100	2	4.407
10	6	4000	85	2	5.086
11	6	4000	100	1	5.260
12	6	6000	100	1.5	5.018
13	7	2000	65	1	4.036
14	7	2000	85	1.5	1.793
15	7	2000	100	2	2.709
16	7	4000	85	2	3.819
17	7	4000	100	1	3.833
18	7	6000	100	1.5	5.125

degree of membership between 0 and 1. Membership functions are mostly expressed descriptive rather than numerical. Fuzzy inference module applies knowledge base of fuzzy IF-THEN rules and membership functions to define functional relations between inputs and outputs and perform reasoning. There are several fuzzy inference systems that can be applied in this stage. Two most famous are Mamdani and Sugeno. Mamdani is the most popular due to its simplicity and intuitive approach. Finally, defuzzification module converts fuzzy values into a numerical real values [11–15].

In this paper Mamdani fuzzy inference was applied to establish functional relations between gas pressure, cutting speed, arc current and cutting height as inputs and bevel angle quality response as output of analyzed process, Fig. 4. Settings of defined Mamdani fuzzy inference system are: and method: min, or method: max, implication: min, aggregation: max, defuzzification method: centroid.

For each input three Gaussian membership functions were defined: L (low), M (medium), H (high), Fig. 5. Bevel angle output was described by five Gaussian membership functions: VL (very low), L (low), M (medium), H (high), VH (very high), Fig. 6.

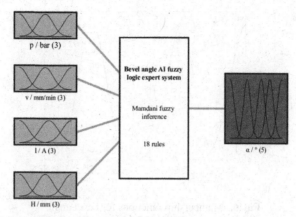

Fig. 4. AI fuzzy logic system for modeling and prediction bevel angle response

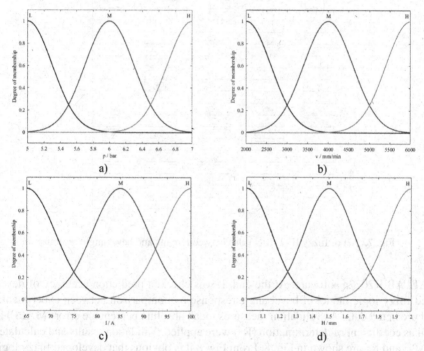

Fig. 5. Membership functions for: a) gas pressure, b) cutting speed, c) arc current, d) cutting height

In order to establish cause-effect connections between inputs and output set of 18 fuzzy IF-THEN rules was defined. There rules are graphically presented in Fig. 7 and in Table 2.

Finally, defuzzification module converts fuzzy output data into a real non-fuzzy values. Whole development procedure of bevel angle fuzzy logic model was conducted in

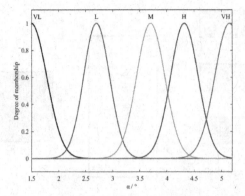

Fig. 6. Membership functions for bevel angle

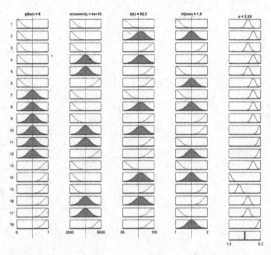

Fig. 7. Set of fuzzy IF-THEN rules between inputs and bevel angle response

MATLAB R2022a software. At the end, it was checked prediction accuracy of developed fuzzy logic model of bevel angle response by comparison between experimental and predicted data. As validation measures mean absolute percentage error (MAPE) as well as coefficient of determination (R^2) were applied. Validation results and calculated MAPE and R^2 are shown in Fig. 8. From Fig. 8 it is obvious that developed fuzzy logic model has high prediction accuracy (R^2: 0.9695, MAPE: 2.83%). Thus it can be furtherly used for analysis of process parameters effects as well as for creating AI fuzzy logic expert system for prediction of bevel angle quality response depending on various process parameters values inside analyzed experimental space.

Table 2. Fuzzy IF-THEN rules

1	If (p is L) and (v is L) and (I is L) and (H is L) then (α is M)
2	If (p is L) and (v is L) and (I is M) and (H is M) then (α is H)
3	If (p is L) and (v is L) and (I is H) and (H is H) then (α is M)
4	If (p is L) and (v is M) and (I is M) and (H is H) then (α is H)
5	If (p is L) and (v is M) and (I is H) and (H is L) then (α is M)
6	If (p is L) and (v is H) and (I is H) and (H is M) then (α is H)
7	If (p is M) and (v is L) and (I is L) and (H is L) then (α is H)
8	If (p is M) and (v is L) and (I is M) and (H is M) then (α is H)
9	If (p is M) and (v is L) and (I is H) and (H is H) then (α is H)
10	If (p is M) and (v is M) and (I is M) and (H is H) then (α is VH)
11	If (p is M) and (v is M) and (I is H) and (H is L) then (α is VH)
12	If (p is M) and (v is H) and (I is H) and (H is M) then (α is VH)
13	If (p is H) and (v is L) and (I is L) and (H is L) then (α is H)
14	If (p is H) and (v is L) and (I is M) and (H is M) then (α is VL)
15	If (p is H) and (v is L) and (I is H) and (H is H) then (α is L)
16	If (p is H) and (v is M) and (I is M) and (H is H) then (α is M)
17	If (p is H) and (v is M) and (I is H) and (H is L) then (α is M)
18	If (p is H) and (v is H) and (I is H) and (H is M) then (α is VH)

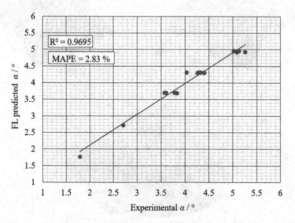

Fig. 8. Comparison between FL predicted and experimental data of bevel angle

4 Results

In order to discuss influence of process parameters and their interactions on bevel angle cut quality response developed fuzzy logic expert system was applied to create 3D response surface plots. These plots covered all analyzed experimental space and present bevel angle changes depending on two variable parameters values while other two parameters were kept constant. From these plots it is also possible to derive few conclusions regarding optimal process conditions that lead to as vertical cut as possible. 3D bevel angle response surface plots are presented in Fig. 9.

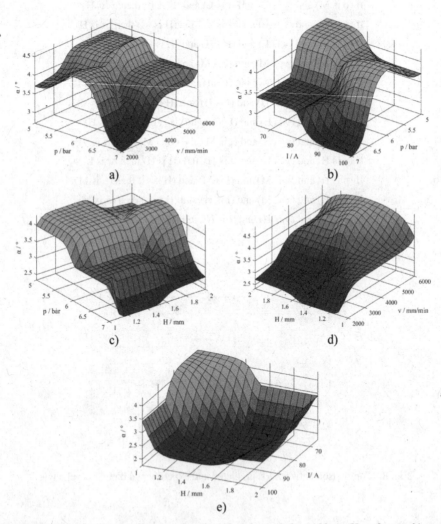

Fig. 9. Process parameters effects on bevel angle when: a) $I = 100$ A, $H = 2$ mm, b) $v = 2000$ mm/min, $H = 2$ mm, c) $v = 2000$ mm/min, $I = 100$ A, d) $p = 7$ bar, $I = 100$ A, e) $p = 7$ bar, $v = 2000$ mm/min

From Fig. 9 it can be observed that cutting speed, arc current and gas pressure have the most significant effect on the bevel angle values, while cutting height has lower importance. Bevel angle was defined by top and bottom kerf widths. Consequently, the lower difference between top and bottom kerf width results with more perpendicular cut and finally better cut quality. From Fig. 9 it is visible that higher cutting speed as well as lower arc current lead to the larger bevel angle. This can be explained by lower heat energy input in the cutting zone that results with decrease of the kerf width. In these conditions bevel angle increase due to more noticeable decrease of the bottom kerf width than top kerf width and larger difference between them. From Fig. 9 it is obvious that higher values of gas pressure results with the lower bevel angle. Plasma gas contributes to more focused plasma jet and blows molten metal away form the cutting zone. Accordingly, higher gas pressure decreases difference between top and bottom kerf width and leads to the lower bevel angle values and more perpendicular cut. Figure 9 c) describes that low gas pressure (5 bar) and high cutting height (2 mm) brings greater deflection and lack of focus and coherence of the plasma jet at constant parameters 2000 mm/min and 100 A. This leads to the lower heat input in the workpiece and consequently larger difference between top and bottom kerf width and bevel angle response.

Above statements were defined according to conducted experimental investigations and generated AI fuzzy logic expert system. In order to identify more precisely parameters effects as well as their interactions on bevel angle cut quality response it is desirable to perform additional experimental trials that will cover whole experimental space. Consequently, fuzzy logic expert system will be upgraded with these new results and will be able to predict and analyze process response more reliable.

5 Conclusion

In this paper experimental investigations in plasma jet manufacturing process of aluminum alloy 5083 thickness 8 mm were performed. Research goal was to examine influence of process parameters gas pressure, cutting speed, arc current and cutting height on bevel angle cut quality response as well as to get experimental data for creation AI fuzzy logic expert system. Based on conducted experimental trials and developed fuzzy logic model several findings were derived:

- Artificial intelligence fuzzy logic technique proved as a very useful tool to describe manufacturing processes such as plasma manufacturing process where due to its complexity and process noises application of traditional mathematical modeling and optimization procedures is not possible.
- Fuzzy logic technique represents good approach to define functional relations between process inputs and outputs and derive useful conclusions especially in cases where lack of experimental data and incomplete information are present as it is situation in this paper.
- Mamdani fuzzy inference system, Gaussian membership functions, set of defined fuzzy IF-THEN rules and defuzzification centroid method represent good settings to create artificial fuzzy logic expert system for prediction bevel angle.
- Prediction accuracy of developed fuzzy logic expert system was confirmed by comparison between experimental and predicted response data.

– By analyzing 3D response surface plots that were derived from fuzzy logic expert system gas pressure, cutting speed and arc current were identified as the most significant parameters that affect bevel angle response while cutting height has unnoticeable influence.
– Decrease of cutting speed, increase of the arc current and gas pressure result with more perpendicular cut and lower bevel angle due to higher heat input in the cutting zone, more uniform top and bottom kerf widths as well as more focused and coherent plasma jet.
– Developed AI fuzzy logic expert system represents good foundation for upgrading it with further more detailed experimental investigations in order to cover whole experimental space and to perform more precisely bevel angle response predictions depending on various inputs values.
– Generated AI fuzzy logic expert system enables inclusion of other cut quality responses such as kerf width, surface roughness, dross height, material removal rate in analysis in order to perform multi objective optimization and to achieve better understanding and control of plasma manufacturing process.

References

1. Kadirgama, K., Noor, M.M., Harun, W.S.W., Aboue-El-Hosein, K.A.: Optimisation of heat affected zone by partial swarm optimisation in air plasma cutting operation. J. Sci. Ind. Res. **69**, 439–443 (2010)
2. Hamid, A., Novareza, O., Dwi Widodo, T.: Optimization of process parameters and quality results using plasma arc cutting in aluminium alloy. J. Eng. Manag. Indust. Syst. **7**, 7–14 (2019)
3. Patel, S.B., Vyas, T.K.: Parametric investigation of plasma arc cutting on aluminium alloy 6082. In: Proceedings of the International Conference on Ideas, Impact and Innovation in Mechanical Engineering, Pune, India, pp. 87–93 (2017)
4. Kumar Das, M., Kumar, K., Barman, K.T., Sahu, P.: Optimization of process parameters in plasma arc cutting of EN31 steel based on MRR and multiple roughness characteristics using grey relational analysis. Procedia Mater. Sci. **5**, 1550–1559 (2014)
5. Peko, I., Marić, D., Nedić, B., Samardžić, I.: Modeling and optimization of cut quality responses in plasma jet cutting of aluminium alloy EN AW-5083. Materials **14**, 5559 (2021)
6. Peko, I., Nedić, B., Dunđer, M., Samardžić, I.: Modelling of dross height in plasma jet cutting process of aluminium alloy 5083 using fuzzy logic technique. Tehnički vjesnik **27**, 1767–1773 (2020)
7. Peko, I., Nedić, B., Đorđević, A., Veža, I.: Modelling of Kerf width in plasma jet metal cutting process using ANN approach. Tehnički vjesnik **25**, 401–406 (2018)
8. Peko, I., et al.: Prediction of surface roughness in plasma jet cutting process using neural network model. In: Proceedings of the 15th International Conference on Tribology SERBIATRIB 2017, Kragujevac, Serbia, pp. 520–525 (2017)
9. Peko I., Marić, D., Šolić, T., Matić, T., Samardžić, M., Samardžić, I.: Fuzzy logic modelling of dross height in plasma jet cutting of shipbuilding aluminium alloy 5083. In: Proceedings of the 10th International Scientific and Expert Conference TEAM 2022, Slavonski Brod, Croatia, pp. 267–274 (2022)
10. Peko, I., Marić, D., Dragičević, M., Šolić, T.: Investigation of the parameters effects on the kerf width in plasma jet cutting process of aluminium 5083 using fuzzy logic technique.

In: Proceedings of the 10th International Scientific and Expert Conference TEAM 2022, Slavonski Brod, Croatia, pp. 275–283 (2022)

11. Dragičević, M., Begović, E., Peko, I.: Multiobjective optimization of MQLC turning process parameters using grey-fuzzy approach. J. Mech. Eng. **16**, 3–13 (2019)

12. Dragičević, M., Begović, E., Peko I.: Optimization of dry turning process parameters using Taguchi method combined with fuzzy logic approach. In: Proceedings of 16th International Conference on Tribology, Kragujevac, Serbia, pp. 429-435 (2019)

13. Madić, M., Ćojbašić, Ž, Radovanović, M.: Comparison of fuzzy logic, regression and ANN laser kerf width models. UPB Sci. Bullet. Ser. D: Mech. Eng. **78**, 197–212 (2016)

14. Madić, M., Radovanović, M., Ćojbašić, Ž, Nedić, B., Gostimirović, M.: Fuzzy logic approach for the prediction of dross formation in CO_2 laser cutting of mild steel. J. Eng. Sci. Technol. Rev. **8**, 143–150 (2015)

15. Kovač, P., Rodić, D., Pucovsky, V., Savković, B., Gostimirović, M.: Application of fuzzy logic and regression analysis for modelling surface roughness in face milling. J. Intell. Manuf. **24**, 755–762 (2013)

Internet of Things in Education: Opportunities and Challenges

Krešimir Rakić(⊠) 🆔

Faculty of Mechanical Engineering, Computing and Electrical Engineering,
University of Mostar, Matice hrvatske b.b., 88000 Mostar, Bosnia and Herzegovina
kresimir.rakic@fsre.sum.ba

Abstract. The basic concept of Internet of Things is the ability to upgrade every-day objects with identification, sensor, network, and processing capabilities that will enable them to communicate with each other, as well as with other devices and services via the Internet. Improved in this way, these objects become smart objects, because they require minimal or even no human intervention to generate, exchange, collect, analyze, and manage data. The numerous possibilities of IoT provide great potential for its application in various areas of human life. In this paper, a comprehensive review of IoT implementation research is given, with a special emphasis on its application in education. The opportunities and advantages that IoT provides to educational institutions and all stakeholders in the learning and teaching process are listed and categorized. Challenges that institutions face when introducing IoT in their daily work are also listed, as well as suggestions for possible solutions for each of the challenges.

Keywords: Education · Internet of Things · Digital Age

1 Introduction

The birth of the personal computer in the 1970s, the graphical user interface in the 1980s, the World Wide Web in the 1990s and today the Internet of Things have launched our global society into the so-called information age. The information age is a period in human history that began in the middle of the 20th century. It is characterized by a sudden transition from traditional industries to an economy centered on information technology [1]. For the vast majority of people, this digital change is happening independently of their conscious perception. They are faced with ever-changing demands and needs. They need digital identification cards to communicate with state institutions. For everyday communication with family, friends, and colleagues, accessing and exchange of information, they need a smartphone. For the same reason, they also maintain pages on social networks. At the same time, the technologies and processes behind these changes have become smaller, more complex, and more hidden in our everyday physical environment [2].

D. Vasić and M. Kundid Vasić (Eds.): MoStart 2023, CCIS 1827, pp. 104–117, 2023.
https://doi.org/10.1007/978-3-031-36833-2_8

Today, the information amount every day exceeds the previous days' situation. This fact is reflected in the explosion of media channels and products, the accelerated informatization of society, the development of education and the growing interest in information-related occupations. Living in the information age, we have become an information society. The information society is a term for a society in which the creation, distribution, use, dissemination, integration, and management of information have become the most important cultural, economic, and political activity. The goal of the information society is to achieve a global competitive advantage, using information technology in a creative and useful way [3]. What is not explicitly stated in above definition is the pervasive nature of some digital information technologies, as well as our personal and professional dependence on computers and the Internet. When talking about the information society, people most likely talk of the incredibly fast ways in which digital communication has developed in the recent decades, and on the impact it has had on their lives and habits [4].

In 2020, the amount of data on the Internet hit 40 zettabytes. A zettabyte is about a trillion gigabytes [5]. Most of this data is first captured and created by humans - by typing, pressing a capture key, taking a digital picture, or scanning a barcode. However, people have limited time, attention, and accuracy, which implies that they should not be the first choice for collecting data about things in the real world. People, just like the environment in which they are living, are physical. Our society is based on physical things, not on ideas or information. Ideas and information are important, but not as much as the things. Yet, today's information technology depends so much on data coming from humans that our computers know more about ideas than things. If we could train computers to know about things, based on data they collected independently, directly from those things, without our help, we could track and count everything, greatly reducing waste, losses, costs, and without the ever-present possibility of human error. We would know when to replace, repair, or recall things and, in general, manage them better and more efficiently. But, in fact, we can. The solution to this problem is the Internet of Things.

This paper describes the concept of the Internet of Things, its characteristics, possible areas of application in everyday life, with a special emphasis on its application in education.

2   Internet of Things

The term Internet of Things (IoT) was first mentioned in 1999 during a presentation on Radio Frequency Identification (RFID) at Procter & Gamble. The term was coined by Kevin Ashton, a technology pioneer who cofounded the Auto-ID Center at the Massachusetts Institute of Technology [6]. This center, among other things, created a global standard system for RFID and other sensors.

The basic concept of IoT is the ability to upgrade everyday objects with identification, sensor, network, and processing capabilities, enabling them to communicate with each other, as well as with other devices and services via the Internet, to achieve their purpose [7]. Improved in this way, these objects are given the label of "smart objects" because they require minimal or even no human intervention to generate and exchange data, while, at the same time, they can collect, analyze, and manage data [8].

IoT represents an improvement in the use of existing technologies: Radio Frequency Identification (RFID) technology, sensor networks, device communication, etc., in terms of the number and type of devices, as well as the connection of networks of these devices via the Internet [9]. Over the past decade, IoT has attracted significant attention from academia and industry due to the new opportunities this contemporary technology provides. IoT describes a world where smart objects are connected to the Internet and communicate with each other, with minimal human intervention. The ultimate goal of IoT research and application is to create a "better world for all people", in which the objects around us will know what we like, what we want and what we need. Accordingly, they will act without explicit instructions.

In its periodic report, Cisco predicts that in the next 10 years IoT will generate up to 500 billion devices connected to the Internet and each other [10]. This change will contribute improved productivity, generate new revenue streams, and create unprecedented business models.

Additionally, the technology is never static. Constant progress, increasing expectations and tasks set before technology motivate scientists and researchers to reach new benchmarks. Moreover, during recent years, there has been a great increase in the research and application of several essential technologies, closely related to IoT, such as cloud computing, big data, etc. Together, these technologies provide almost infinite possibilities in a wide variety of human activities.

The areas of application of IoT technologies are numerous and diverse, and IoT solutions are expanding every day and today find their place in almost all areas of human activity [11, 12]. Some of the most referenced IoT application areas are listed below.

2.1 Applications of Internet of Things

The numerous possibilities of IoT provide enormous potential for its applications with a significant social, economic, and environmental impact, and the realization of some new concepts that would not exist without IoT. The increasing presence of these concepts in public, business and to people's private lives, their vivid advantages over traditional equivalents, the dependence that we, as a society, are slowly developing for them, are gradually taking on visionary proportions and placing them high on the priority list of human efforts to achieve a better life for all [13]. Some of the concepts based on IoT are, among others, Smart Mobility/Transportation, Smart Grids, Smart Homes/Buildings/Cities, Public Safety and Environmental Monitoring, Medicine and Healthcare, Agriculture and Cultivation, etc.

Another highly prominent area of application is the smart industry, in which the IoT is a communication channel for the collaboration of smart manufacturing systems, with each other and with people. This application is referred to as Industry 4.0 [14], and this change with which IoT is entering the industry in a big way is often identified as the Fourth Industrial Revolution.

Smart Mobility/Transportation. Smart Mobility/Transportation represents a flexible and multimodal transport system that should enable seamless, efficient, and flexible travel by different driving modes. It represents the basis of the Internet of Vehicles (IoV) concept, which seeks to improve road safety by preventing or reducing the number of traffic accidents and providing new solutions for an optimized mode of transportation. Some of the problems faced by this IoT application are related to wireless networks and communication [15, 16], smart and self-driving vehicles [17, 18], fleet tracking [19, 20], problem solving traffic jams [21], etc.

Smart Grid. Smart Grid is an electricity supply network that uses digital communication technology to detect and respond to local changes in usage. It channels energy according to the previously set requirements of end users. A Smart Grid is an electricity supply network that uses digital communication technology to detect and respond to local changes in usage. It channels energy according to the previously set requirements of end users. Some of the applications of IoT in this area are smart infrastructure and its monitoring [22, 23], the way of communication in a smart grid [24], systems for managing renewable energy sources [25], etc.

Smart Houses/Buildings. Smart houses or buildings represent a common living environment, equipped with heating, lighting and other electronic devices that can be controlled remotely either via a smartphone or via a computer. Smart cities are municipalities that use information and communication technologies to improve the quality of government services and the well-being of citizens. Some of the main research directions carried out in this context include the integration of RFID technology in households [26, 27], computer architecture proposals for managing IoT devices [28, 29], the integration of IoT with Cloud Computing and web services [30, 31], solutions such as monitoring the availability of parking spaces in real-time, intelligent street lighting [32], etc.

Public Safety and Environmental Monitoring. Public Safety and Environmental Monitoring, using IoT technology, includes observing weather conditions, protecting endangered species, monitoring water quality and other parameters that are directly or indirectly related to our environment using sensor-enriched applications and other devices to monitor changes in the environment. Some of the research in this area includes exploring suitable network architecture, communication protocols and web services [33–35], using RFID and/or wearable technology to monitor environmental parameters [36, 37], combining IoT services, Cloud Computer Science, Geoinformatics, Remote Sensing and GPS for environmental monitoring and management [38], etc.

Medicine and Healthcare. The application of IoT in medicine and healthcare is often called the Internet of Medical Things (IoMT) and represents a systematic way of connecting healthcare services with IT systems via, and medical devices with built-in Wi-Fi systems that enable Machine-to-Machine communication. Some of the topics of research on the use of IoT in medicine and healthcare include identifying the communication requirements of different processes and their integration in the form of web services [39], using Cloud Servers to collect large amounts of data as a basis for further research [40], applications based on wearable RFID technology [41], networked sensor platforms for monitoring individual physical and mental health [42, 43], proactive health analytics for disease prevention [44], etc.

Agriculture and Cultivation. Trends in the development of agriculture increasingly rely on modern technologies, including IoT. Smart devices are increasingly being considered and used to assess parameters that contribute to plant growth, and agricultural activities are carried out in accordance with their readings. And according to observations they perform agricultural activities. Some research directions in this field include intelligent agricultural management [45], application of Wireless Sensor Networks (WSN) to read climate conditions [46, 47], combining Cloud Computing and IoT techniques for synergistic effect [48, 49], automation in agriculture [50, 51], etc.

Industry 4.0. In recent years, the concept of IoT has gained increasing influence in the field of industry, labeling it as Smart Industry or Industry 4.0. The requirements of modern industry, with their intensity and needs, direct the development of IoT. Some of the research on the use of IoT in industry includes the development of frameworks for connecting heterogeneous devices with different functionalities, work scheduling and decision making [52–55], predictive maintenance of industrial equipment [56], resource-based data access methods [57], using in-depth knowledge of various public logistics services with the aim of real-time information sharing and visibility [58], etc.

In addition to all the above-mentioned areas of human activity, in whose current research IoT finds its place, the area of education is of particular importance for this paper. Below are presented the possibilities of applying IoT in education, as well as the challenges that arise.

3   Internet of Things in Education

The digital age, in which we live and work, has led to the fact that technology has entered practically every pore of human life and activity. For society to be successful in any aspect of its activity, some of which we have listed above, a large number of highly educated experts are needed who know modern technological achievements, follow all changes and trends in technological research and know how to apply them in their daily work to the benefit of the whole society. IoT technology brings changes in modern teaching practice, but also changes the infrastructure of educational institutions [59]. The term IoT can be viewed in two ways in education, due to its use as a technological tool to improve the infrastructure of educational institutions, but also as a subject for teaching the basic concepts of computer science [60].

One of the basic requirements that today's economy puts before the education system is exactly the production of experts of these profiles in the field of science, technology, engineering and mathematics, fields that we often combine under the STEM label, experts who will know IoT technology [61]. Numerous higher education institutions are responding to this demand by offering elective courses related to IoT to graduate students in computer science and engineering [62–64].

Microcontrollers (such as Arduino) [65, 66] and single-board computers (such as Raspberry Pi) [67, 68] have, with their affordable price and wide range of possibilities and compatible sensors and actuators, enabled quality education in the field of IoT. This kind of modern education is no longer reserved only for the richest societies and the most prestigious universities, enabling, in this way, potential economic growth worldwide.

However, we will leave the offer of courses dealing with IoT technology and its application to universities and colleges. We will deal with another aspect of integrating IoT into all levels of education. Given that education is a widespread and systematically organized activity, it intertwines to a greater or lesser extent with the previously mentioned areas. In this way, some of the numerous directions of research mentioned before can be considered in education as well. Below is an overview of the possibilities of using IoT in education.

3.1 Smart Campus

University campuses are, as a rule, connected to the Internet. Using sensors, RFID, Near-Field-Communication (NFC), Quick Response (QR) tags and other IoT technologies, numerous campus facilities, such as open spaces, buildings, parking lots, classrooms and laboratories, doors, windows, printers, projectors, etc., can be turned into smart objects [69]. Smart campus can be a collection of several smart things in one system. Some possibilities for applying IoT in establishing a smart campus are listed below.

Safe Teaching and Learning Environment. A safe learning environment is one of the cornerstones of good education, enabling students and teachers to participate in learning and teaching without hesitation. IoT enables a wide range of applications that can increase security and protection within educational institutions and thus make the lives of students much more comfortable [70]. Video surveillance tools that can identify suspicious persons, IoT-enabled security systems such as wireless door locks, facial recognition devices, RFID technology in conjunction with automated access control [71], etc. will help provide enhanced security not only to students but also teachers and staff [72]. IoT can also help improve online security by protecting all systems as well as sensitive student data using firewalls and authentication mechanisms [73].

Improved Energy Efficiency. By controlling campus HVAC systems, IoT technology can significantly reduce electricity and water usage costs. Systems that automatically adjust the lighting in the campus and classrooms, according to weather conditions and the time of day and the presence of students in the classroom, will contribute to lower operating costs [74–76]. By collecting information from individual water heating, lighting, and air conditioning systems over time, it is possible to analyze them, predict needs and optimize them using artificial intelligence algorithms.

Smart Parking. There is a growing need to improve campus access control and surveillance [77]. By using IoT technology, it is possible to improve this process and realize an automatic entry, exit and parking management system. The system can include automatic recognition of vehicle plates, identification cards or RFID tags of teachers and staff, and detect the presence of vehicles in the parking lot [78, 79]. Based on that information, the system can regulate access to the campus and suggest the optimal parking spot.

3.2 Smart Classroom

The concept of a smart classroom represents an environment enriched with advanced learning aids based on the latest technology or connected smart things such as microphones, cameras, and various sensors. These sensors can be used to measure student satisfaction with the teaching process as well as many other related things, thus providing ease and comfort for classroom management and creating better learning and teaching environments [80]. Some applications of IoT for creating and managing a smart classroom are listed below.

Smart Classroom Management. Classroom management refers to the approach a teacher uses to control and manage the classroom in which he teaches. The use of smart devices can provide him with information about whether he should speak louder, whether students are losing interest, or their concentration is declining [81]. The use of IoT devices for the purpose of teaching and learning is increasingly gaining momentum in the modern educational process. Some of the most used IoT devices in the classroom are interactive whiteboards, tablets and mobile devices, virtual and augmented reality equipment [82], 3-D printers, student ID cards or wearable technology, etc. A smart classroom can provide information to the teacher about what students want to learn and how they want to learn, which is useful feedback. It helps students understand the real purpose of using technology, which also facilitates the learning process [83].

Smart Classroom Attendance System. Data on classroom attendance at universities is a reference in showing the credibility of each student, which teachers use as input data for student evaluations as well as material for evaluating the success of teaching and learning process [84]. Recording students' attendance at classes is a long-term task if it is done in the traditional way. However, the use of IoT technology, which collects and records the presence of each individual student based on student ID cards, RFID tags or NFC technology in smartphones, can save time and effort [85, 86].

Student Tracking, Engagement Improvement and Lecture Quality Feedback in Real Time. An educational institution's information system can collect data on student activity and offer a personalized learning plan, as well as topics or resources that could help students [87]. Teachers can track whether their students have completed an assignment and their overall progress in the course. Classrooms based on IoT devices provide an interactive platform for students. Immersive learning methods arouse students' interest and excite them to participate in group tasks and activities. Mobile apps are better for teaching some topics because students can simultaneously access their textbooks and digital content by scanning a barcode or QR code [88]. Student understanding is directly related to the quality of lectures. Feedback from students about the classes they attend can play a key role in improving the quality of lectures. IoT technology for monitoring and observing students' reactions to the lecture provides the teacher with real-time feedback [89].

3.3 Challenges and Possible Solutions

The mentioned possibilities of using IoT technology in creating a better and safer environment for learning and teaching represent an evolutionary step in comparison to traditional, frontal, *ex-cathedra* teaching. However, there are still some real limitations and challenges. We list some of them below.

Technology Is (Still) Not Accessible to Every Student. IoT implementation can be hampered by unequal access to technology among students. To achieve the full functionality of IoT in education, it is necessary to use technology by students, both in the educational institution and at home (the flipped classroom model). The solution to this challenge is the procurement of devices for teachers and students by an educational institution or educational authority, which entails the costs of installing the equipment, maintaining it, training teachers, and hiring technical staff to operate the IoT system.

Another, equally important, need is that of a reliable high-speed Wi-Fi connection that provides bandwidth for audio and video streaming of multimedia content. Educational institutions can provide this level of connectivity, but administrative authorities must accept the potential benefits of this approach and invest in high-level public connectivity.

IoT involves a large amount of collected data that must be properly stored and organized. Local data storage systems, which educational institutions often rely on, are sometimes inadequate or outdated. This makes the data potentially unstable, exposed to attacks or natural disasters. By using Internet-connected systems and cloud-based storage systems, it is possible to store a huge amount of data while simultaneously keeping copies in multiple locations to further secure the data.

Security and Privacy. With the greater presence of IoT technology in educational institutions, the amount of data about students stored on the Internet is also increasing, thus leading to increased concerns about the security and privacy of students. This data is a potential target of cyber threats such as data stealing, phishing stacks, man-in-the-middle attacks, ransomware, etc.

In order to ensure data privacy and security on the Internet, it is important that educational institutions invest in technologies and tools that enable the use of protective measures and contingency plans in the event of cyber-attacks, data breaches or other threats, which will require a highly skilled technical team. Students, teachers, and staff need to be educated on the importance of Internet security to protect themselves from data breaches. If the educational institution does not use the advanced, necessary technologies to preserve the privacy and security of its and students' data, it can become disastrous for your institution in terms of money, fame and trust of students and parents in the institution itself.

System Complexity and Management. IoT is still a relatively new concept and ongoing efforts, and research are being made to improve its effectiveness and usage. The systematic introduction of IoT in education represents a transformation of the functioning of the entire system that can lead to an increase in complexity for students, teachers and management who are used to traditional ways. If educational institutions want a successful implementation of IoT, they must make strict rules and decisions to make this transformation. facilitated, and encourage all stakeholders to use educational technology.

In addition, the educational institution must ensure that both its IT equipment and teaching approaches support the use of IoT in the classroom. Certain devices and applications are not compatible and can make it difficult or even impossible to build reliable and accessible IoT settings. Although the risks and potential obstacles associated with the technology used are a potential landmine, educational organizations can gain significant benefits from researching and experimenting with different IoT capabilities.

Costs. Implementing IoT in an educational institution, in whole or in part, involves high costs for the systems, devices, software, hardware and power to run them. Setting up equipment and its installation, as well as periodic maintenance, require the engagement of expert professionals and technical teams trained in the field of data science and data management, installation and maintenance, software development, security, etc. This becomes a big challenge, especially for smaller and publicly funded institutions, schools.

Researchers and institutions around the world are making constant efforts to develop new and improved ways to make IoT-enabled systems more accessible and easier to implement. With extra effort, it is possible to find IoT systems within the budget, the implementation and maintenance of which can be managed by a small team of experts, either within the institution or on a contract basis.

4 Conclusion

IoT technology and its almost endless possibilities have proven their value in education, both for students and for teachers and educational institutions in general. IoT enables the collection of meaningful and relevant data in real time and, indirectly, more effective planning and fine-tuning and improvement of curricula. These technologies help stimulate student learning and make it more engaging. They enable teachers to digitize the teaching process, with greater efficiency.

Although there are many advantages of IoT in education, there are also challenges regarding availability, security, management, cost, etc. As IoT technology is still in development, a lot of research is being done on its applicability and how to use it in large numbers. human activities, among them education. New, more efficient and productive systems, which will appear as a result of these researches, will alleviate the mentioned problems in, we hope, the near future.

References

1. Castells, M.: The Information Age: Economy, Society and Culture. Blackwell, Oxford (1996). ISBN 978-0631215943
2. Zandbergen, D.: We live in an Information Age: What does that actually mean? (2013). https://waag.org/en/article/we-live-information-age-what-does-actually-mean. Accessed 25 Mar 2023
3. Zadeh, S.K., Veisi, A.G., Zadeh, M.K.: Do we live in an information society? Does it matter? Int. J. Adv. Res. 1(3), 362–366 (2013). ISSN NO 2320-5407
4. Ou, M.S.: Do We Live in an "Information Society"? Library and Information Science Foundation, University of London (2016)
5. HealthIT Webpage. How Big is the Internet, and How Do We Measure It? (2020). https://healthit.com.au/how-big-is-the-internet-and-how-do-we-measure-it. Accessed 25 Mar 2023
6. Ashton, K.: That "Internet of things" thing. RFID J. 22(7), 97–114 (2009)
7. Gubbi, J., Buyya, R., Marušić, S., Palaniswami, M.: Internet of Things (IoT): a vision, architectural elements, and future directions. Futur. Gener. Comput. Syst. 29(7), 1645–1660 (2013)
8. Stankovski, S., Ostojic, G., Laslo, T., Stanojevic, M., Babic, M.: Challenges of IoT payments in smart services. In: Katalinic, B. (ed.) Proceedings of the 30th DAAAM International Symposium, pp. 0004–0009. Published by DAAAM International, Vienna, Austria (2019). ISBN 978-3-902734-22-8, ISSN 1726-9679

9. Majstorovic, V., Rakic, K.: Internet of Things and social media: tools of a successful information organization. In: Katalinic, B. (ed.) Proceedings of the 28th DAAAM International Symposium, pp. 0295–0298. Published by DAAAM International, Vienna, Austria (2017). ISBN 978-3-902734-1-2, ISSN 1726-9679

10. Cisco Internet of Things. (2017). https://www.cisco.com/c/r/en/us/internet-of-everything-ioe/internet-of-things-iot/index.html. Accessed 27 Aug 2017

11. Atzori, L., Iera, A., Morabito, G.: The Internet of Things: a survey. Comput. Netw. **54**(15), 2787–2805 (2010)

12. Efremov, S., Pilipenko, N., Voskov, L.: An integrated approach to common problems in the Internet of Things. Procedia Eng. **100**, 1215–1223 (2015)

13. Khanna, A., Kaur, S.: Internet of Things (IoT), applications and challenges: a comprehensive review. Wireless Pers. Commun. **114**(2), 1687–1762 (2020). https://doi.org/10.1007/s11277-020-07446-4

14. Shrouf, F., Ordieres, J., Miragliotta, G.: Smart factories in Industry 4.0: a review of the concept and of energy management approached in production based on the Internet of Things paradigm. In: Proceedings of the 2014 IEEE International Conference on Industrial Engineering and Engineering Management, pp. 697–701. IEEE (2014)

15. Zorzi, M., Gluhak, A., Lange, S., Bassi, A.: From today's Intranet of things to a future Internet of things: a wireless-and mobility-related view. IEEE Wirel. Commun. **17**(6), 44–51 (2010)

16. Hank, P., Müller, S., Vermesan, O., Van Den Keybus, J.: Automotive ethernet: in-vehicle networking and smart mobility. In: Proceedings of the Conference on Design, Automation and Test in Europe, pp. 1735–1739, EDA Consortium (2013)

17. Kyriazis, D., Varvarigou, T., White, D., Rossi, A., Cooper, J.: Sustainable Smart City IoT applications: heat and electricity management & eco-conscious cruise control for public transportation. In: 2013 IEEE 14th International Symposium and Workshops on a World of Wireless, Mobile and Multimedia Networks (WoWMoM), pp. 1–5. IEEE (2013)

18. Somov, A., Dupont, C., Giaffreda, R.: Supporting Smart-City mobility with cognitive Internet of Things. In: Future Network and Mobile Summit (FutureNetworkSummit), pp. 1–10. IEEE (2013)

19. Lee, S., Tewolde, G., Kwon, J.: Design and implementation of vehicle tracking system using GPS, GSM, GPRS technology and smartphone application. In: IEEE World Forum on Internet of Things (WF-IoT), pp. 353–358. IEEE (2014)

20. Vermesan, O., et al.: Internet of Things strategic research and innovation agenda. In: Vermesan, O., Friess, P. (eds.) Internet of Things - From Research and Innovation to Market Deployment, pp. 7–142. River Publishers, Aalborg (2014)

21. Ma, X., Yu, H., Wang, Y., Wang, Y.: Large-scale transportation network congestion evolution prediction using deep learning theory. PLoS ONE, **10**(3) (2015)

22. Karnouskos, S., De Holanda, T.N.: Simulation of a smart grid city with software agents. In: Third UKSim European Symposium on Computer Modeling and Simulation, EMS 2009, pp. 424–429. IEEE (2009)

23. Bressan, N., Bazzaco, L., Bui, N., Casari, P., Vangelista, L., Zorzi, M.: The deployment of a smart monitoring system using wireless sensor and actuator networks. In: 2010 First IEEE International Conference on Smart Grid Communications (SmartGridComm), pp. 49–54. IEEE (2010)

24. Zhang, Y., Yu, R., Nekovee, M., Liu, Y., Xie, S., Gjessing, S.: Cognitive machine-to-machine communications: visions and potentials for the smart grid. IEEE Network **26**(3), 6–13 (2012)

25. Yun, M., Yuxin, B.: Research on the architecture and key technology of Internet of Things (IoT) applied on smart grid. In: 2010 International Conference on Advances in Energy Engineering (ICAEE), pp. 69–72. IEEE (2010)

26. Darianian, M., Michael, M.P.: Smart home mobile RFID-based Internet-of-Things systems and services. In: International Conference on Advanced Computer Theory and Engineering, ICACTE 2008, pp. 116–120. IEEE (2008)
27. Jie, Y., Pei, J.Y., Jun, L., Yun, G., Wei, X.: Smart home system based on IoT technologies. In: 2013 Fifth International Conference on Computational and Information Sciences (ICCIS), pp. 1789–1791. IEEE (2013)
28. Chong, G., Zhihao, L., Yifeng, Y.: The research and implement of smart home system based on Internet of Things. In: 2011 International Conference on Electronics, Communications and Control (ICECC), pp. 2944–2947. IEEE (2011)
29. Li, X., Lu, R., Liang, X., Shen, X., Chen, J., Lin, X.: Smart community: an Internet of Things application. IEEE Commun. Mag. **49**(11), 68–75 (2011)
30. Soliman, M., Abiodun, T., Hamouda, T., Zhou, J., Lung, C.-H.: Smart home: integrating Internet of Things with web services and cloud computing. In: 2013 IEEE 5th International Conference on Cloud Computing Technology and Science (CloudCom), vol. 2, pp. 317–320. IEEE (2013)
31. Aazam, M., Khan, I., Alsaffar, A.A., Huh, E.N.: Cloud of Things: integrating Internet of Things and cloud computing and the issues involved. In: Proceedings of 2014 11th International Bhurban Conference on Applied Sciences & Technology (IBCAST) Islamabad, Pakistan, 14th–18th January 2014, pp. 414–419. IEEE (2014)
32. Wortmann, F., Flüchter, K.: Internet of things. Bus. Inf. Syst. Eng. **57**(3), 221–224 (2015)
33. Kelly, S.D.T., Suryadevara, N.K., Mukhopadhyay, S.C.: Towards the implementation of IoT for environmental condition monitoring in homes. IEEE Sens. J. **13**(10), 3846–3853 (2013)
34. Castellani, A.P., Gheda, M., Bui, N., Rossi, M., Zorzi, M.: Web services for the Internet of Things through CoAP and EXI. In: 2011 IEEE International Conference on Communications Workshops (ICC), pp. 1–6. IEEE (2011)
35. Oliveira, L.M., Rodrigues, J.J.: Wireless sensor networks: a survey on environmental monitoring. JCM **6**(2), 143–151 (2011)
36. Jia, X., Feng, Q., Fan, T., Lei, Q.: RFID technology and its applications in Internet of Things (IoT). In: 2012 2nd International Conference on Consumer Electronics, Communications and Networks (CECNet, pp. 1282–1285. IEEE (2012)
37. Swan, M.: Sensor Mania! The Internet of Things, wearable computing, objective metrics, and the quantified self 2.0. J. Sens. Actuator Netw. **1**(3), 217–253 (2012)
38. Kantarci, B., Mouftah, H.T.: Trustworthy sensing for public safety in cloud-centric Internet of Things. IEEE Internet Things J. **1**(4), 360–368 (2014)
39. Bui, N., Zorzi, M.: Health care applications: a solution based on the Internet of Things. In: Proceedings of the 4th International Symposium on Applied Sciences in BioMedical and Communication Technologies, p. 131. ACM (2011)
40. Doukas, C., Maglogiannis, I.: Bringing IoT and Cloud Computing towards pervasive healthcare. In: 2012 6th International Conference on Innovative Mobile and Internet Services in Ubiquitous Computing (IMIS), pp. 922–926. IEEE (2012)
41. Amendola, S., Lodato, R., Manzari, S., Occhiuzzi, C., Marrocco, G.: RFID technology for IoT-based personal healthcare in smart spaces. IEEE Internet Things J. **1**(2), 144–152 (2014)
42. Yang, G., Xie, L., Mäntysalo, M., Zhou, X., Pang, Z., Da Xu, L., et al.: A health-IoT platform based on the integration of intelligent packaging, unobtrusive bio-sensor, and intelligent medicine box. IEEE Trans. Industr. Inf. **10**(4), 2180–2191 (2014)
43. Hassanalieragh, M., et al.: Health monitoring and management using Internet-of-Things (IoT) sensing with cloud-based processing: opportunities and challenges. In: 2015 IEEE International Conference on Services Computing (SCC), pp. 285–292. IEEE (2015)
44. Ukil, A., Bandyoapdhyay, S., Puri, C., Pal, A.: IoT healthcare analytics: the importance of anomaly detection. In: 2016 IEEE 30th International Conference on Advanced Information Networking and Applications (AINA), pp. 994–997. IEEE (2016)

45. Yan-e, D.: Design of intelligent agriculture management information system based on IoT. In: 2011 International Conference on Intelligent Computation Technology and Automation (ICICTA), vol. 1, pp. 1045–1049. IEEE (2011)

46. Liqiang, Z., Shouyi, Y., Leibo, L., Zhen, Z., Shaojun, W.: A crop monitoring system based on wireless sensor network. Procedia Environ. Sci. **11**, 558–565 (2011)

47. Li, S.: Application of the Internet of Things technology in precision agriculture irrigation systems. In: 2012 International Conference on Computer Science & Service System (CSSS), pp. 1009–1013. IEEE (2012)

48. Bo, Y., Wang, H.: The application of Cloud Computing and the Internet of Things in agriculture and forestry. In: 2011 International Joint Conference on Service Sciences (IJCSS), pp. 168–172. IEEE (2011)

49. Tong Ke, F.: Smart agriculture based on Cloud Computing and IOT. J. Convergence Inf. Technol. **8**(2) (2013)

50. Zhao, J., Zhang, J., Feng, Y., Guo, J.: The study and application of the IOT technology in agriculture. In: 2010 3rd IEEE International Conference on Computer Science and Information Technology (ICCSIT), vol. 2, pp. 462–465. IEEE (2010)

51. Kaloxylos, A., Eigenmann, R., Teye, F., Politopoulou, Z., Wolfert, S., Shrank, C., et al.: Farm management systems and the future internet era. Comput. Electron. Agric. **89**, 130–144 (2012)

52. Kovatsch, M., Mayer, S., Ostermaier, B.: Moving application logic from the firmware to the cloud: towards the thin server architecture for the Internet of Things. In: 2012 6th International Conference on Innovative Mobile and Internet Services in Ubiquitous Computing (IMIS), pp. 751–756. IEEE (2012)

53. Palattella, M.R., Accettura, N., Grieco, L.A., Boggia, G., Dohler, M., Engel, T.: On optimal scheduling in duty-cycled industrial IoT applications using IEEE802. 15.4 e TSCH. IEEE Sens. J. **13**(10), 3655–3666 (2013)

54. Bi, Z., Da Xu, L., Wang, C.: Internet of Things for enterprise systems of modern manufacturing. IEEE Trans. Industr. Inf. **10**(2), 1537–1546 (2014)

55. Reaidy, P.J., Gunasekaran, A., Spalanzani, A.: Bottom-up approach based on Internet of Things for order fulfillment in a collaborative warehousing environment. Int. J. Prod. Econ. **159**, 29–40 (2015)

56. Durkop, L., Trsek, H., Jasperneite, J., Wisniewski, L.: Towards autoconfiguration of industrial automation systems: a case study using Profinet IO. In: 2012 IEEE 17th Conference on Emerging Technologies & Factory Automation (ETFA), pp. 1–8. IEEE (2012)

57. He, W., Da Xu, L.: Integration of distributed enterprise applications: a survey. IEEE Trans. Industr. Inform. **10**(1), 35–42 (2014)

58. Qiu, X., Luo, H., Xu, G., Zhong, R., Huang, G.Q.: Physical assets and service sharing for IoT-enabled Supply Hub in Industrial Park (SHIP). Int. J. Prod. Econ. **159**, 4–15 (2015)

59. Veeramanickam, M.R.M., Mohanapriya, M.: IoT enabled futurus smart campus with effective e-learning: I-Campus. GSTF J. Eng. Technol. (JET) **3**(4), 8–87 (2016)

60. Elyamany, H.F., Al Khairi, A.H.: IoT-academia architecture: a profound approach. In 2015 IEEE/ACIS 16th International Conference on Software Engineering, Artificial Intelligence, Networking and Parallel/Distributed Computing (SNPD), pp. 1–5. IEEE (2015)

61. Al-Emran, M., Malik, S.I., Al-Kabi, M.N.: A survey of Internet of Things (IoT) in education: opportunities and challenges. In: Hassanien, A.E., Bhatnagar, R., Khalifa, N.E.M., Taha, M.H.N. (eds.) Toward Social Internet of Things (SIoT): enabling technologies, architectures and applications. SCI, vol. 846, pp. 197–209. Springer, Cham (2020). https://doi.org/10.1007/978-3-030-24513-9_12

62. Maenpaa, H., Varjonen, S., Hellas, A., Tarkoma, S., Mannisto, T.: Assessing IoT projects in university education-a framework for problem-based learning. In: 2017 IEEE/ACM 39th

International Conference on Software Engineering: Software Engineering Education and Training Track (ICSE-SEET, pp. 37–46. IEEE (2017)

63. Raikar, M.M., Desai, P., Naragund, J.G.: Active learning explored in open elective course: Internet of Things (IoT). In: Proceedings of IEEE 8th International Conference on Technology for Education, T4E 2016. IEEE (2017)

64. Silvis-Cividjian, N.: Teaching Internet of Things (IoT) literacy: a systems engineering approach. In: 2019 IEEE/ACM 41st International Conference on Software Engineering: Software Engineering Education and Training (ICSE-SEET), pp. 50–61. IEEE (2019)

65. Plaza, P., et al.: Arduino as an educational tool to introduce robotics. In: 2018 IEEE International Conference on Teaching, Assessment, and Learning for Engineering (TALE), pp. 1–8. IEEE (2018)

66. Bashir, A., Alhammadi, M., Awawdeh, M., Faisal, T.: Effectiveness of using Arduino platform for the hybrid engineering education learning model. In: 2019 Advances in Science and Engineering Technology International Conferences (ASET), pp. 1–6. IEEE (2019)

67. Zhong, X., Liang, Y.: Raspberry Pi: an effective vehicle in teaching the Internet of Things in computer science and engineering. Electronics 5(3), 56 (2016)

68. Mullett, G.J.: Teaching the Internet of Things (IoT) using universally available Raspberry Pi and Arduino platforms. In: 2016 ASEE Annual Conference & Exposition (2016)

69. Cață, M.: Smart University, a new concept in the Internet of Things. In: 2015 14th RoEduNet International Conference - Networking in Education and Research (RoEduNet NER), pp. 195–197. IEEE (2015)

70. Alhaddad, M.M.: Improving security performance in smart campuses. ResearchBerg Rev. Sci. Technol. 2(4), 17–28 (2019)

71. Qiu, Y., Chen, J., Zhu, Q.: Campus access control system based on RFID. In: 2012 IEEE International Conference on Computer Science and Automation Engineering, pp. 407–410. IEEE (2012)

72. Campbell, A.: Role and Impact of IoT in Education (2022). https://www.helpwire.app/blog/iot-in-education/. Accessed 25 Mar 2023

73. Van Hoojidonk, R., Zandbergen, D.: IoT in Education: A Better-Connected and More Collaborative Future for Students and Teachers (2022, 2013). https://blog.richardvanho oijdonk.com/en/iot-in-education-a-better-connected-and-more-collaborative-future-for-stu dents-and-teachers/. Accessed 25 Mar 2023

74. Shyr, W.J., Zeng, L.W., Lin, C.K., Lin, C.M., Hsieh, W.Y.: Application of an energy management system via the Internet of Things on a university campus. EURASIA J. Math. Sci. Technol. Educ. 14(5), 1759–1766 (2018)

75. Moura, P., Moreno, J.I., López López, G., Alvarez-Campana, M.: IoT platform for energy sustainability in university campuses. Sensors 21(2), 357 (2021)

76. Tanasiev, V., Pătru, G.C., Rosner, D., Sava, G., Necula, H., Badea, A.: Enhancing environmental and energy monitoring of residential buildings through IoT. Autom. Constr. 126, 103662 (2021)

77. Shoup, D.: Parking on a Smart Campus: Lessons for Universities and Cities. UCLA (2005)

78. Anuar, F., Lingas, N.: Smart campus initiative: car entrance, exit and parking management prototype development. In: AIP Conference Proceedings, vol. 2643(1). AIP Publishing LLC (2023)

79. Sari, M.W., Ciptadi, P.W., Hardyanto, R.H.: Study of smart campus development using Internet of Things technology. IOP Conf. Ser. Mater. Sci. Eng. 190(1) (2017). IOP Publishing

80. Kassab, M., DeFranco, J., Laplante, P.: A systematic literature review on Internet of Things in education: benefits and challenges. J. Comput. Assist. Learn. 36(2), 115–127 (2020)

81. Rytivaara, A.: Collaborative classroom management in a co-taught primary school classroom. Int. J. Educ. Res. 53, 182–191 (2012)

82. Cunningham, E.: IoT in Education: Tech Makes Gains in K-12 Schools. https://edtech
    magazine.com/k12/article/2021/12/iot-education-tech-makes-gains-k-12-schools-perfcon.
    Accessed 25 Mar 2023
83. Chang, C.H.: Smart classroom roll caller system with IoT architecture. In: 2011 2nd Interna-
    tional Conference on Innovations in Bio-Inspired Computing and Applications, pp. 356–360.
    IEEE (2011)
84. Santoso, B., Sari, M.W.: Design of student attendance system using Internet of Things (IoT)
    technology. J. Phys. Conf. Ser. **1254**(1) (2019). IOP Publishing
85. Kariapper, R.K.A.R.: Attendance system using RFID, IoT and machine learning: a two factor
    verification approach. Syst. Rev. Pharm. **12**(3), 314–321 (2021)
86. Alotaibi, S.J.: Attendance system based on the Internet of Things for supporting blended
    learning. In: 2015 World Congress on Internet Security (WorldCIS), p. 78 (2015)
87. Orehovački, T., Plantak Vukovac, D., Džeko, M., Stapić, Z.: Evaluating relevant UX dimen-
    sions with respect to IoT ecosystem intended for students' activities tracking and success
    prediction. In: Zaphiris, P., Ioannou, A. (eds.) LCT 2018. LNCS, vol. 10924, pp. 279–293.
    Springer, Cham (2018). https://doi.org/10.1007/978-3-319-91743-6_22
88. Cheng, Y.W., Wang, Y., Chen, N.S.: A framework for designing an immersive language learn-
    ing environment integrated with educational robots and IoT-based toys. In: Foundations and
    Trends in Smart Learning: Proceedings of 2019 International Conference on Smart Learn-
    ing Environments, pp. 1–4. Springer, Cham (2019). https://doi.org/10.1007/978-981-13-690
    8-7_1
89. Gligorić, N., Uzelac, A., Krco, S.: Smart classroom: real-time feedback on lecture qual-
    ity. In: 2012 IEEE International Conference on Pervasive Computing and Communications
    Workshops, pp. 391–394. IEEE (2012)

Artificial Intelligence for Knowledge Visualization: An Overview

Robert Rozić[1]([⊠]) [iD], Robert Slišković[2][iD], and Marko Rosić[3][iD]

[1] Faculty of Science and Education, University of Mostar, Mostar,
Bosnia and Herzegovina
robert.rozic@fpmoz.sum.ba
[2] University of Mostar, Mostar, Bosnia and Herzegovina
robert.sliskovic@sum.ba
[3] Faculty of Science, University of Split, 21000 Split, Croatia
marko.rosic@pmfst.hr

Abstract. Artificial Intelligence (AI) has transformed the way we interact with data and information. The growing volume of data and knowledge has made knowledge visualization (KV) important tool for understanding and analyzing complex datasets. AI has the potential to significantly improve KV by automating tasks such as data processing, pattern recognition, and visualization design. This paper provides a comprehensive overview of the current state-of-the-art on the application of AI for KV, as well as the challenges related to visualizing complex datasets. Different KV approaches, such as information visualization, ontologies and concept mapping are examined. We explore various AI techniques used to enhance these methods, including natural language processing (NLP), machine learning (ML), and deep learning (DL). Finally, we discuss the limitations and promising areas for future research in this field.

Keywords: Knowledge Visualization · Artificial Intelligence · Information Visualization · Concept Mapping · Data Analysis · Data Visualization · Big data · Semantic Web · Ontology

1 Introduction

The rapid development of internet technology in recent years has led to a massive increase in data generation, resulting in the emergence of big data and data lakes. These technologies are becoming widespread across various domains, including business, finance, healthcare, and education. However, volume and complexity of data produced present significant challenges in extracting meaningful insights and actionable knowledge. To address these challenges, knowledge visualization has evolved as an essential tool for effectively presenting complex data.

In recent years, there has been a growing interest in using artificial intelligence (AI) to improve KV. AI techniques, such as NLP, ML, and deep learning, can automatically identify patterns and relationships within large datasets and

D. Vasić and M. Kundid Vasić (Eds.): MoStart 2023, CCIS 1827, pp. 118–131, 2023.
https://doi.org/10.1007/978-3-031-36833-2_9

generate visualizations that can help in better understanding of information. The application of AI in KV has potential to transform various domains by enabling more efficient and effective data analysis and decision-making processes.

Presenting data and information visually enables users to detect patterns, establish connections, and acquire insights that might be difficult to acquire otherwise. Creating effective KVs is complex task that demands not only understanding of underlying data, but also cognitive processes involved in data analysis.

This paper aims to provide a comprehensive review of the current state-of-the-art in AI-based KV. We examine the literature on various data and knowledge visualization types and application of AI techniques, including natural language processing (NLP), machine learning (ML), and deep learning, to enhance these visualizations. Additionally, we address the challenges and limitations associated with employing AI for KV and suggest potential future research directions to overcome these obstacles.

2   Background

To understand opportunities in applying AI techniques for KV, we provide the necessary background information for understanding the challenges and opportunities in applying AI techniques to KV. We begin by discussing knowledge-based systems, followed by an overview of big data and data lakes, and finally, we delve into different knowledge representation methods.

> Information does not equal knowledge. For information to become knowledge, we need to interpret and understand it. Visualization in general responds directly to this need. However, even after producing a visual representation, we must address issues involving exploration, navigation, and interpretation of the data [8].

This quote highlights the importance of presenting information visually and ensuring that the resulting representation is easy to explore, navigate, and interpret.

2.1   Knowledge Based Systems

Knowledge-based systems are computer programs that rely on a knowledge base to solve complex problems or provide insights. These systems make use of formalized domain-specific knowledge, which is typically represented using a variety of techniques such as rules, frames, or semantic networks. Knowledge-based systems have been extensively used in areas like expert systems, decision support systems, and intelligent tutoring systems.

The rise of AI and machine learning has brought about advancements in knowledge-based systems, enabling them to learn from data and adapt to new information. These advancements have made it possible to develop more sophisticated systems that can tackle increasingly complex problems and provide valuable insights for decision-making processes.

2.2 Big Data and Data Lakes

"If you think of a Data Mart as a store of bottled water, cleansed and packaged and structured for easy consumption, the Data Lake is a large body of water in a more natural state. The contents of the Data Lake stream in from a source to fill the lake, and various users of the lake can come to examine, dive in, or take samples." (James Dixon, founder and former CTO of Pentaho) [11]. In other words, data lakes contain vast amounts of raw, unprocessed data, which can be difficult to work with using traditional analytical tools. KVs powered by AI and machine learning techniques, can help to transform this data into meaningful insights and actionable knowledge.

Big data refers to the large and complex datasets that are generated by various sources, such as social media, sensors, and transaction records. The key characteristics of big data are often described using the 5 V's: volume, variety, velocity, veracity, and value. The sheer volume of data, coupled with its diversity, rapid generation, and varying levels of quality, presents unique challenges for processing, analysis, and visualization.

Data lakes are a popular solution for storing and managing big data. They are large-scale storage repositories that can accommodate raw data in various formats, such as structured, semi-structured, and unstructured data. Data lakes enable organizations to consolidate their data sources and provide a flexible environment for data processing, analysis, and visualization.

2.3 Knowledge Representation and Reasoning (KRR)

Knowledge representation and reasoning is the field of artificial intelligence (AI) dedicated to representing information about the world in a form that a computer system can use to solve complex tasks such as diagnosing a medical condition or having a dialog in a natural language [19]. It is process of encoding information in a format that can be easily processed and understood by both humans and machines. Various knowledge representation methods have been developed to structure and organize information in meaningful ways. Effective knowledge representation is essential for AI systems, as it provides the foundation for reasoning and decision-making processes. Various techniques have been developed for representing knowledge, and some of the most commonly used methods are:

Semantic Networks. A graphical representation of knowledge that uses nodes to represent concepts and edges to represent relationships between those concepts. Semantic networks are useful for capturing hierarchical and associative information [33].

Frames. A structured representation of knowledge that organizes information into "frames," which are data structures containing slots for attributes and values. Frames are particularly useful for representing objects, their properties, and relationships between objects [27].

Rule-Based Systems. A method of knowledge representation that uses a set of rules or production rules to express relationships between entities and actions. Rule-based systems are often used in expert systems and can represent complex reasoning processes [6].

Ontologies. Ontologies are formal representations of concepts, relationships, and properties within a specific domain. They provide a structured vocabulary and a set of rules for defining and reasoning about the relationships between concepts [14].

Probabilistic Graphical Models (PGM). A class of knowledge representation methods that use graphs to model the probabilistic relationships between variables [17].

Concept Maps and Mind Maps. Visual representation techniques that display relationships between concepts and ideas in a hierarchical or associative manner. These maps facilitate learning, understanding, and knowledge organization by visually depicting connections between concepts [28].

3 Literature Review

In this section, we give a general review of various methods and technologies such as ontologies, semantic web, concept maps, and mind maps, used in KV. Following this, we will provide a comprehensive overview of the significant contributions and advancements in that field using AI techniques. We will explore how these AI techniques have been applied to tasks like clustering, pattern recognition and text-to-image generation. We discuss the advantages and drawbacks of these approaches and look at how they have been used across different fields.

3.1 Ontologies and Semantic Web

Gruber (2003) defined an ontology as "an explicit specification of a conceptualization," highlighting the importance of representing objects, concepts, and entities believed to exist in a specific domain, along with the relationships that hold among them [14].

These technologies provide a structured and machine-readable representation of knowledge, enabling more sophisticated reasoning and analysis capabilities. Studies have explored their application in various visualization techniques, including knowledge graphs, interactive visualizations, and ontology-based visualizations.

Berners-Lee, Hendler, and Lassila (2001) introduced the concept of the semantic web, which aimed to create a universally accessible, machine-readable web of information, linking data and metadata to facilitate a new level of information discovery and usage [4]. The semantic web was designed to leverage ontologies as a means of providing structured, interoperable, and semantically rich data representations.

Rosic, Stankov, and Glavinic (2002) discuss the potential benefits of integrating personal agents and Semantic Web in distance education systems, particularly their Distributed Tutor Expert System (DTEx-Sys). They highlight how personal agents can help users avoid information overload and adapt to their needs, while the Semantic Web can enable agents to understand the content of the documents they access. [31] In a later study, Glavinić, Stankov, Zelić, and Rosić (2008) delve deeper into the application of intelligent tutoring in the Semantic Web and Web 2.0 environments within the TExSys model. They propose a multi-agent architecture where agents in these environments can exchange data and communicate, enhancing the system's functionality and extending intelligent tutoring through mobile, collaborative, and social dimensions [12].

Alani et al. (2003) presented the Artequakt project, which combines a knowledge extraction tool with an ontology to achieve continuous knowledge support and guide information extraction. The extraction tool searches online documents and extracts knowledge that matches the given classification structure, generating machine-readable output that is automatically maintained in a knowledge base. RDF schemas [26] play a critical role in this process, as they offer a flexible and expressive means of representing complex relationships and dependencies between entities [2].

Allemang and Hendler (2008) provided a practical guide to building and using ontologies in the Semantic Web. Their work covered the modeling of information in RDF, RDFS, and OWL and offered guidance on best practices for creating and managing ontologies in real-world applications [3].

Lohmann et al. (2015) introduced WebVOWL, a responsive web application for the visualization of ontologies based on the Visual Notation for OWL Ontologies (VOWL) and open web standards. WebVOWL renders ontologies in a force-directed graph layout according to the VOWL specification and offers interaction techniques that allow users to explore and customize their visualizations [21] (Table 1).

3.2 Concept Maps and Mind Maps

Cañas et al. (2005) studied the integration of knowledge and information visualization through concept maps. The authors highlighted the difference between information visualization, a well-established field, and KV, a relatively new area of research. They demonstrated how concept maps can be used to organize repositories of information in a manner that is easily browsable and can improve searching algorithms on the Web. The paper also discussed the role of information in complementing knowledge models and enhancing the construction of concept maps [7] (Figs. 1).

Eppler (2006) compared concept maps with three other visualization formats: mind maps, conceptual diagrams, and visual metaphors. The author discussed the application parameters, advantages, and disadvantages of each format for learning and knowledge sharing. Eppler argued that the combination of these

Table 1. Summary of literature on KV in Ontologies and Semantic Web

Authors	Publication Year	Contribution
Gruber	1993	Defined the term "ontology" in the context of artificial intelligence
Berners-Lee et al.	2001	Introduced the concept of the Semantic Web and its components
Rosic et al.	2002	Explored the integration of personal agents and Semantic Web in distance education systems, focusing on the Distributed Tutor Expert System (DTEx-Sys)
Alani et al.	2003	Presented the Artequakt project, which links a knowledge extraction tool with an ontology for continuous knowledge support
Alleman & Hendler	2008	Provided a practical guide to building and using ontologies in the Semantic Web
Lohmann et al.	2015	Introduced WebVOWL, a web application for ontology visualization based on VOWL and open web standards

four visualization types can maximize the strengths of each one. The paper also discussed the implications of using these visualization formats in classroom and meeting contexts [10].

Concept maps have been used as a means of assessing learners' knowledge and constructing individualized learning paths in adaptive e-learning systems. Volarić et al. (2017) presented a semi-automatic tool for teaching programming using concept maps as an ontology. The system assessed learners' knowledge and constructed a student model, based on which it decided which concepts to include in the teaching process. The CM Tutor module was used to evaluate learners' performance through qualitative and quantitative means. The results showed good effectiveness of the system, demonstrating the potential of concept maps for constructing individualized learning paths [36].

Grubišić et al. (2017) investigated the use of knowledge indicators in concept map-based Intelligent Tutoring Systems (ITSs) to enhance learners' self-reflection and awareness during the learning process. They introduced a common set of knowledge indicators and analyzed their relationship with learner performance across three different courses. The results and learners' feedback suggested that incorporating these knowledge indicators into dashboard-like visualizations within integrated ITSs could improve the overall learning experience [15] (Table 2).

3.3 Artificial Intelligence

Humphrey, Cunningham, and Witten (1998) explored KV techniques for machine learning, specifically addressing the limitations of standard forms such as decision trees, production rules, and decision graphs in helping end-users comprehend the knowledge generated by machine learning systems. The authors

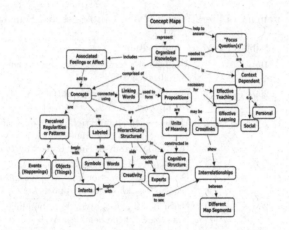

Fig. 1. Concept map about concept map [9]

map these questions onto visualization tasks and create new graphical representations that show the flow of examples through a decision structure. These techniques offer enhanced support to users, allowing them to better understand the properties of their data sets [16].

KV in NLP has gained increased attention in recent years as researchers seek to develop techniques to analyze textual data and generate visual representations of the underlying themes and structures. NLP techniques have been employed in various ways, including the creation of topic models and visualizations of document collections, as well as the generation of concept maps and knowledge graphs from textual sources.

One of the foundational approaches in KV is Latent Dirichlet Allocation (LDA), a generative probabilistic model for collections of discrete data such as text corpora. LDA is a three-level hierarchical Bayesian model that models each item in a collection as a finite mixture over an underlying set of topics. This approach has been used to create visualizations of document collections, revealing underlying themes and structures [5].

Van der Maaten and Hinton (2008) introduced a technique called t-SNE (t-Distributed Stochastic Neighbor Embedding) that visualizes high-dimensional data by assigning a location in a two or three-dimensional map to each data point. T-SNE significantly improves upon the original Stochastic Neighbor Embedding technique by optimizing it and reducing the tendency to crowd points together in the map's center. The authors demonstrated t-SNE's superior performance compared to other non-parametric visualization techniques, such as Sammon mapping, Isomap, and Locally Linear Embedding [23].

Stula et al. (2010) proposes a novel approach to modeling and simulating complex systems using agent-based fuzzy cognitive maps (ABFCMs). The ABFCM combines the strengths of fuzzy cognitive maps and multi-agent systems to enable the use of different inference algorithms in each node, making it more suitable for simulating real-world systems with diverse behavior concepts [34].

Table 2. Summary of literature on KV in CM and MM

Authors	Publication Year	Contributions
Cañas et al.	2005	Explored concept maps' role in integrating knowledge and information visualization, and enhancing construction of knowledge models
Eppler	2006	Compared concept maps, mind maps, conceptual diagrams, and visual metaphors, and demonstrated their complementary use in educational settings
Volarić et al.	2017	Developed an adaptive tool for teaching programming using concept maps in an e-learning system, demonstrating the potential of concept maps for constructing individualized learning paths
Grubišić et al.	2017	Proposed a set of knowledge indicators for enhancing learners' self-reflection and awareness in concept map-based ITSs, and explored their relationships with learner performance

Fig. 2. Word2Vec[1]

Mikolov et al. (2013) introduced two novel model architectures for computing continuous vector representations of words from very large data sets, known as word2vec. These vector representations have been used in various NLP tasks, including word similarity, text classification, and collaborative filtering [25]. Ma and Zhang (2015) further explored the use of word2vec for processing big text data and proposed a method for reducing data dimensionality by clustering similar words together [22] (Fig. 2).

McInnes, Healy, and Melville (2018) proposed UMAP (Uniform Manifold Approximation and Projection), a novel manifold learning technique for dimension reduction. UMAP is based on a theoretical framework rooted in Riemannian geometry and algebraic topology, resulting in a practical and scalable algorithm for real-world data. The algorithm is competitive with t-SNE in terms of visualization quality while arguably preserving more global structure and offering better run time performance [24].

Liu et al. (2018) developed Data Illustrator, a novel visualization framework that augments vector design tools with lazy data binding for expressive visualization authoring. The framework extends interaction techniques in modern vector design tools, enabling direct manipulation of visualization configurations and parameters. The authors demonstrated the expressive power of Data Illustrator through various examples, and a qualitative study showed that designers could effectively use the framework to compose visualizations [20].

The development of Generative Pre-trained Transformer (GPT) models has significantly advanced the field of natural language understanding. Radford et al. (2018) introduced a framework that combines unsupervised pre-training with supervised fine-tuning to achieve strong natural language understanding using a single task-agnostic model [29].

Moreover, GPT models can be applied to natural language processing tasks related to KV, such as text summarization, topic modeling, and sentiment analysis. These tasks can be useful for pre-processing textual data before visualizing it, enabling more focused and informative visualizations. In addition, GPT models can be used to generate human-readable descriptions of visualizations, helping users better understand and interpret the information presented in the visual form.

Vig (2019) introduced a tool called BertViz, which visualizes the attention mechanism in the BERT and GPT models. BertViz allows users to observe the self-attention mechanism and the interactions between different attention heads and layers, providing a clearer understanding of how these models process and generate text. The author showcased several examples of how BertViz can be used to analyze the models' performance on various NLP tasks, such as sentence classification, named entity recognition, and text generation [35].

Another relevant study is that of Lee et al. (2020), who proposed BioBERT, a novel domain-specific language representation model for creating a hierarchical knowledge graph from biomedical textual sources using deep learning techniques. Their approach adapts the Bidirectional Encoder Representations from Transformers (BERT) for biomedical text mining by pre-training it on large-scale biomedical corpora [18] (Fig. 3).

Generative adversarial networks (GANs) are a type of artificial intelligence algorithm that has been successfully applied to a wide variety of tasks, including image generation. The recent text-to-image generation approach proposed by Ramesh et al. (2021) [30] leverages the power of GANs to achieve high-quality image synthesis from textual data. GANs have also shown potential in generating more interpretable and meaningful hierarchical knowledge graphs and visualizations for end-users [13].

Ramesh et al. (2021) introduced a groundbreaking approach to zero-shot text-to-image generation using a transformer-based model. The authors leveraged the power of autoregressive transformers, combined with a large-scale dataset and model size, to achieve high-quality image generation from text descriptions. This approach outperforms previous domain-specific models and demonstrates the ability to perform complex tasks such as image-to-image

Fig. 3. Text-to-Image generation [30]

translation without requiring specialized methods. The study emphasizes the role of scale in improving generalization and suggests that further progress in the field can be driven by leveraging scale in model architecture, dataset size, and computational resources [30].

4   Discussion

The growing interest in KV emphasizes the importance of focusing on equipping systems with knowledge rather than prescribing their actions.

> "Don't tell the program what to do, tell it what to know" Smith (1985) [32].

This quote highlights the need for developing systems that are capable of processing and understanding vast amounts of knowledge, which is where KV plays a crucial role.

The literature review revealed that the application of deep learning techniques, such as dimensionality reduction, clustering, and pattern recognition, has made a significant contribution to KV. Algorithms like t-SNE and UMAP have improved visualization quality and scalability, allowing for a better understanding of complex data. However, there is still a need to develop new algorithms that preserve both local and global structures while offering better performance (Table 3).

Additionally, recent advancements in AI, particularly in NLP, have led to the development of sophisticated KV techniques. Semantic web technologies, ontologies, concept maps, and mind maps have also played a significant role in KV by enabling more sophisticated reasoning, analysis capabilities, and

Table 3. Summary of literature on KV in AI

Authors	Publication Year	Contributions
Humphrey et al.	1998	Developed new graphical representations to improve user understanding of decision structures in machine learning
Blei et al.	2003	Introduced Latent Dirichlet Allocation (LDA) for modeling and visualizing topics in document collections
Van der Maaten & Hinton	2008	Developed t-SNE for high-dimensional data visualization with improved performance
Stula et al.	2010	Introduced an agent-based fuzzy cognitive map (ABFCM) that combines fuzzy cognitive maps (FCM) with multi-agent systems (MAS) technology.
Mikolov et al. & Dean	2013	Proposed two novel model architectures for efficiently estimating word representations in vector space
Ma & Zhang	2015	Utilized Word2Vec to process big text data, clustering similar words together to reduce data dimension
McInnes et al.	2018	Proposed UMAP, a manifold learning technique for dimension reduction with better runtime performance
Liu et al.	2018	Created Data Illustrator, a framework for expressive visualization authoring in vector design tools
Radford et al.	2018	Introduced Generative Pre-trained Transformer (GPT) models, which learn effective text representations through unsupervised pre-training, improving natural language understanding and enabling transfer learning for diverse tasks
Vig	2019	Introduced BertViz, a tool for visualizing attention mechanisms in BERT and GPT models
Lee et al.	2020	Introduced BioBERT, a domain-specific language representation model pre-trained on biomedical corpora for creating hierarchical knowledge graphs
Goodfellow et al.	2020	Introduced Generative Adversarial Networks (GANs) for generative modeling and successfully applied them to a wide variety of tasks, including image synthesis for knowledge visualization
Ramesh et al.	2021	Developed a transformer-based approach for zero-shot text-to-image generation, achieving high-quality synthesis and diverse capabilities through model and dataset scale

enhanced knowledge acquisition. The use of pre-trained language models, such as BioBERT, has been adapted to specific domains to improve information extraction and knowledge graph generation.

Furthermore, the text-to-image generation approach proposed by Ramesh et al. (2021) [30] offers a promising direction for future research. It demonstrates a wide range of capabilities, including generating visual representations from textual data, which can be particularly useful in creating knowledge graphs and visualizations that aid in understanding and interpreting complex information.

Overall, there is still room for improvement in applying deep learning techniques to generate more interpretable and meaningful hierarchical knowledge graphs and visualizations for end-users, and future research should focus on developing new algorithms and approaches to overcome these challenges.

5   Conclusion and Future Work

In this paper, we have provided a comprehensive review of KV, emphasizing the impact of AI on the field's future. Through this review, we have identified several gaps and limitations in existing research, which can serve as potential directions for future work.

As AI technologies, such as ChatGPT and image-generating algorithms like DALL-E continue to evolve, we can expect further advancements in KV. Future research should explore interdisciplinary approaches and emerging technologies to enhance the effectiveness of such tools.

However, it is important to recognize that the reviewed literature has not addressed the interoperability of different visualization techniques and approaches across different domains. Furthermore, a clear comparison of advantages and disadvantages of the discussed methods is not possible due to the heterogeneity of the research area and the absence of appropriate metrics.

In conclusion, this review highlights the potential of AI techniques to significantly enhance KV in various domains, providing a solid foundation for future research to build upon. We anticipate that advancements in AI will lead to the development of more sophisticated and powerful KV tools, enabling better understanding and interpretation of complex, high-dimensional data.

References

1. Alammar, J.: The illustrated word2vec. https://jalammar.github.io/illustrated-word2vec/. Visited 4 Apr 2023
2. Alani, H., et al.: Automatic ontology-based knowledge extraction from web documents. IEEE Intell. Syst. **18**(1), 14–21 (2003)
3. Allemang, D., Hendler, J.: Semantic Web for the Working Ontologist: Modeling in RDF, pp. 14–50. RDFS and OWL-Morgan Kaufmann Publishers (2008)
4. Berners-Lee, T., Hendler, J., Lassila, O.: The semantic web. Sci. Am. **284**(5), 34–43 (2001)
5. Blei, D.M., Ng, A.Y., Jordan, M.I.: Latent Dirichlet allocation. J. Mach. Learn. Res. **3**(Jan), 993–1022 (2003)
6. Buchanan, B.G., Duda, R.O.: Principles of rule-based expert systems. In: Advances in Computers, vol. 22, pp. 163–216. Elsevier (1983)
7. Cañas, A.J., et al.: Concept maps: integrating knowledge and information visualization. In: Tergan, S.-O., Keller, T. (eds.) Knowledge and Information Visualization. LNCS, vol. 3426, pp. 205–219. Springer, Heidelberg (2005). https://doi.org/10.1007/11510154_11
8. Carpendale, M.S.T., Cowperthwaite, D.J., Fracchia, F.D.: Extending distortion viewing from 2D to 3D. IEEE Comput. Graphics Appl. **17**(4), 42–51 (1997)

9. Derbentseva, N., Safayeni, F., Cañas, A.J.: How to teach dynamic thinking with concept maps. Teach. Teach. Strateg. Innov. Probl. Solving, 207–227 (2008)
10. Eppler, M.J.: A comparison between concept maps, mind maps, conceptual diagrams, and visual metaphors as complementary tools for knowledge construction and sharing. Inf. Vis. **5**(3), 202–210 (2006)
11. Foote, K.D.: A brief history of data lakes, June 2020. https://www.dataversity.net/brief-history-data-lakes/. Visited 4 Apr 2023
12. Glavinić, V., Stankov, S., Zelić, M., Rosić, M.: Intelligent tutoring in the Semantic Web and Web 2.0 environments. In: Lytras, M.D., et al. (eds.) WSKS 2008. CCIS, vol. 19, pp. 172–177. Springer, Heidelberg (2008). https://doi.org/10.1007/978-3-540-87783-7_21
13. Goodfellow, I., et al.: Generative adversarial networks. Commun. ACM **63**(11), 139–144 (2020)
14. Gruber, T.R.: A translation approach to portable ontology specifications. Knowl. Acquis. **5**(2), 199–220 (1993)
15. Grubišić, A., et al.: Knowledge tracking variables in intelligent tutoring systems. In: Proceedings of the 9th International Conference on Computer Supported Education-CSEDU, vol. 1, pp. 513–518 (2017)
16. Humphrey, M., Cunningham, S.J., Witten, I.H.: Knowledge visualization techniques for machine learning. Intell. Data Anal. **2**(1), 333–347 (1998). https://doi.org/10.1016/S1088-467X(98)00029-8, https://www.sciencedirect.com/science/article/pii/S1088467X98000298
17. Koller, D., Friedman, N.: Probabilistic Graphical Models: Principles and Techniques. MIT Press (2009)
18. Lee, J., et al.: BioBERT: a pre-trained biomedical language representation model for biomedical text mining. Bioinformatics **36**(4), 1234–1240 (2020)
19. Levesque, H.J., Brachman, R.J.: A fundamental tradeoff in knowledge representation and reasoning. Laboratory for Artificial Intelligence Research, Fairchild, Schlumberger (1984)
20. Liu, Z., et al.: Data illustrator: augmenting vector design tools with lazy data binding for expressive visualization authoring. In: Proceedings of the 2018 CHI Conference on Human Factors in Computing Systems, pp. 1–13 (2018)
21. Lohmann, S., Link, V., Marbach, E., Negru, S.: WebVOWL: web-based visualization of ontologies. In: Lambrix, P., et al. (eds.) EKAW 2014. LNCS (LNAI), vol. 8982, pp. 154–158. Springer, Cham (2015). https://doi.org/10.1007/978-3-319-17966-7_21
22. Ma, L., Zhang, Y.: Using Word2Vec to process big text data. In: 2015 IEEE International Conference on Big Data (Big Data), pp. 2895–2897. IEEE (2015)
23. Van der Maaten, L., Hinton, G.: Visualizing data using t-SNE. J. Mach. Learn. Res. **9**(11) (2008)
24. McInnes, L., Healy, J., Melville, J.: UMAP: uniform manifold approximation and projection for dimension reduction. arXiv preprint arXiv:1802.03426 (2018)
25. Mikolov, T., Chen, K., Corrado, G., Dean, J.: Efficient estimation of word representations in vector space. arXiv preprint arXiv:1301.3781 (2013)
26. Miller, E.: An introduction to the resource description framework (13), 3–11 (1998)
27. Minsky, M.: A framework for representing knowledge (1974)
28. Novak, J.D., Cañas, A.J.: The theory underlying concept maps and how to construct and use them (2008)
29. Radford, A., Narasimhan, K., Salimans, T., Sutskever, I., et al.: Improving language understanding by generative pre-training (2018)

30. Ramesh, A., et al.: Zero-shot text-to-image generation. In: International Conference on Machine Learning, pp. 8821–8831. PMLR (2021)
31. Rosic, M., Stankov, S., Glavinic, V.: Application of semantic web and personal agents in distance education system. In: 11th IEEE Mediterranean Electrotechnical Conference (IEEE Cat. No. 02CH37379), pp. 542–546. IEEE (2002)
32. Smith, R.G.: Knowledge-based systems concepts, techniques, examples. Canadian High Technology Show (1985)
33. Sowa, J.F.: Semantic networks. Encycl. Artif. Intell. **2**, 1493–1511 (1992)
34. Stula, M., Stipanicev, D., Bodrozic, L.: Intelligent modeling with agent-based fuzzy cognitive map. Int. J. Intell. Syst. **25**(10), 981–1004 (2010)
35. Vig, J.: BertViz: a tool for visualizing multihead self-attention in the BERT model. In: ICLR Workshop: Debugging Machine Learning Models (2019)
36. Volarić, T., Vasić, D., Brajković, E.: Adaptive tool for teaching programming using conceptual maps. In: Hadžikadić, M., Avdaković, S. (eds.) Advanced Technologies, Systems, and Applications. LNNS, vol. 3, pp. 335–347. Springer, Cham (2017). https://doi.org/10.1007/978-3-319-47295-9_27

Digital Tools and Pre-reading Skills

Suzana Tomaš[1]($\boxtimes$) (iD), Marijana Vrdoljak[1] (iD), and Mateja Prka[2]

[1] Faculty of Humanities and Social Sciences in Split, Poljička cesta 35, 21000 Split, Croatia
`{suzana,marijanav}@ffst.hr`
[2] Dječji vrtić "Pučišća", Park Hrvatskih branitelja 1, 21412 Pučišća, Otok Brač, Croatia

Abstract. Everyday activities enable a child to develop and adopt pre-reading skills which are the base for learning how to read. Digital technology and numerous available digital tools provide different possibilities for learning, researching and acquiring knowledge. Considering how important pre-reading skills are for children and their education from the very early age, this paper researches the application of digital tools with the purpose of acquiring pre-reading skills and their impact on children in daily work in the institution of early and preschool education. This paper focuses on pre-reading skills of sound synthesis, sound analysis, syllables recognition and segmentation, creating the connection between a sound and a letter, connecting the first sound in a word and recognizing rhyme and rhyming. With the help of digital apps and games, children developed their pre-reading skills during the period of four months, and they improved in all tested categories.

Keywords: digital tools · pre-reading skills · digital game

1 Introduction

The development of pre-reading skills is of extreme importance in the kindergarten, especially considering the preparation of children for later successful learning of how to read. Pre-reading skills can be developed through different activities which are suitable for children's age and individual needs. Pre-reading skills present a precondition, necessary knowledge and skill enabling a child to easily and quickly reach the level of "reading with understanding smoothly" [1]. These are the skills which precede the process of learning how to read [2]. A child acquires pre-reading skills every day, naturally, with the help of a parent spending time with a child, talking, reading and discussing the read material with a child, playing, expanding child's vocabulary, providing child with the new knowledge about the world and opportunities to actively develop speaking and retelling skills, skills of handling a book and writing instruments. This way a child will be prepared to learn how to read and to read [1]. The following are considered as pre-reading skills: understanding told story and simple retelling, understanding the function of reading, writing and text characteristics, understanding the process of transforming speech into text, recognizing sounds in a word, separating words into sounds and combining sounds into words, recognizing alphabet letters and connecting them with

D. Vasić and M. Kundid Vasić (Eds.): MoStart 2023, CCIS 1827, pp. 132–143, 2023.
https://doi.org/10.1007/978-3-031-36833-2_10

sounds, understanding the substitute of letters with sounds in a word and writing [1]. One of the preconditions for the development of reading skills is phonological awareness referring to recognizing, creating and handling smaller parts of words, and it is reflected through, for example, recognizing the words that rhyme, counting syllables, separating the beginning and the end of a word, and separating the sounds in a word [3]. Furthermore, phonological awareness is defined as metacognitive understanding that the words which are being read or listened to have internal structure [3]. Phonological awareness is developed according to levels, from the awareness of larger units or syllables, onset, rhymes to the higher level of awareness or understanding smaller units, phonemes, in all their positions within a word. The phonological awareness development is universal, and the speed at which the language is developed depends on language characteristics that are visibility, linguistic forms complexity, phoneme position and pronunciation [3]. It is necessary to start developing pre-reading skills from a child's birth and at the latest by the time a child turns three. This is done during everyday activities, child's play and communication with adults, not by mechanical teaching. In order for the pre-reading skills to properly develop, children need the surrounding that is quality and rich in content. They also need suitable teaching in order to make the awareness of sounds and application of alphabet principle easier [4]. While practicing reading technique, one goes through the process of understanding the meaning of words, sentences and whole texts which is automatized with time and which the reader begins to recognize as a unit, and larger sentence parts. In this way, the reader is directed to understand the sense of a read text. The author Čudina Obradović defines four phases in adopting the reading technique: the phase of unique recognition that means logographic strategy typical for beginners' reading where a whole written word denotes a spoken word. A child makes many mistakes at that phase as learnt words are a part of a text and as child reads the text by recognizing the learnt words and guessing the meaning of other words. The phase of initial sound division is a phase when a child starts paying attention to letters – sounds making up a word. Children guess those which are unknown to them from the meaning and according to the first letter – sound in a word. The awareness of the elements a word consists of increases. The phase of translating letters into sounds is the most important and most difficult phase in learning how to read as it requires sound division and sounds memorization. In this phase children recognize letters and translate them into their substitution. In other words, children apply alphabet strategy. Their capability of reading becomes flexible, and children are capable of reading every word including those whose meaning they do not know. Some children discover phonological system and method of separating and combining words during the process of learning how to read, and there are some children who need to be taught or who cannot master this which leads to difficulties in reading. The phase of complex translating of graphical units into sound units means the usage of orthographic strategy during which children notice familiar written unites and do not divide words into graphemes. In this phase, children are skilled readers reading easily and quickly what they know as linguistic and written units from before. They are capable of making letter-sound division of the new and unknown units quickly [4]. Pre-reading skills are the key for successful understanding and interpretation of written texts. In digital surrounding they become a challenge. Digital tools provide different possibilities for reading and approaching the text. Simultaneously, they present a challenge which requires the development of other digital skills.

2 Pre-reading Skills with the Help of Digital Tools

This paper describes the development of pre-reading skills with the help of digital tools. The application of digital tools in a kindergarten presents an introduction of a new toy with a cause and a consequence to children. This helps children understand how technology impacts them in everyday life. The extent to which digital tools can improve learning among children aged three to six depends on teachers, the tools they choose to use, the way they choose to use them and when they choose to use them. Teachers must have clear instructions, examples and support for their own professional learning in order to make decisions on the nature and volume of the usage of digital tools in the process of learning. These decisions are influenced by factors such as personal level of teacher's trust in digital tools in the process of learning and teaching in the early childhood. Therefore, this paper presents how digital tools enable the introduction, adoption and development of pre-reading skills. Applied digital tools are taken from ICT-AAC project [5] (Fig. 1).

Fig. 1. ICT-AAC website

Research with the application of digital tools included eight different digital tools from ICT-AAC project and educational and entertaining website RasTURam.com [6]. They enable learning, adopting and further development of pre-reading skills in an interesting manner adjusted to children's age. Three digital tools were selected from the ICT-AAC project and five digital tools containing several levels depending on children's capabilities and knowledge were taken from the RasTURam.com website [6].

ICT-AAC is a project focusing on the transfer of knowledge and development of the new assisted communication services. In other words, it is a competence network based on information and communication technology intended to persons with complex communicational needs. Assisted communication methods are based on the use of graphical and textual symbols which indicate certain objects, concepts and actions. They are based on information and communication technology, and they refer to services using specific knowledge and capabilities related to communication based on symbols and implemented between persons and between persons and devices. This means creating "tools" for communication of persons with complex communicational needs such as combining sentences/phrases for both learning and fun. They proved to be extremely efficient when it comes to encouragement and improvement in using the language, literacy, learning, employment and quality of life of the persons with complex communicational needs. ICT-AAC project includes children, youth and adults involved in the programs of care, education and rehabilitation in the Republic of Croatia. Digital tools used in this research are: Pamtilica, Slovarica, Glaskalica Table 1 (Fig. 2).

Table 1. Digital tools ICT-AAC

Digital tool	Features of the digital tools	Number of players
Pamtilica	To establish the connection between a letter and a sound The game can be played in three different ways: by matching two equal sounds, by matching the beginning sound and a suitable symbol, and by matching two equal symbols	one or two players
Slovarica	The connection between visual symbols and new phonological forms made easier	one player
Glaskalica	To learn phonological awareness The game includes the recognition of the first, last and all sounds in a word	one player

Fig. 2. Glaskalica game

RasTURam.com is an entertainment website intended for children and youth with developmental difficulties and to all those who wish to learn and adopt educational and everyday skills in a fun and simple manner. There is a possibility of choosing easy, medium or difficult level. The offered games refer to letters, writing, riddles, memory and other possibilities. The following educational children's games were chosen from the RasTURam.com website as they can be used to adopt, develop and strengthen pre-reading skills [6] (Figs. 3 and 4).

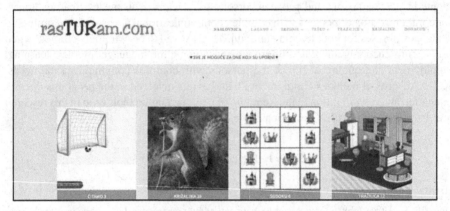

Fig. 3. RasTURam.com website

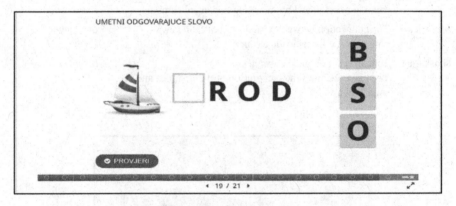

Fig. 4. Umetni slovo game

The game entitled Umetni slovo provides the possibility of choosing the game Umetni slovo 1, Umetni slovo 2, Umetni slovo 3, and it offers the tasks with the concepts ranging from easier to more difficult ones that are the concepts ranging from three to four sounds to five and more sounds. The task is to select suitable location for a letter. Each of these games includes the image of a symbol for which the sound from the group of selected sounds has to be chosen. There is a possibility to check the accuracy of your choice when a yellow star appears on the screen. After this, you continue with other concepts. At the end of the game, total score is presented as well as solutions if a child wishes to see correct answers where the task was solved incorrectly. There is also the possibility of repeating the game. In the game entitled Umetni slovo 1, suitable letter corresponding to the beginning of the concept has to be selected. These are words with three or four sounds. It contains the image of a concept for which the first sound has to be chosen from the group of three sounds. New concepts follow until a child reaches the total number of twenty-one offered concepts. Umetni slovo 2 is a higher level game requiring suitable letter in different places in a word. Letters have to be put at the beginning, in the middle and at the end of a word. These are words consisting of three to six letters, and there are eleven different concepts. Umetni slovo 3 contains words consisting of three sounds. Suitable letter has to be put in the middle or at the end of a word, and the game consists of fifteen different concepts. Prepisujemo is the game where a child needs to copy the subject word or put it at the right location. There is a concept above the square that has to be filled in, and there are six different sounds from which a child has to select or copy the correct ones. There is no image of the symbol or the possibility to check the accuracy of this task. The game includes the words consisting of four and five sounds, and there are fifteen different concepts. The game provides the possibility of checking the solutions in order for a child to see if and when a child made a mistake. Pišemo riječi is a game which requires you to combine the words accompanied by an image of a symbol, and which provides you with a number of squares corresponding to the number of sounds in a word. It includes the following games: Pišemo riječi – 3 slova, Pišemo riječi – 4 slova, Pišemo riječi – 5 slova, Pišemo riječi – 6 slova. They differ in the number of letters that have to be put in the right place as well as in the number of words within each game. Therefore, Pišemo riječi – 3 slova offers seventeen different concepts, Pišemo riječi – 4 slova contains fourteen concepts, Pišemo riječi – 5 slova contains fifteen concepts, whereas Pišemo riječi – 6 slova includes the greatest number of concepts – twenty. Mixed letters are provided below the squares, and they have to be properly organized. Organized word can be checked by selecting the icon Check. If a word is not properly organized, than the letters which are not at their right location become red instead of black and they are marked with an x. Letters which are at their right location become green, and they are marked with a tick. This way a child can see whether he/she chose the right order of the letters for a certain concept and a child can repeat the word. Slogovi 1 is a game including words with over four letters with two syllables accompanied by the image of an offered word. Syllables are located below the squares. Some are put in correct order, and some are not. However, all have to be placed at the right place. A child has to order the syllables so that they form a word required by an image. Apart from the mentioned, there is a Check icon below the task accompanied by a yellow star. Syllables which are correctly organized become green and contain a tick sign, while the incorrect ones become red and contain an x mark. Just as in the previous games, in this game a child obtains a yellow star for a correct answer. Also, there is a possibility of additional try. The game contains twenty tasks and the possibility of presenting correct/incorrect solutions. Čitamo and Čitamo 2 are games which require a child to read the word and record it with a help of a microphone. Both games contain ten concepts. Čitamo 1 includes concepts with three to four letters and Čitamo 2 includes concepts with four letters. Furthermore, it contains the icon Press for Speech and an icon with which a child can visually check what was read as well as what should be read.

3   Research Methodology

3.1   Research Goal

The goal of this research is to understand if the use of digital tools allows the development of pre-reading skills in children aged three to six.

3.2   Research Sample

The research was implemented in the "Pućišća" kindergarten at the island of Brač, more precisely. Kindergarten "Jerulica" Pražnica with regular six-hour program for children of mixed ages from 3 to 6. The research included 10 children from "Jerulica" kindergarten, and they developed pre-reading skills with the help of digital tools. There were 3 preschool children aged 6, 3 children aged 5, and 4 children aged 3. In accordance with the Act on Preschool Education, the kindergarten implemented compulsory preschool program which children have to attend before starting elementary school [7]. Parents signed consent for their children to participate in this study.

3.3   Research Instrument

Research instrument for this research were worksheets for children (initial and final), digital tools for the development of pre-reading skills and satisfaction questionnaire for children. The worksheet contained six questions related to different pre-reading skill areas, and within each question there were tasks which helped to establish initial level of development of pre-reading skills considering a child's age. The worksheet contained sound synthesis tasks (combining sounds in a word), sound division tasks (separating words in sounds), syllable recognition and segmentation, creating the connection between a sound and a letter, connecting the first sound in a word, and recognizing and combining rhyme and pictures. Each child was individually tested. The same worksheet was applied at the end of the research as an instrument testing the final level of pre-reading skills after the activities were implemented. Next research instrument were digital tools with different content and learning possibilities focusing on the development of pre-reading skills in children. Satisfaction questionnaire contained questions on whether the children liked learning with digital tools, how they felt while learning, what they liked the most while using digital tools, and what digital tool they liked the most. Children gave oral answers to these questions.

3.4   Research Course

The research which included initial check, digital tools application, final check and satisfaction questionnaire lasted from November 2021 to April 2022. Initial testing in the two subject kindergartens started in November 2021 with the help of a worksheet. The research with the application of digital tools in "Jerulica" kindergarten started in December 2021. It included eight different digital tools from the ICT-AAC project [5] and from the educational and entertainment website RasTURam.com [6]. A laptop and two tablets with selected digital tools intended for the development of pre-reading skills, or developing, encouraging and improving sound synthesis, sound division, syllable recognition and segmentation, creating the connection between a sound and a letter, connecting the first sound in a word and recognizing and combining rhyme, were available to children in the kindergarten. The children had the opportunity to use digital tools when they wished. It is important to emphasize that, due to coronavirus pandemics and other diseases, some children were absent from the kindergarten and therefore, unable to take part in the activities focusing on the development of pre-reading skills.

3.5 Research Results

Results of the Pre-reading Skills Initial Check

Initial inspection of pre-reading skills included the field of sound synthesis, sound analysis, syllable recognition and segmentation with the words ranging from one-syllable and two-syllable words to the words with more syllables, creating the connection between a sound and a letter, connecting the first sound in a word with an image of the requested word, and recognizing and making rhyme. The children's results are shown in the Tables 2.

Table 2. Results of the initial testing of children attending "Jerulica" Pražnica kindergarten

Children N	Sound synthesis	Sound analysis	Syllable recognition and segmentation	Creating the connection between a sound and a letter	Connecting the first sound in a word	Recognizing and making rhyme
6 years N = 3	22/36 (54.54%)	14/24 (58.33%)	51/57 (94.73%)	33/33 (100%)	14/18 (77.77%)	7/18 (38.88%)
5 years N = 3	0/36 (0%)	2/24 (8.33%)	31/57 (54.38%)	31/33 (93.93%)	0/18 (0%)	0/18 (0%)
4 years N = 1	1/12 (8.33%)	0/8 (0%)	16/19 (84.21%)	10/11 (90.90%)	1/6 (16.66%)	0/6 (0%)
3 years N = 3	0/36 (0%)	0/24 (0%)	22/57 (38.59%)	28/33 (84.84%)	4/18 (22.22%)	3/18 (16.66%)

Initial testing results show that, as expected, the best results in the pre-reading skills testing were achieved by six-year old or preschool children. Out of seven preschool children, two had negative results in the tasks referring to sound synthesis. Other preschool children solved the tasks very well and experienced very few obstacles in words with five and more sounds. Children below six years of age did not achieve any results in dividing the words into sounds which means that they did not develop sound analysis skill. Final check was implemented after the activity for the development of pre-reading skills was done.

Results of Pre-reading Skills Final Check
Identical worksheet from the initial check was used in the final check as well. After five months of developing pre-reading skills with digital tools in Jerulica kindergarten, the results shown in the Tables 3 were obtained.

Table 3. The results of the final testing of children attending "Jerulica" kindergarten

Children N	Sound synthesis	Sound analysis	Syllable recognition and segmentation	Creating the connection between a sound and a letter	Connecting the first sound in a word	Recognizing and making rhyme
6 years N = 3	29/36 (80%)	16/24 (66.66%)	57/57 (100%)	33/33 (100%)	18/18 (100%)	18/18 (100%)
5 years N = 3	1/36 (2.77%)	0/24 (0%)	32/57 (56.14%)	33/33 (100%)	4/18 (22.22%)	4/18 (22.22%)
4 years N = 1	0/12 (0%)	0/8 (0%)	19/19 (100%)	8/11 (72%)	0/6 (0%)	6/6 (100%)
3 years N = 3	1/36 (2.77%)	0/24 (0%)	54/57 (94.73%)	28/33 (84%)	5/18 (27.77%)	2/18 (11.11%)

Pre-reading skills were best developed and adopted by children of preschool age that are six years old children. Preschool children showed improvement in the activities focusing on combining sounds in a word. Small improvement could also be noticed with younger children when working with three or four letter words such as eye, nose, hand, mum. Sound analysis was poorly developed during the research if compared to the initial situation, especially among younger children. Older children improved their results. Improvement was not recorded in case of words with five or more sounds as the situation was the same as the initial one. Pursuant to the levels of phonological awareness development in children with regular speech-language development [8] considering their age, pre-reading skills of combining and dividing sounds in a word were developed among six-year-old children. This is in accordance with the results achieved by six-year-olds within the testing. Therefore, younger children are not expected to develop the above stated pre-reading skills. There is improvement in syllable recognition and segmentation among all tested children. When it comes to creating the connection between a sound and a letter, it can be noticed that children are very good at making the connection between a sound and a letter visually. Recognition of the first sound in a word is developed in children aged 5.5 [8] in accordance with the levels of phonological awareness development among children with regular speech-language development. This can be seen from the results obtained by tested children of that age, unlike the results obtained by younger children. It is noticed that younger children connect the first sound in a word with some of the concepts although this happens with the concepts such as car and cat which was also the case in the initial testing. Recognizing and making rhyme is developed in children aged 3 and 4 [8]. When recognizing and making rhyme, it was noticed that children younger than six connect the concepts with images which correspond to the next described image; they do not connect it with rhyme. For example, they connect the image of an animal with another animal, the image of grass with a goal, which does not correspond to the rhyme. After comparing the results of initial and final testing of pre-reading skills in children from both groups, it can be concluded that there is no difference, and that children in both groups made improvement in developing pre-reading skills. In "Jerulica" kindergarten greater improvement was recorded in the field of syllable recognition and segmentation, and in the field of making rhymes, among preschool children, but also among younger children. In accordance with the results shown in the Tables 2 and 3, we can notice improvement or stagnation ranges of the groups in certain fields.

3.6 Results Interpretation

The results of the initial and final check of pre-reading skills in children from both groups indicate the fact that pre-reading skills can be developed with the help of digital tools. The same is confirmed by the authors Segers and Verhoeven [9], who implemented a one-year research with 100 six-year old children as regards to early literacy in the first grade of elementary school. Their research showed significant positive correlation between the time children spent playing digital games which include letters and activities developing pre-reading skills and phonological awareness, and improvement in sound analysis and graphemes recognition. Apart from the mentioned, in accordance with the obtained results, we can conclude that digital tools intended for learning can be used as valuable tools in adopting pre-reading skills. The conclusions from this research are confirmed by Persson [10], who states that serious games and digital tools are becoming more and more popular, not just for fun, but as efficient educational tools which might be integrated in educational work. This is proved by a research implemented in 2017 at the sample of 47 children aged 5 to 7. The research showed that the use of SMARTBoard and iPad can improve pre-reading skills such as letter recognition, naming, speed and metalinguistic awareness in kindergarten [11]. Also, it is important to mention that the research from 2022 showed that children can develop reading skills with the help of educational game for Androids which was designed using ADDIE model. This educational game was designed in a manner that it provides children with the activities developing pre-reading and reading skills (connecting letters, identifying syllables and connection between the syllables, combining words in a sentence). It was proved efficient for the development of the above mentioned skills after it was used with 26 children [12].

Results of the Satisfaction Questionnaire as Regards to the Usage of Digital Tools for Children.
Children attending "Jerulica" kindergarten and using digital tools in the pre-reading skills research took part in the questionnaire examining satisfaction after using digital tools for children. When asked whether they liked learning via digital tools, all ten children (100%) answered positively. Children chose Glaskalica (50%) and Pamtilica (50%) as

their favourite digital tools. Responses to the question what they liked the most while they used digital tools can be seen in the Table 4.

Table 4. The results of the questionnaire examining satisfaction with digital tools in "Jerulica" Pražnica kindergarten

Satisfaction with learning via digital tools	Pamtilica	Glaskalica
"Because I could play, I liked to play on a tablet, we could share it, and we were careful with it. If you are at preschool age, you go and play those games. Because I am preschool age next year and I want to teach my brain, I have to teach it to learn letters	"Pamtilica because I had cards there, I learned letters – R, and then you had image rabbit. I could play with a friend. We looked forward to this game. We had to watch images."	"I liked Glaskalica the most because of the letters. Glaskalica because I can learn letters and words and because I think how to guess the missing letters."
"When I can move my fingers on tablet, I can guess letters, I can play. I liked to play games at tablet. Because I just press what I like and it speaks. I liked that I am good at it, it was all new."	"I liked it the most, because I learned while I played, and I liked it the most."	"Glaskalica because I could press letters and if I did it correctly, it told me. If it's not correct, it also told me. I could guess and chose what letter I want to guess."

4   Conclusion

The development of pre-reading skills is a part of children's everyday life. In children's surrounding, it prepares them for learning how to read and for reading itself. By adopting skills, children will advance and acquire new skills which are necessary for reading. In order for this to be realized, parents play an important role as they read to children, tell stories, talk to them, play with children and therefore, expand their vocabulary and broaden their knowledge. Furthermore, children's surrounding has the same role as it is an important factor in the development of pre-reading skills in children, as well as teachers and participants in the institutions of early and preschool education. Preschool period is the period when children develop their pre-reading skills which are of extreme importance for children's future success in reading. Considering that the phonological awareness develops according to levels and at certain age, children have to be encouraged to take an active role in the process of reading and writing and to enjoy it. The results of the implemented research with children attending Jerulica kindergarten indicate that children can use digital tools to develop pre-reading skills. Furthermore, the results confirm that all methods of learning new knowledge and expanding the existing knowledge are welcome and positively impact the development of pre-reading skills in children.

References

1. Čudina – Obradović, M.: Čitanje prije škole: priručnik za roditelje i odgojitelje. Školska knjiga, Zagreb (2002)
2. Kozlov, J., i Kanjić, S.: Poticanje razvoja predčitačkih vještina kod djece u godini pred polazak u školu. Dijete, vrtić, obitelj **11**(39), 13–17 (2005)
3. Ivšac Pavliša, J., i Lenček, M.: Fonološke vještine i fonološko pamćenje: neke razlike između djece urednoga jezičnoga razvoja, djece s perinatalnim oštećenjem mozga i djece s posebnim jezičnim teškoćama kao temeljni prediktor čitanja. Hrvatska revija za rehabilitacijska istraživanja, vol. 47 (1), pp. 1–16. Edukacijsko-rehabilitacijski fakultet Sveučilišta u Zagrebu (2011)
4. Čudina – Obradović, M.: Igrom do čitanja: igre i aktivnosti za razvijanje vještina čitanja. 2nd edn. Školska knjiga, Zagreb (2008)
5. ICT-AAC. http://www.ict-aac.hr/index.php/hr/, (Accessed 10 Dec 2022)
6. RasTURam. https://rasturam.com/, (Accessed 10 Dec 2022)
7. Zakon o predškolskom odgoju i obrazovanju. https://www.zakon.hr/z/492/Zakon-o-pred%C5%A1kolskom-odgoju-i-obrazovanju, (Accessed 20 Jan 2023)
8. Banjan Baketić, I.: Predvještine čitanja i pisanja. http://logoterapia.hr/dijagnostika-i-terapija/predcitacke-vjestine/, (Acessed 27 Jan 2022)
9. Segers, E., Verhoeven, L.: Long-term effects of computer training of phonological awareness in kindergarten. J. Comput. Assist. Learn. **21**(1), 17–27 (2005)
10. Persson, N. Serious Games: Present and Future (Dissertation). http://urn.kb.se/resolve?urn=urn:nbn:se:umu:diva-89200, (Accessed 12 Dec 2022)
11. Protti Coto, M., Cannon Díaz, B. Y., Heredia Escorza, Y.: Development of Pre-Reading Skills Using iPad and SMARTBoard Technologies. http://hdl.handle.net/11285/632855, (Accessed 13 Jan 2023)
12. Rakimahwati, R., Hanifa, N., Aryani, N.: Android based educational game development to improve early childhood reading ability. AL-ISHLAH: Jurnal Pendidikan **14**(2), 1123–1134 (2022)

Detecting Academic Fraud at Online Tests During COVID-19 Using Machine Learning-Based Methods

Tomislav Volarić[1]([✉]) [iD], Goran Martinović[2] [iD], and Hrvoje Ljubić[1] [iD]

[1] University of Mostar, Trg hrvatskih velikana 1, Mostar, Bosnia and Herzegovina
{tomislav.volaric,hrvoje.ljubic}@fpmoz.sum.ba
[2] Faculty of Electrical Engineering, Computer Science and Information Technology,
Josip Juraj Strossmayer University of Osijek, Osijek, Croatia
goran.martinovic@ferit.hr
https://www.sum.ba/

Abstract. The first step in eliminating academic dishonesty (in e-learning systems) is to detect fraudulent activities. There are various approaches that deal with this problem, but only few of them are based on human-computer interaction (HCI). Accordingly, we have developed a novel data acquisition model that collects information about student HCI activities. This model was applied within an open-source module, named Student Activity Tracker, available as chromium web browser extension. During the COVID-19 pandemic (in academic year of 2019/2020.), an experiment was conducted with 54 volunteer participants that performed online tests from home. As a result, 500k raw logs were collected and later processed and used to develop four machine learning models. The main contribution of this research is the proof of an obvious correlation between HCI activities and fraudulent behaviour even on such a small sample. Also, we believe that this module can help other researchers to create new data sets and build new more advanced models.

Keywords: Academic dishonesty · Online test · Fraud detection · Machine learning · Human computer interaction · COVID-19

1 Introduction

The problem of cheating on tests is probably as old as testing itself. Over time, the methods and cheating techniques have changed and improved. This problem within the academic community was seriously addressed almost half a century ago by various authors [1] and even much earlier [2]. Technology development has brought new ways of teaching and testing, and thus new ways of cheating have developed. This confirms that this is an activity that never stops [3]. Although e-learning has brought many benefits, adaption to e-learning has not been easy and it is a process that is still ongoing. Despite that, it seems that student creativity was not lacking and it did not take long to adapt traditional methods of cheating

D. Vasić and M. Kundid Vasić (Eds.): MoStart 2023, CCIS 1827, pp. 144–158, 2023.
https://doi.org/10.1007/978-3-031-36833-2_11

to the digital environment. It is clear that academic fraud is a serious problem in online tests, even much more challenging than in the classroom. Obviously, certain rules in this environment change significantly and many of the things we know about student behavior during tests are no longer valid or are just partially valid. In this sense, our research is aimed to find a correlation between cheating and student behaviour activities on the computer. As very little research has been reported on this topic, with the arrival of the COVID-19 pandemic this problem became more attractive for solving. Although research presented in this paper is primarily focused on computer science students and it would definitely not help in testing some other professions such as music art, it does provide some valuable insights into student behavior while doing online tests. Focus of this research is on online tests written on a personal computer or notebook, while the possibility of writing tests on a mobile device was not considered. Mobile devices have become an unavoidable topic in e-learning because they enable learning and testing from anywhere and anytime [4] so this should be considered in future research.

This paper is divided into five chapters. After Introduction, the second chapter looks into theoretical background and related work that has been done prior to our research. This chapter is split into a 7 distinct subsections (Academic dishonesty, Fraud triangle, Plagiarism, Code plagiarism, Student collaboration, Outlier detection in online tests and Continous authentication). In third chapter we describe the machine learning and its methods that has been used in this paper. In this chapter, unsupervised learning is intentionally omitted, and only supervised learning and classification algorithms that are used later in paper are described. In fourth chapter, experiment setup and results are described, also as environment, participants and data collection model. This is leading to the final chapter where results are discussed also with limitations of this research. At the end there is a conclusion and plans for future work.

2   Related Work

Despite the fact that e-learning has existed for several decades, it has not received sufficient and necessary attention from a large number of educational institutions worldwide. With the appearance of the COVID-19 pandemic, one of the most important topics in 2020. year became teaching through technology. The concept of e-learning is quite broad because "e" stands for electronics, so educational content delivered via radio transmitters can be also considered as a e-learning. However, it is clear that the term e-learning today stands for something much more formal and serious, where the two-way communication is presumption.

During the pandemic, e-learning enabled educational institutions to successfully continue and finish the school and academic year. Hybrid learning, which was dominant until the pandemic became, turned into complete online learning. Therefore, previous research has not been focused on testing in uncontrolled environments. The question is whether it is possible to properly evaluate someone's knowledge in an unsupervised environment. It is not enough to rely on trust and academic ethics because, as mentioned earlier, cheating on tests is not uncommon even in controlled conditions (in the classroom) although it has been shown that results in a controlled and uncontrolled environment strongly correlate [5].

2.1 Academic Dishonesty

Most students have cheated somehow at least once in their lives [6–9]. Demographically, gender has the greatest impact on cheating, specifically - men cheat more than women [10]. In order to completely eliminate cheating on tests, the academic community must work in an organizational and technical sense [11]. The authors [12] divided cheating motives of undergraduate students into three groups, (i) individual factors, (ii) institutional policies and (iii) peer pressure.

In fact, cheating most often occurs under pressure and it is on this basis that higher education institutions try to identify and prevent cheating [13]. However, sometimes it is difficult to establish whether it is accidental or deliberate cheating, and to reveal who copied from whom [14]. All this is true in the e-environment, but we also have some new issues when it comes to an uncontrolled environment, which is currently a rather unexplored topic from a technical, pedagogical and psychological aspect.

2.2 Fraud Triangle

When it comes to talk about fraudulent behavior, in whatever direction the story goes, the term "fraud triangle" is unavoidable. This triangle encompasses three concepts - motivation, opportunity, rationalization, and was developed by Donald Cressey, an American criminologist [15]. Although this research focus was on financial fraud, it was shown to have an equally influential effect on student cheating - it was most notable in the "motivation" variable [13]. Few years ago, this research was continued in the paper [16]. The results showed that, even today, all the elements of this triangle are intertwined and have a very large impact on the work of companies. Furthermore, the triangle is extended to a quadrilateral with new element - fraud-inhibiting inner voice. This (inner) voice weakens over time and makes it easier for the subject to commit fraud. Numerous authors agree on how all of the above can be applied to test behavior [13,15,17]. It is interesting to point out that the chances for cheating are increased if the student does not find the course interesting (if dislikes the course) [18].

2.3 Plagiarism

Although not directly related to the research topic, something that is impossible to avoid when talking about academic dishonesty is plagiarism. Plagiarism is the copying of someone's work without author attribution. This problem has been addressed by many researchers on various e-learning systems [19–21]. One new approach is presented in [22] and serves to detect potentially plagiarized documents in academia. HyPlag checks the correlation of images, citation patterns, mathematical statements, and text that are analyzed separately and then combined into one.

2.4   Code Plagiarism

The topic of code-plagiarism is often mentioned among computer science students. There are numerous approaches to finding copied and plagiarized program code. The key items in developing such systems are: (i) a suitable discriminator to indicate the presence of plagiarism, (ii) a suitable method for comparing these discriminators, and (iii) an appropriate measurement of similarity. [23] A Moodle plugin introduced in [23] has ability to show the percentage between two program source codes and also shows the contents of these similarities. This plugin uses an SMS system that sends notifications to alert the student about the plagiarism detection process. Similar plugin presented in [24], named Moss, detects similarity between two code and is integrated with GCC compiler which reduces time cost and make it easier for teachers to do grading.

In [25] the authors developed an application called FLEXauth that uses machine and deep learning methods to detect plagiarism, with the best results with random forest algorithm and the worst with a deep neural network. This is due insufficiently large sample. A slightly different approach was used in a study in which the authors used the locality sensitive hashing (LSH) technique to accelerate the detection of plagiarism in the model-driven software components [26]. This extremely interesting approach consists of 3 steps. In the first step, a robust hash is applied to the repository, then an LSH classification group is created, and finally, an attempt is made to find plagiarism using pairwise comparison. Due to a similar task, AI agent Jack Watson [27] was employed. Agent is browsing the Internet in order to discover paid projects. The authors who developed Jack Watson believe that this type of cheating is particularly dangerous and very difficult to detect. In this paper, we do not deal with this type of cheating, but only cheating during the test.

2.5   Student Collaboration

Collaboration among students during the test is a serious problem within the classroom and it has been shown that students are more likely to collaborate if they know each other, i.e. if they are friends [28]. Assumption is that the same phenomenon has spread to online tests, but the methods and techniques are somewhat newer and more modern. This interaction is most often accomplished using social media and other available tools that are much harder to detect and disable in an unsupervised environment than in a classroom.

The authors from Morocco [29] asked three research questions: (i) why students participate in online cheating, (ii) how cyber-cheating supports collective movement, and (iii) what is the correlation between the latter two. They presented a model called the Collective Action Cyber-Cheating Model that integrates collective action and social learning theories. An interesting continuation of our research would be if we were to go in this direction.

One way to detect student collaboration is to check for internal plagiarism [30] by comparing students' work to find similarities between them. Problem arises if the test is reduced to a series of correct/incorrect questions and a fill blank space in sentence where is correct answer expected to be the same for all students. This problem have already been addressed by numerous authors, but only individual students results were analysed [31]. It would be valuable if their results are compared in pairs to find an indication of collaboration.

2.6 Outlier Detection in Online Tests

It is possible to detect outliers with only one variable - response time [32]. There are quite different approaches to this problem in the literature. Some authors use machine [25,33] and deep learning, while some use probabilistic models [34]. The authors of [35] believe that one of the key elements is the environment in which the tests are held. Testing in an uncontrolled environment makes it very difficult to apply the solutions from previous research. Access control has been reduced, the availability of various materials and devices has been increased, and reliable authentication and monitoring of collaboration between students have been disabled.

By collecting and analyzing HCI activities created by interacting with the mouse and keyboard, it is possible to detect the emotional state of the student [36,37], which is a fundamental task for the development of adaptive systems [38]. The development of such systems, such as intelligent tutoring systems, in any case, represents a continuation of the development and future of e-learning systems.

2.7 Continuous Authentication

User authentication is the first step and a fundamental prerequisite for a valid test design. Globally, authentication can be divided into static and continuous [39]. It is quite obvious that static authentication (username and password) is not good enough in general, and especially when creating tests because providing user data is an easily circumvented factor and is not a sure indicator that this person is doing the test. A term that is increasingly appearing in the literature is continuous authentication [40,41] which has already been applied in several educational software solutions [42], and we believe that it will be an unavoidable element, in the coming years, of any e-learning system.

There are numerous studies that have applied the basic principles of continuous authentication in e-learning systems [43], some even on mobile devices [44] where they have reduced the impact of head movements and light changes on reducing facial recognition accuracy.

Also, the thing that we do not deal with, and a very important aspect is the recognition of suspicious activities via a video camera. Recognizing suspicious movements and generating descriptions of recorded video clips in which two students exchange information and cheat on a test were explored in [45] using the divide-and-rule method with relatively good results. In the paper [46], continuous authentication is achieved in two ways: (i) by checking the smart card and (ii) by recording the face of the student who was previously registered at the checked place, at the university respectively, in such a way that the student is photographed several times. The entire testing process is stored and can be subsequently sent for review and automatic checking and detection of cheating is achieved using machine learning algorithms.

3   Background

Machine learning is a branch of artificial intelligence (AI) and computer science that uses statistical techniques in order to give the computer the ability to learn with the help of a data set without explicit programming of all possible usage scenarios. The term "machine learning" was first used by Arthur Samuel in 1959. Machine learning has actually evolved from the study of pattern recognition and artificial intelligence theory. The goal of machine learning is to enable the development of systems that make data-driven decisions. Machine learning has two main branches; supervised and unsupervised learning. The main difference between supervised and unsupervised learning is primarily in the data being processed. Supervised learning requires sample that have input and output data, while unsupervised learning requires only input data, as the output data is completely unknown. The other type of machine learning branching is so-called machine learning tasks, i.e. regression, classification, clustering and unsupervised transformations. Regression and classification are in fact tasks of supervised learning, and grouping and transformation of data are tasks of unsupervised learning. Alpaydin defined machine learning as computer programming in a way that optimizes some performance criteria based on data examples or previous experience. Machine learning takes on a role when classical programming cannot meet the needs of a system, for example in complex problems or in problems for which one cannot give a (simple) explanation understandable to a computer. In this paper, the emphasis is on supervised learning.

3.1   Supervised Learning

The group of algorithms that build a "generalized" model of knowledge from samples of input and output data is called supervised learning. The requirement of supervised learning is that each sample has to be an ordered pair, with input data on the first coordinate and output on the second. The success of an algorithm is often closely related to the size of the data set, so a larger set often implies better results. Accordingly, there are two ways to improve results; (i) tuning the algorithm and (ii) extending the data set. In the literature, supervised learning is divided into regression and classification. The task of classification is to assign a sample to one of two (binary classification) or more (multi-variable classification) classes. For example, building a "spam filter" is a classification problem. As only two classes are possible, i.e."spam" and "not spam", it is obviously a binary classification. In classification, we can say that the output variable is discrete because it cannot happen that our output is partly "spam" and partly "not spam". If the output variable is not discrete, but it is from a set of real numbers then it is probably a regression task. For example, to build a mathematical model that calculates the value of real estate, we must use regression because the output will be in the form of a decimal number e.g. $2340.70. The output data can be roughly divided into quantitative and qualitative, i.e. (i) numerical and (ii) categorical. Numerical data are divided into discrete (e.g. 5 people, 20 d, 2 dogs) and continuous (e.g. 5.12 kg, 23.8 cm, $250.32). Although numbers are usually associated with categorical data, these numbers have no mathematical (numerical) meaning. Categorical data are divided into nominal and ordinal. The difference is that the nominal data do not require respect for the hierarchy, i.e. the classes are independent of each other. Examples of nominal data are categories such as "eye color" or "blood type". Ordinal data are mostly presented as a combination of discrete and numerical data and are not so intuitive at first glance. Star rating from 1 to 5, where some intermediate value is possible, e.g. 3 and a half stars is an example of ordinal data [47].

3.2   Classification

A set of supervised learning methods and algorithms that group data into classes is called a classification. The classification can be binary (two possible classes) or multi-class (at least three classes) classification. The task of classification is to associate a class label with a sample i.e. to find a function that would approximately divide the data into similar groups (classes). Classification is the basic task of data analysis and pattern recognition, which presupposes the construction of classifiers. A classifier is nothing more than a function that assigns a class label to test patterns (which are described by attributes). There are various approaches to building classifiers, which are based on their functional representation, such as decision trees, decision lists, neural networks and many others.

Logistic Regression. Logistic regression is a family of functions $h : R^n \to [0,1]$ whose task is to calculate the probability that a sample belongs to a class. Although the very name of this method implies that it is a regression method, it is still a classification method. Logistic regression is based on the logistic sigmoidal function $\theta_{sig} : R \to [0,1]$ defined by the equation below:

$$\theta_{sig}(y) = \frac{1}{1 + e^{-\beta y}}$$

K-NN Algorithm. Undoubtedly, one of the best known and simplest algorithms from this group is the k-nearest neighbors (k-NN) algorithm. As its name suggests, the goal of the algorithm is to predict the class of a test sample based on adjacent samples. It can be said that simplest case occurred when $k = 1$, i.e. when the algorithm is looking for (one) nearest neighbor. Then, the output value of the prediction is the class to which the nearest neighbor belongs. For more complex cases, i.e. $k > 1$, the so-called voting is used in order to select the correct output [48].

Although it is mainly a classification algorithm, k-NN can also be used for regression problems. Such algorithms are called versatile algorithms. In the literature, regression k-NN is also called k-neighbors regression. k-NN is a very simple and relatively accurate algorithm, the built model is easy to understand and does not require excessive parameter tuning to get some (reasonably) good results. However, it is very computationally demanding, memory-consuming, while giving poor results on data sets with a large number of features. It is also relatively slow in the prediction phase [49].

Decision Trees. Tree structures are often used in machine learning. Tree-based algorithms include stratifying or segmenting predictor space into several simple regions. These methods are simple and useful to interpret, and are known as decision trees. Decision trees are used for classification and regression problems. Decision trees whose task is classification are sometimes called classification trees, and in regression they are regression trees. Both are mostly very similar, while classification trees giving qualitative outputs and regression ones giving quantitative outputs. There are numerous advantages of this algorithm; Decision trees are easy to explain and make decisions the way people often do. Also, decision trees are easy to visualize and interpret. On the other hand, these methods are usually not competitive compared to some other methods of supervised learning and there is a risk of over-specialization of the model [50].

Random Forest. As already mentioned, decision trees are not as accurate as some other machine learning methods, so they need improvement. Random forests are one such improvement of decision trees. In addition to random forests, there are other alternative methods that can provide better results, such as bagging and boosting, which are general-purpose methods and are not exclusively related to decision trees. These three methods belong to the group of so-called ensemble methods, which describes learning multiple trees in order to achieve better results.

4 Experiment Setup and Results

4.1 Participants and Materials

The experiment was conducted in summer semester of academic year 2019/2020, concretely from April 15 to May 15, and counted 56 participants. Participants were attenders of the following courses: "Computer Science Practicum 2" (first year of pre-graduate studies), "Data Structures and Algorithms" (second year of pre-graduate studies) and "Introduction to e-learning systems" (first year of graduate study). All three courses are attended within the study of informatics (or at combined studies that involve the study of Informatics). Participation in the experiment was voluntary and the results of the individual student had no impact on student's grades or the perception of his knowledge by the lecturer. For the purpose of the experiment, a special e-course was created at the e-learning platform named SUMARUM. Furhtermore, within the e-course, two tests were designed (initial and final). The questions was formed from general knowledge about computer science, which made it not possible for older students to have an advantage over younger students with their knowledge due to the larger number of taken courses over time, although our ultimate goal is not to assess their knowledge. The tests are designed in such a way that all participants should know the answers to approximately the same extent, regardless of the level of study (pre-graduate/graduate).

4.2   Experiment Setup

The experiment consisted of an initial and a final test. Both tests had 15 questions each and the total duration of the test was limited to a maximum of 18 min. Although the questions in the final test were different from the initial ones, they were similar and of approximately equal weight. The idea of the whole experiment was to have a control and experimental group. The control group performed both tests without cheating, while the experimental group performed the initial test normally and the final test had the task to cheat. The experimental group was further divided in the final test. This group was divided into three smaller groups, a group that cheats (i) via a mobile device (ii) via same browser in which performing test and (iii) via other browsers or sources of knowledge. This was done to get a wider range of the data collected and to get more realistic results. In the first group (mobile device cheating), we rely mostly on inactivity time as a variable that could indicate cheating, second group should be easy to detect cheating behaviour because we inject Javascript code in every loaded page, and final group that is using other browser on the same device could be detected with inactivity time and focus changes of browser.

The most of questions (six of them) were essays because in this way activities such as text marking and copy/paste come to the fore, and the possibility of a random answering and random correct answer is reduced. 60 students did the initial test, but the final one was done by 54 students. After the correction of the tests, the database events were queried and filtered according to the already mentioned student activities monitored by the extension. Two students made some environment configuration mistakes, so final data set consists of 52 students who took both tests, had the extension correctly installed and turned on the both tests. From these 52 students, 23 belong to the control group and the remaining 29 are from the experimental group. In the experimental group, 10 of them used the Google Chrome browser when copying, 8 students copied using a mobile device. The remaining 11 used other browsers.

Our hypothesis is that a student who has a large number of suspicious activities (compared to the control group) tries to cheat on the test. What activities are suspicious is defined in Table 1.

4.3   Environment and Data Acquisition

In order to detect behavior changes, certain activities need to be identified and stored. For this purpose, software consisting of a client[1] and server application[2] were developed. The client application is actually a chromium extension that injects custom Javascript code into every running webpage (but only at the agreed time and when the user is logged and backend is activated). The extension name is Student Activity Tracker (SAT) and it uses the plain Javascript events to collect data about student activities and then uses the VueJS and Axios plugin to send that data to the backend. On the backend side, restful API is written in PHP Framework Lumen 7.0.3 which is part of Laravel and it runs on a cloud environment, more precisely on Ubuntu 20.04.3 server on which PHP 7.2 is installed. The database is MySQL 8.0 and the webserver is Nginx 1.18.0. The database model consists of 3 tables - events, event_types and errors. User authentication was performed using eduID identity issued by the IT center of the University of Mostar, which students normally use to log in to the e-learning system SUMARUM.

Table 1. Detailed information about events, types of events and their units

Activity	Measure units	Activity category	Additional information
Mouse movement	coordinates array	Normal	separate request
Mouse click	click	Normal	left/right//double
Mouse scroll	movement	Normal	up/down/left/right
Keyboard click	touch	Normal	separate into categories
Activity time	second	Normal	if no events
Screen size (at login)	ordered pairs	Normal	height and width
Enabled cookies	boolean	Normal	accepted
Operating system	string	Normal	win/lin/mac
Text manipulations	unit	Suspicious	cut, copy, paste
Inactivity time	second	Suspicious	no events
Text highlighting	string	Suspicious	number of characters
Opened new tab/site	unit	Suspicious	do not prohibit
Browser toggled focus	unit	Suspicious	lost/returned
Total time (calculated)	seconds	Neutral	test duration
Time per page (calculated)	seconds	Neutral	duration per question

4.4   Experiment Results

After the tests were performed, data collected and filtered, we made a final data as a table that consists of 52 rows and 17 columns. Columns are marking text,

---

[1] https://github.com/hljubic/sat_client.
[2] https://github.com/hljubic/sat_backend.

manipulations on text, mouse clicks, mouse scrolling, activity time, inactivity time, mouse moves, keyboard presses, authorization, focus toggles, operating system, cookies enabled, screen size, window size, multiple tabs, final grade and group. The last column was used as a binary classification output (0 is control group, 1 is experimental). After lot of iterations and feature selection, final training set used only 6 columns - marking text, manipulations on text, activity and inactivity time, multiple tabs and focus toggles. To fully balance data set, synthetic minority over-sampling technique (SMOTE) [51] was used. Six new examples were made in minority class, which makes a total of 58 samples in new augmented data set.

On this augmented data set, four machine learning models were trained using the Python programming language and the SciKit-learn library. All models used k-fold cross-validation for $k = 10$. Data was preprocessed with StandardScaler[3]. The used machine learning algorithms are as follows: (i) logistic regression, (ii) decision trees, (iii) random forest and (iv) k-nearest neighbors. In logistic regression, an accuracy of 96.67% was achieved, decision trees had an accuracy of 93.87%, random forest was 95.1% and k-NN had an accuracy of 89.6%.

5 Conclusion and Future Research

It is possible to detect academic fraud in an uncontrolled testing environment using a non-invasive method such as this extension. The results of these machine learning models that are shown in previous chapter cannot be taken as completely relevant because the data set is extremely small, over-fitting can occur and it is relatively easy to achieve high accuracy without good generalization. Nevertheless, these results give hope that it is possible to detect suspicious behaviors in real time with this extension and machine learning algorithms, even on a such small data set.

It is important to mention that the results of the experiment were negatively affected by certain problems. The first problem is that all students took the tests from home, in an uncontrolled environment, and it is more likely that some students will deviate from the designed scenario of experiment. Also, at the moment we can't be completely sure if the right person is doing the test, so it would be good to include some kind of biometrics or other monitoring methods such as a camera and a microphone. If the student uses printed material for cheating, these activities are also not possible to monitor.

Second problem is that the test was not formally evaluated. This fact surely decreased motivation for some students in experimental group to give enough effort when cheating (to hide their suspicious activities).

Third problem is that it is a web-browser extension that cannot track activities outside of the browser itself. This means that a student can have more windows or tools open, especially if there are multiple screens and thus accomplish cheating without detecting strange behavior. Here, we rely only on one

[3] https://scikit-learn.org/stable/modules/generated/sklearn.preprocessing.StandardScaler.html.

variable, that is inactivity time. If the desktop service or application was developed instead of web browser extension it would be possible to get more valuable data about other used tools while doing test. On the other hand, it is not possible to gather as much detail about surfing through a web browser as it is done this way. The best option would be to use both approaches, but this would make it much more difficult to develop and also to prepare the test environment, especially for different operating systems.

The future direction of the research is to involve a much larger number of students in experiment, at least 10 times more, but also to include a whole range of professions, not just computer science. Second, expand the geographical area where students come from, not only to Bosnia and Herzegovina, but to the region or even better to the world-wide. Also, the plan is to upgrade this extension to work with an intelligent tutoring system CMTutor [52]. From the side of prediction, instead of machine learning we plan to use deep neural networks because they have proven to be superior to the algorithms used in this paper. Furthermore, the plan is to use generative adversarial networks (GANs) [53] to augment the collected data and create a balanced data set instead of using SMOTE for the task. The experiment should have been conducted in more controlled conditions to avoid errors and unplanned scenarios and thus lost some valuable data.

Acknowledgements. The authors are grateful to the project of digital transformation of education in Bosnia and Herzegovina schools that teach in the Croatian language for supporting this research.

References

1. Hilbert, G.A.: Academic fraud: Prevalence, practices, and reasons. J. Prof. Nurs. **3**(1), 39–45 (1987)
2. Bird, C.: The influence of the press upon the accuracy of report. Psychol. Sci. Public Interest **22**(2), 123 (1927)
3. Muhsin, K., et al.: An analyis of student's academic fraud behavior. Adv. Soc. Sci. Educ. Humanities Res. **164**(1), 34–38 (2018)
4. Luo, Z., Zhang, T.: A mobile service platform for trustworthy e-learning service provisioning. Int. J. Depend. Trustworthy Inform. Syst. (IJDTIS) **1**(3), 1–13 (2010)
5. Gholami, A., Zhang, L.Y.: Student behaviour in unsupervised online quizzes: A closer look. In: Proceedings of the 23rd Western Canadian Conference on Computing Education (2018)
6. Hollinger, R.C., Lanza-Kaduce, L.: Academic dishonesty and the perceived effectiveness of countermeasures: An empirical survey of cheating at a major public university. NASPA J. **33**(4), 292–306 (1996)
7. Choi, J.: Cheating behaviors and related factors at a Korean dental school. Korean J. Med. Educ. **31**(3), 239 (2019)
8. Witherspoon, M., Maldonado, N., Lacey, C.H.: Academic Dishonesty of Undergraduates: Methods of Cheating. Online Submission (2010)
9. Jones, D.L.R.: Academic dishonesty: Are more students cheating? Bus. Commun. Q. **74**(2), 141–150 (2011)
10. Mustaine, E.E., Tewksbury, R.: Southern college students' cheating behaviors: An examination of problem behavior correlates. Deviant Behav. **26**(5), 439–461 (2005)

11. Keresztury, B., Cser, L.: New cheating methods in the electronic teaching era. Procedia. Soc. Behav. Sci. **93**, 1516–1520 (2013)
12. Akbulut, Y., et al.: Exploring the types and reasons of Internet-triggered academic dishonesty among Turkish undergraduate students: Development of Internet-Triggered Academic Dishonesty Scale (ITADS). Comput. Educ. **51**(1), 463–473 (2008)
13. Widianingsih, L.P.: Students cheating behaviors: The influence of fraud triangle. Rev. Integrat. Bus. Econ. Res. **2**(2), 252 (2013)
14. Li, Z., Zhu, Z., Yang, T.: A multi-index examination cheating detection method based on neural network. In: 2019 IEEE 31st International Conference on Tools with Artificial Intelligence (ICTAI). IEEE (2019)
15. Cressey, D.R.: Other people's money; a study of the social psychology of embezzlement (1953)
16. Schuchter, A., Levi, M.: The fraud triangle revisited. Secur. J. **29**(2), 107–121 (2016)
17. Choo, F., Tan, K.: The effect of fraud triangle factors on students' cheating behaviors. Advances in accounting education. Emerald Group Publishing Limited (2008)
18. Anderman, E.M., Won, S.: Academic cheating in disliked classes. Ethics Behav. **29**(1), 1–22 (2019)
19. Sabonchi, A.K.S., Görür, A.K.: Plagiarism detection in learning management system. In: 2017 8th International Conference on Information Technology (ICIT). IEEE (2017)
20. Osman, A.H., Barukab, O.M.: SVM significant role selection method for improving semantic text plagiarism detection. Int. J. Adv. Appli. Sci. **4**(8), 112–122 (2017)
21. McGowan, U.: Plagiarism detection and prevention: Are we putting the cart before the horse. In: Proceedings of the HERDSA Conference (2005)
22. Meuschke, N., et al.: HyPlag: a hybrid approach to academic plagiarism detection. In: The 41st International ACM SIGIR Conference on Research & Development in Information Retrieval (2018)
23. Tresnawati, D., Syaichu, A.: Plagiarism detection system design for programming assignment in virtual classroom based on Moodle. Procedia. Soc. Behav. Sci. **67**, 114–122 (2012)
24. Kaya, M., Ayşe Özel, S.: Integrating an online compiler and a plagiarism detection tool into the Moodle distance education system for easy assessment of programming assignments. Comput. Appli. Eng. Educ. **23**(3), 363–373 (2015)
25. Opgen-Rhein, J., Küppers, B., Schroeder, U.: An application to discover cheating in digital exams. In: Proceedings of the 18th Koli Calling International Conference on Computing Education Research (2018)
26. Martínez, S., Wimmer, M., Cabot, J.: Efficient plagiarism detection for software modeling assignments. Comput. Sci. Educ. **30**(2), 187–215 (2020)
27. Graziano, R., et al.: Jack Watson: Addressing contract cheating at scale in online computer science education. In: Proceedings of the Sixth (2019) ACM Conference on Learning@ Scale (2019)
28. Topîrceanu, A.: Breaking up friendships in exams: A case study for minimizing student cheating in higher education using social network analysis. Comput. Educ. **115**, 171–187 (2017)
29. Parks, R.F., et al.: Why students engage in cyber-cheating through a collective movement: A case of deviance and collusion. Comput. Educ. **125**, 308–326 (2018)
30. Oberreuter, G., et al.: Approaches for intrinsic and external plagiarism detection. Proc. PAN **4**(5), 63 (2011)

31. Sheridan, D., Witherden, S.: Detecting cheaters using a learning management system. In: EdMedia+ Innovate Learning. Association for the Advancement of Computing in Education (AACE) (2004)

32. Ueno, M.: Online outlier detection system for learning time data in E-learning and It's evaluation. In: Proceedings of of Computers and Advanced Technology in Education (CATE2004), 248–253 (2004)

33. Zopluoglu, C.: Detecting examinees with item preknowledge in large-scale testing using extreme gradient boosting (XGBoost). Educ. Psychol. Measur. **79**(5), 931–961 (2019)

34. Li, L., Qiu, C., Fang, A.: Detection of test cheating by outlier analysis approach using probability estimation. In: Proceedings of the International Conference on Artificial Intelligence, Information Processing and Cloud Computing (2019)

35. Wang, J., et al.: Analysis on test cheating and its solutions based on extenics and information technology. Proc. Comput. Sci. **55**, 1009–1014 (2015)

36. Khan, I.A., Brinkman, W.-P., Hierons, R.: Towards estimating computer users' mood from interaction behaviour with keyboard and mouse. Front. Comput. Sci. **7**(6), 943–954 (2013)

37. Estrada, J., Buhia, J., Guevarra, A., Forcado, M.R.: Keyboard and mouse: tools in identifying emotions during computer activities. In: Jung, J.J., Kim, P., Choi, K.N. (eds.) BDTA 2017. LNICST, vol. 248, pp. 115–123. Springer, Cham (2018). https://doi.org/10.1007/978-3-319-98752-1_13

38. Pentel, A.: Emotions and user interactions with keyboard and mouse. In: 2017 8th International Conference on Information, Intelligence, Systems & Applications (IISA). IEEE (2017)

39. Bours, P., Barghouthi, H.: Continuous authentication using biometric keystroke dynamics. In: The Norwegian Information Security Conference (NISK), vol. 2009 (2009)

40. Frank, M., et al.: Touchalytics: On the applicability of touchscreen input as a behavioral biometric for continuous authentication. IEEE Trans. Inform. Foren. Sec. **8**(1), 136–148 (2012)

41. Deutschmann, I., Nordström, P., Nilsson, L.: Continuous authentication using behavioral biometrics. IT Professional **15**(4), 12–15 (2013)

42. Fenu, G., Marras, M., Boratto, L.: A multi-biometric system for continuous student authentication in e-learning platforms. Pattern Recogn. Lett. **113**, 83–92 (2018)

43. Bhandwalkar, K.T., Hanwate, P.S.: Continuous user authentication using soft biometric traits for E-learning. Int. J. Innovative Res. Sci. Eng. Technol. **3**(4), 231–235 (2014)

44. Asep, H.S.G., Bandung, Y.: A design of continuous user verification for online exam proctoring on M-learning. In: 2019 International Conference on Electrical Engineering and Informatics (ICEEI). IEEE (2019)

45. Arinaldi, A., Fanany, M.I.: Cheating video description based on sequences of gestures. In: 2017 5th International Conference on Information and Communication Technology (ICoIC7). IEEE (2017)

46. Ghizlane, M., Hicham, B., Reda, F.H.: A new model of automatic and continuous online exam monitoring. In: 2019 International Conference on Systems of Collaboration Big Data, Internet of Things & Security (SysCoBIoTS). IEEE (2019)

47. Ljubić, H.: Predviđanje ishoda učenja pomoću neuronskih mreža u okruženje konceptualnih mapa

48. Müller, A.C., Guido, S.: Introduction to machine learning with Python: a guide for data scientists. O'Reilly Media, Inc. (2016)

49. Bronshtein, A.: A quick introduction to K-Nearest Neighbors Algorithm. Noteworthy-The Journal Blog (2017)
50. James, G., Witten, D., Hastie, T., Tibshirani, R.: An Introduction to Statistical Learning. STS, vol. 103. Springer, New York (2013). https://doi.org/10.1007/978-1-4614-7138-7
51. Chawla, N.V., et al.: SMOTE: synthetic minority over-sampling technique. J. Artifi. Intell. Res. **16**, 321–357 (2002)
52. Volarić, T.: Model oblikovanja i isporuke znanja u inteligentnom sustavu za upravljanje učenjem. Sveučilište u Splitu (2017)
53. Goodfellow, I., et al.: Generative adversarial nets. In: Advances in Neural Information Processing Systems 27 (2014)

Changes in Legal Education in the Digital Society of Artificial Intelligence

Franjo Vučić(✉) iD

University of Mostar, Trg Hrvatskih Velikana 1, Mostar, Bosnia and Herzegovina
franjo.vucic@sum.ba
https://www.sum.ba/

Abstract. As artificial intelligence (AI) becomes increasingly prevalent in the legal industry, it is essential to consider its impact on legal education and law practice. This paper examines the changes in legal education in the digital society of AI. We first draw an analogy between the importance of introducing AI in law and Justinian's Code, which led to the development of new forms of legal learning and sophisticated academic and professional legal texts. Similarly, AI allows for analyzing large amounts of legal data and provides new knowledge about legal trends and risks. AI tools like machine learning algorithms can automate routine legal tasks and accelerate legal research. However, AI also présents challenges related to transparency, accountability, ethics, and privacy, which require new legal education and practice approaches. Law students need to be aware of the impact of AI on the law and society and be equipped with the necessary skills to work with it. Furthermore, legal professionals need to understand the implications of AI to create appropriate legal frameworks to mitigate potential risks while avoiding impeding innovation. Overall, this paper highlights the need for a new paradigm in legal education and practice that considers the evolving role of AI in the legal industry.

Keywords: Legal education · Artificial Intelligence · AI related Legal Skills · Legal technology · Insurance Law · Legal reasoning

1 Introduction

Since electrification, the story of the twentieth century has been the race between education and technology [1]. Artificial Intelligence (AI) has been increasingly applied in various fields, including law student education, to solve complex problems, increase efficiency, and improve accessibility. However, the use of AI in these fields has also raised serious concerns regarding privacy and ethical issues. It is transforming various industries, and the legal profession is no exception. The use of AI in the legal field is becoming increasingly prevalent, with its potential to automate routine tasks, streamline legal research, and enhance decision-making. As AI technologies continue to advance, it is crucial to understand their implications for legal education and law practice. Over the course of a generation,

D. Vasić and M. Kundid Vasić (Eds.): MoStart 2023, CCIS 1827, pp. 159–176, 2023.
https://doi.org/10.1007/978-3-031-36833-2_12

algorithms have gone from mathematical abstractions to powerful mediators of daily life. In evolving from static computer programs hand-coded by engineers to the products of machine learning, these technologies have made our lives more efficient, more entertaining, and, sometimes, better informed. At the same time, complex algorithms are increasingly crushing the basic rights of individual citizens [2]. According to the European Commission's Ethics Guidelines for Trustworthy AI, ethical principles, such as transparency, accountability, and fairness, must be integrated into the design and deployment of AI systems to ensure they are human-centric and promote the common good. In addition, the General Data Protection Regulation (GDPR) sets out strict rules on processing personal data, including data processed by AI systems. Artificial Intelligence and Law (AI and Law), a research field since the 1980s with roots in the previous decades, is about to experience a revolution [3]. This paper explores the changes in legal science and legal education in the digital society of artificial intelligence. The paper's objectives are to examine the impact of AI on the legal profession, to identify the challenges and opportunities posed by these developments, and to propose recommendations for legal education and the practice of law. Overall, this paper aims to contribute to the growing body of literature on the impact of AI on the legal profession and to provide insights into the challenges and opportunities presented by AI for legal education and practice.

2   The Impact of AI on the Future of Law and Legal Education

Experts say the rise of artificial intelligence will make most people better off over the next decade, but many have concerns about how advances in AI will affect what it means to be human, to be productive and to exercise free will [4].

An interesting analogy can be drawn between the importance of introducing AI into law and the Justinian Code [5]. Just as the Code was a massive and sophisticated corpus of Roman law that posed information overload challenges to students, teachers, and practitioners of law, AI enables the analysis of large amounts of legal data and provides new insights into legal trends and risks. The Code led to the development of new forms of legal education and sophisticated academic and professional legal texts, so too does AI lead to the development of new forms of legal education and the automation of routine legal tasks. The Code presented challenges in terms of information overload, and so too does AI pose challenges around issues of transparency, accountability, ethics, and privacy.

The Justinian Code influenced the development of canon law and much of what is understood as law in the Western world today, and similarly, AI has the potential to impact the development of law through predictive law, the automation of legal services, and legal chat bots. AI tools, such as machine learning algorithms, can be used to automate routine legal tasks such as document search and analysis, classification, and prediction. This technology also enables faster and more precise searching of legal literature, facilitating and expediting legal research. Tools such as Contract Express, DocuSign, Neota Logic, Juro, and LawGeex are all used to automate routine legal tasks such as generating legal documents, signing documents, verifying legal validity, and analyzing and searching documents.

There are two possible futures for the professions. Both of these rest on technology. The first is reassuringly familiar to most professionals-it is simply a more efficient version of what we have today. In the future, professionals of many different types use technology largely to streamline and optimize their traditional ways of working. In the language of economists, technologies "complement" them in these activities. The second future is a different proposition. Here, increasingly capable systems and machines, either operating alone or designed and operated by people who look quite unlike doctors and lawyers, teachers and accountants, and others, gradually take on more of the tasks we associate with those traditional professionals. New technologies instead, in the words of economists, "substitute" for professionals in these activities [6].

AI tools can also be used to automate routine legal tasks such as generating legal documents, verifying legal validity, and predicting court decisions. This can save time and reduce costs for lawyers. Blockchain technology allows for decentralized and transparent transaction records, which is helpful for legal science as it enables easier tracking and proof of legal transactions, increasing transparency and security. Technologies such as e-document tracking and digital discovery can expedite and simplify judicial and administrative proceedings. Technologies like AI bring new legal issues related to data privacy, cyber security, and intellectual property that lawyers must understand and be trained to work with. These are all new challenges for lawyers. AI does offer a lot of business value, but much of that value isn't glamorous or visible. Products and processes will be made somewhat better and easier to use. Decisions will be better informed. We'll continue-and perhaps even accelerate a bit-the fantastic progress that we've seen over the last couple of decades in data and analytics [7].

It is also unclear what law students need to learn about technology. Law firms have long called for law schools to graduate "practice-ready" students but even firms seem confused about the kinds of technology the firms will require, whether to develop the technology in-house or rely on external suppliers and the skills and knowledge that would best prepare law students for evaluating and using the new technologies [8].

Therefore, new approaches to legal education are needed to acquire the necessary skills to understand AI. Law students need to be aware of the impact of AI on law and society. A particular challenge is terminology used in technical fields such as neural networks, machine learning, and others. Lawyers need to be aware of the implications of AI to create an appropriate legal framework to reduce potential public risks of AI while avoiding obstructing innovation. There are already some academic areas, such as law and technology or IT law, that are attempting to offer legal frameworks for addressing challenges around artificial intelligence. However, AI has enormous potential to improve the management of legal resources for lawyers.

The incorporation of Artificial Intelligence (AI) in legal education is becoming increasingly important due to the significant impact that AI is having on the legal profession. The use of AI in the legal industry has been rapidly growing in recent years, with the potential to automate routine legal tasks, improve legal research, and provide more efficient and effective legal services. Therefore, legal students must have the necessary knowledge and skills to work alongside these emerging technologies.

By introducing AI in legal education, students can gain a deeper understanding of how AI can be used in the legal industry, the benefits it can provide, and the ethical and privacy considerations that must be addressed. Furthermore, incorporating AI in legal education can help students develop critical thinking and problem-solving skills needed to evaluate the appropriateness and effectiveness of AI applications in various legal scenarios.

Legal professionals with knowledge and skills in AI will be better equipped to adapt to changes in the legal profession and utilize AI effectively to streamline their work and provide better services to clients. Moreover, as the use of AI in the legal industry continues to grow, legal professionals will need to understand how to work with AI and ensure its use adheres to ethical and legal standards.

Incorporating AI in legal education is essential to prepare future legal professionals for the challenges and opportunities that AI presents. Legal education must adapt to the changing nature of the legal industry to equip students with the necessary skills and knowledge to work alongside AI effectively. This requires legal education to cultivate versatile professionals who have the ability of legal thinking and legal application and can analyze and use artificial intelligence technology to adapt to the demands of the new era [10]. But in the long run, it is difficult to foresee anything other than a much smaller need for conventional lawyers [11].

2.1 The Impact of Artificial Intelligence on Risk Assessment, Claims Processing, and Fraud Detection

We may be living in the dawn of the age of artificial intelligence today. Consequently, the legal landscape surrounding our lives will require rethinking, as the case was with every big leap in technology [12].

Artificial Intelligence (AI) has the potential to revolutionize the legal industry by providing new tools to analyze large amounts of legal data, and to identify legal trends and risks.

One area in which AI can be particularly useful is Insurance Law. One of the primary ways in which AI is impacting insurance law is through the use of predictive analytics. Insurance companies can now use machine learning algorithms to analyze vast amounts of data to predict the likelihood of future events, such as accidents, illnesses, or property damage. This technology allows insurance companies to set premiums and determine coverage based on a more accurate risk assessment. For example, a car insurance company can use data on a driver's age, driving record, and the make and model of their car to predict the likelihood of an accident occurring. By using this information, the company can set premiums that reflect the actual risk of insuring that driver, rather than relying on broad categories such as age and gender.

While predictive analytics can improve risk assessment accuracy, it raises legal and ethical questions. For example, some argue that using data such as a person's zip code or credit score to determine their insurance premiums may lead to discrimination against certain groups. This issue has already been raised in the healthcare industry, where predictive analytics has been criticized for discriminating against people with certain medical conditions.

Another way in which AI is impacting insurance law is through the use of chatbots and other automated systems to handle insurance claims. Instead of relying on human adjusters to assess claims, insurance companies use AI-powered chatbots to interact with customers and process claims. These systems use natural language processing to understand and respond to customer inquiries, and machine learning algorithms to identify fraudulent claims. This technology can significantly reduce the time and cost of processing claims, and improve customer satisfaction.

However, using chatbots and other automated systems also raises legal and ethical questions. For example, if a chatbot denies a claim without a human adjuster reviewing it, the insured may not receive a fair assessment. Similarly, if the chatbot makes an error in processing the claim, the insurance company could be held liable for any damages that result.

AI is also impacting insurance law by enabling insurers to automate underwriting. Underwriting is how an insurance company assesses the risk of insuring a particular individual or entity. By using machine learning algorithms to analyze data, insurers can more accurately assess risk and determine appropriate coverage and premiums. This technology can help insurers to avoid costly mistakes and reduce the time and resources needed to underwrite policies.

However, using AI in underwriting also raises legal and ethical questions. For example, if an algorithm is used to determine coverage and premiums, it may not consider individual circumstances that could affect risk. This could lead to individuals being unfairly denied coverage or charged higher premiums than they should be.

AI is impacting insurance law by enabling insurers to detect better and prevent fraud. Insurance fraud is a significant problem, costing the industry billions of dollars annually. By using machine learning algorithms to analyze data, insurers can identify patterns that may indicate fraud, such as unusually high claim amounts or multiple claims from the same individual. This technology can help insurers detect fraud earlier and reduce the overall cost to the industry.

The use of AI to detect fraud also raises legal and ethical questions. For example, if an algorithm identifies a claim as fraudulent, but is later determined to be legitimate, the insured may suffer significant harm. Similarly, if an algorithm identifies specific groups of people as more likely to commit fraud, it could lead to discrimination against those groups. The ability of AI to learn from its personal experience, through ML for instance, leads to independent and autonomous decision-making that are characteristics of legal personality [9].

2.2   AI's Potential to Automate Routine Legal Tasks

Artificial Intelligence (AI) has the potential to automate routine legal tasks, saving time and reducing costs for lawyers. Routine tasks such as document analysis, classification, and prediction can be automated using machine learning algorithms. For example, Contract Express, DocuSign, Neota Logic, Juro, and LawGeex are all used to automate routine legal tasks such as generating legal documents, signing documents, verifying legal validity, and analyzing and searching documents. Fuelled by developments in automation and AI, the proliferation of 'legal tech' highlights that legal services are no longer immune to innovation [13]. One of the most significant advantages of AI in legal practice is its ability to process vast amounts of data in a fraction of the time it would take a human. For instance, AI-powered contract review tools can scan through large volumes of contracts, analyze clauses, and extract relevant data in a matter of hours, while this task would take lawyers days or even weeks to complete. Additionally, AI can assist with legal research, providing faster and more precise searching of legal literature and case law, which can facilitate and expedite legal research. AI-based tools such as natural language processing (NLP) are already changing different practices, from discovery processes to contract review and prediction [14].

AI can also be used for legal document automation. Legal document automation involves creating standardized templates that can be quickly customized to meet clients' specific needs. This process can significantly reduce the time and cost of drafting legal documents. For example, AI-powered document assembly platforms such as ContractExpress can help lawyers generate contracts and other legal documents more efficiently.

For example, a recent report looking at technological innovation in legal services highlights that legal technologies, such as document assembly, automation, and AI, are expected to disrupt the BMs of legal services firms by creating new and enhanced services, bringing new ways to engage and interact with clients, but also challenging their current structure and economic model [15].

Moreover, AI can also automate routine legal tasks such as verifying legal validity, predicting court decisions, and drafting simple legal documents such as wills and contracts. This can save time and reduce costs for lawyers, allowing them to focus on more complex legal tasks that require human intervention.

AI technology is not a substitute for legal professionals, and it should be seen as a tool to assist them in their work. Although AI can automate routine tasks, it cannot replace the critical thinking and judgment skills that lawyers possess. Moreover, AI technology is not infallible, and it is essential to have human oversight to ensure that the results produced by AI systems are accurate and ethical.

The potential of AI to automate routine legal tasks is enormous, allowing lawyers to work more efficiently and effectively. However, integrating AI into legal practice should be done with caution, as it is crucial to maintain the ethical and legal standards underpinning the legal profession. AI should be viewed as a tool to assist lawyers in their work, and lawyers should be trained to work alongside AI technologies to provide better and more effective legal services.

Although, The most recent technology is not focused on replacing the routine tasks of lawyers yet, but rather on facilitating the understanding and analysis of legal material, improving the services that lawyers can provide - and the production of services using these technologies does not depend very much on the economy of scale of large law firms, and also capacitates individual professionals and small business lawyers. If emerging technologies automate routine tasks for lawyers, the problems of the profession would undoubtedly be permanent since their effect would be mainly related to large-scale transactional or litigation practice. These technologies would thus be beneficial to large law firms. But the individual lawyer (or one who works in a small office) will experience a declining market, as technology will replace them in some of the tasks usually done by human lawyers (preparation of declarations of will or contracts, for example), but without offering corresponding opportunities to expand their practice [16].

3 Adapting Legal Education for the Age of AI: Incorporating Technical Skills and Ethics Education

In addition to the standard curriculum, law schools should consider offering specialized courses or certifications in legal technology and innovation. These programs could cover topics such as AI, machine learning, natural language processing, and data analytics to ensure that students have the necessary skills to work alongside emerging technologies in the legal industry [17].

Moreover, law schools should encourage students to develop problem-solving, critical thinking, and interdisciplinary collaboration skills, which are essential in working alongside AI technologies. Law schools can also partner with legal tech companies or other organizations to provide students with practical experience using AI in legal practice [18].

Law schools should educate students on AI's ethical and legal implications and encourage discussions. This includes data privacy, transparency, accountability, and bias in AI algorithms.

The goal of law schools should be to prepare students to work effectively alongside emerging technologies and to be adaptable in the changing landscape of the legal industry. Law students need a fundamental understanding of coding and data to utilize AI in law effectively. This knowledge enables them to comprehend the basic functioning of AI systems, facilitating education about AI and learning from AI [19].

3.1 The Need for New Approaches to Legal Education

The emergence of artificial intelligence (AI) technology in the legal industry has created a need for new approaches to legal education. Traditional legal education has focused on teaching students the doctrine, legal reasoning, and legal analysis needed to practice law. However, in the age of AI, legal education needs to be adapted to include knowledge and skills related to technology and data analytics.

There is little doubt that technology will replace some of the tasks typically performed by lawyers (a recent example of this is the online platform of lawsuits) [20]. To be effective in a world where AI plays an increasingly prominent role in legal practice, students must be equipped with the skills and knowledge needed to work alongside these emerging technologies. Law schools should consider incorporating AI-related topics, such as machine learning, natural language processing, and data analytics, into their curricula. This would help students understand how AI can be used in the legal industry and the ethical and privacy considerations that must be addressed.

Companies are already developing technologies capable of understanding and answering complex legal questions and their answers depend on several factors - mainly applications that use machine learning, extensive legal data analysis, and neural computing to textually analyze all relevant sources and provide a probabilistic answer to that question. Thus, knowing how to qualify a legal relationship to investigate its suitability for different aspects of law, for example, is perfectly achievable by such applications. For lawyers who, beyond dogmatic classifications (between fact, law, and jurisprudence for drafting documents/petitions, for example), also engage in other substantive areas of law (such as tax planning or mediation, for example), technologies that perform dogmatic classifications are closer to the increasing intelligence, freeing the lawyer to focus on more complex legal issues. However, for those whose experience and expertise are limited to such dogmatic classifications, the technology in question will be treated as an AI apparatus that will most likely replace them [21].

Law schools should encourage students to develop skills in problem-solving, critical thinking, and interdisciplinary collaboration, which are essential in working alongside AI technologies. Legal professionals with knowledge and skills in AI will be better equipped to adapt to changes in the legal profession and utilize AI effectively to streamline their work and provide better services to clients. Law schools can also partner with legal tech companies or other organizations to offer students practical experience using AI in legal practice.

Furthermore, law schools should educate students on AI's ethical and legal implications and encourage discussions. This includes data privacy, transparency, accountability, and bias in AI algorithms. The use of AI in the legal industry must adhere to ethical and legal standards. Therefore, lawyers must understand the implications of AI to create an appropriate legal framework to reduce potential public risks of AI while avoiding obstructing innovation.

Lawyers have a role to play in helping their clients prepare for the impact of AI while maintaining ethical standards and achieving legal objectives. The author suggests three ways in which lawyers can do this. Firstly, they can shape advice and policies by familiarizing themselves with the technology and setting standards. This helps clients avoid potential legal issues related to AI and, when necessary, dissuades clients from engaging in certain behaviors. Secondly, lawyers can assist clients in assessing their relationships with the technology sector by identifying and learning from legitimate experts and appreciating the importance of healthy skepticism between governments and technology developers. Finally, lawyers can monitor AI developments in other countries to prevent the temptation to take shortcuts to catch up [22].

As AI technologies replace some legal tasks, students must be prepared to work with these tools effectively. Law schools should emphasize problem-solving, critical thinking, and interdisciplinary collaboration to help students adapt to the changing legal profession. Partnerships with legal tech companies or other organizations can offer students practical experience with AI in legal practice.

Moreover, law schools should promote discussions on AI's ethical and legal implications, including data privacy, transparency, accountability, and bias. Legal professionals must understand AI's implications to create an appropriate legal framework that balances risk reduction and innovation.

In summary, the need for new approaches to legal education is crucial in the age of AI. Legal education must adapt to the evolving legal industry to equip students with the necessary skills and knowledge to work effectively with AI, addressing its challenges and opportunities.

An example of this is a real-world, impactful project for law students that develops AI-related legal skills and could involve creating an AI-powered tool for analyzing contracts and identifying potential risks or areas for negotiation. In this project, students should begin by choosing a specific type of relevant and widely used contract, such as an employment contract, lease agreement, or sales contract. They should then conduct comprehensive research on the chosen contract type to gather relevant information, including applicable laws, regulations, standard clauses, and potential legal issues. Additionally, they need to collect a dataset of sample contracts to serve as the basis for the AI tool's training.

After that, students work with AI technologies, such as machine learning and natural language processing, to develop the contract analysis tool. They need to train the device using the dataset of sample contracts and optimize its performance through iterative testing and feedback. Throughout the project, students will address ethical concerns and privacy issues related to using AI in contract analysis, such as ensuring the tool's accuracy, maintaining user confidentiality, and handling sensitive information.

Students must design a user-friendly interface for the contract analysis tool, ensuring it is accessible and easy for many users, including those with limited legal knowledge or technical skills. They should conduct pilot testing of the contract analysis tool with volunteer users who represent the target audience, such as small business owners, landlords, or human resources professionals. Feedback from the pilot testing will be used to refine the tool and improve its performance.

Finally, upon completing the contract analysis tool, students must develop a plan for promoting it to the public and relevant organizations, such as legal clinics, business associations, and universities. The goal is to maximize the tool's impact by making it widely accessible to those who may benefit from its services.

3.2   Skills and Competencies Required for Law Students and Professionals in the Age of AI

As the legal industry continues to embrace AI technologies, there is a growing need for law students and professionals to acquire new skills and competencies. In addition to traditional legal training, lawyers must be proficient in working alongside AI tools and be able to navigate the latest ethical and legal issues in the AI age. Alarie et al. highlight that to fully realize the advantages of AI tools in the legal field, legal professionals must rethink how legal services are provided at a global level [14].

One of the critical skills that law students and professionals must develop is understanding and working with AI algorithms. This includes understanding the principles behind machine learning and natural language processing, which are fundamental components of many AI tools used in the legal industry. In addition, lawyers must be able to work with large amounts of data and use data analytics to identify patterns and trends. This skill set is essential for lawyers to effectively use AI tools to automate routine legal tasks and to gain insights into complex legal issues. Lawyers of the future will not need to be able to "code," but they will need an intimate and continuing understanding of how to identify and use AI solutions to meet their clients.' needs [23].

Another critical skill is problem-solving. With the increasing use of AI in the legal industry, lawyers must be able to evaluate the appropriateness and effectiveness of AI applications in various legal scenarios. This requires critical thinking and the ability to identify potential ethical and legal issues related to the use of AI. Lawyers must also be able to assess AI outputs' reliability and understand AI algorithms' limitations. Mainly strongly associated with legal reasoning is the legal problem-solving process in which lawyers identify relevant rules, critically apply the directions to the facts of a situation, and predict probable results with a convincing conclusion [24].

In addition to technical skills, lawyers must possess soft skills such as communication and collaboration. With the rise of interdisciplinary teams and the increasing use of AI tools in legal practice, lawyers must be able to work effectively with other professionals, including data scientists and engineers. Lawyers must be able to communicate legal concepts and requirements to non-legal professionals and collaborate with them to achieve legal objectives. The article "The Impact of Artificial Intelligence on Legal Communication" by Enrico Francesconi and Carlo Guarnieri, published in the journal Artificial Intelligence and Law, discusses the impact of AI on legal communication. The authors argue that AI technologies have the potential to revolutionize legal communication by providing new tools for drafting, analyzing, and presenting legal arguments. They note that AI can help lawyers to identify relevant legal precedents, analyze legal documents, and even draft legal briefs and contracts. However, the authors also note that using AI in legal communication raises several ethical and practical issues. For example, they discuss the need for transparency in AI systems, so that lawyers and judges can understand how AI technologies arrive at their conclusions. They also highlight the importance of maintaining professional standards and ethical principles in using AI. The article argues that AI has the potential to enhance legal communication significantly, but that it is essential for lawyers and other legal professionals to carefully consider the ethical and practical implications of AI technologies. By doing so, they can ensure that AI is used responsibly and effectively to support the rule of law and the administration of justice [25].

Law students and professionals must also be aware of AI's ethical and legal implications. They must be able to identify potential biases in AI algorithms and ensure that the use of AI adheres to ethical and legal standards. Lawyers must also be able to assess the privacy and security implications of using AI in legal practice and understand the potential risks and limitations in decision-making processes. Legal reasoning can be seen as a variety of skills required in the law profession, such as analyzing legal principles, organizing data into legal categories, and evaluating ethical principles [26].

To acquire these skills and competencies, law schools must adapt their curriculum to incorporate relevant AI-related topics, such as machine learning, natural language processing, and data analytics. They should also consider offering specialized courses or legal technology and innovation certifications. Law schools should encourage interdisciplinary collaboration and partner with legal tech companies or other organizations to provide students with practical experience in using AI in legal practice.

Legal professionals must engage in continuous learning to keep up with the rapidly changing landscape of AI in the legal industry. This includes attending conferences, participating in workshops and training sessions, and staying up-to-date with new AI tools and developments. The age of AI presents challenges and opportunities for law students and professionals. To succeed in this new era, lawyers must possess diverse skills and competencies, including technical skills related to AI algorithms and data analytics, problem-solving skills, communication and collaboration skills, and an understanding of the ethical and legal implications of AI. Law schools must adapt their curriculum and provide practical experiences to prepare students for the changing legal landscape. Legal professionals must engage in continuous learning to stay up-to-date with new AI tools and developments.

3.3 Existing Initiatives and Programs in Legal Education Related to AI

Several initiatives and programs in legal education related to AI aim to equip law students with the necessary knowledge and skills to work alongside emerging technologies.

One example is the Summer School at the European University Institute in Florence, Italy. The Summer School on AI and Law is held every year. It is jointly hosted by the European University Institute (Florence, Italy) and the University of Pittsburgh School of Law (U.S.A.). It is also sponsored by Cirsfid-University of Bologna (Italy), the University of Groningen (the Netherlands), The University of Konstanz, the University of Swansea, the European Academy of Legal Theory, the University of Utrecht (the Netherlands), and the ERC project CompuLaw [27].

The University of Michigan Law School offers a course called "Artificial Intelligence and Law" that explores the intersection of AI and the legal industry. The course covers topics such as machine learning, natural language processing, and predictive analytics, as well as ethical and regulatory considerations surrounding the use of AI in legal practice. Students engage in hands-on exercises to develop their AI models and learn about the potential impact of AI on the legal profession [28].

ai-and-law-lisbon.com is a platform that promotes the study and discussion of artificial intelligence and its implications for the legal profession. It offers courses, workshops, and events aimed at law students, lawyers, and legal professionals interested in learning about the intersection of AI and the law. The platform is run by the University of Lisbon, the Faculty of Law, and the European Law Students' Association Lisbon. The courses and events cover a wide range of topics, including legal tech, ethics and regulation of AI, data protection, and the impact of AI on legal practice. They also provide resources such as articles, reports, and case studies related to AI and the law. It serves as a hub for the exchange of knowledge and ideas among legal professionals and scholars interested in exploring the potential of AI in the legal field [29].

The program titled "Applied Artificial Intelligence" offered by Alma Mater Europaea - ECM is a post-graduate program that provides students with knowledge and skills related to AI and its practical applications in various fields, including law. The program covers topics such as machine learning, natural language processing, and data analytics, which are relevant to using AI in legal practice. Specifically, the program includes courses on "AI and Law," which cover legal issues related to the use of AI, such as data privacy, transparency, accountability, and bias in AI algorithms. Additionally, the program offers courses on "LegalTech" and "Digital Transformation", which provide students with practical knowledge and skills in using AI and other digital technologies in legal practice [30].

Overall, these initiatives and programs demonstrate the growing recognition of the importance of AI in the legal profession and the need to prepare law students for the changes emerging technologies will bring.

4   Challenges in Implementing Changes in Legal Education in the Digital Society of AI

Implementing changes in legal education in the digital society of AI faces several challenges that must be addressed. Some of these challenges include:

4.1   Resistance to Change

Many legal educators may resist the implementation of AI in legal education due to a lack of understanding or fear of the unknown. They may be skeptical about AI tools' accuracy and ability to replace traditional teaching methods. Are students interested in changes other than those which take them into a practice situation sooner? Are law professors interested in any change which might impinge upon their well-known independence? Can we develop a form of legal scholarship that is meaningful both to the profession and the university community? Finally, is there the remotest chance of the type of funding that will allow radical legal education reform to proceed? These are professor Stevens's questions while writing on the history of legal education [31].

4.2   Challenges in Integrating AI into Legal Education

Integrating AI into legal education requires significant infrastructure, software, and hardware investment. Legal educators need to be trained in using AI tools, which can be time-consuming and costly. In the field of research and development, the dependence on technology and data will determine that the investment in research and development of artificial intelligence technology in the legal field will keep expanding for a long time [32].

4.3   Ethical and Moral Considerations

There are ethical and moral considerations to be taken into account when using AI in legal education. For example, using AI in legal education raises questions about privacy, bias, and discrimination. As with any transformative technology, some AI applications may raise new ethical and legal questions, for example, related to liability or potentially biased decision-making. The ethics of artificial intelligence in general has received much attention [33].

4.4   Legal and Regulatory Issues

There may be legal and regulatory issues related to the use of AI in legal education, such as data protection laws, intellectual property laws, and liability issues. The use of AI in legal education involves the collection, processing, and storage of personal data. Legal educators must comply with data protection laws, such as the General Data Protection Regulation (GDPR), to ensure that personal data is collected and processed lawfully and transparently. The use of AI in legal education can involve the creation of copyrighted works, such as legal documents or research papers. Legal educators must ensure they have the necessary permissions and licenses to use and distribute copyrighted works. The use of AI in legal education can raise liability issues if AI tools produce inaccurate or biased results. Legal educators must take steps to ensure that AI tools are accurate and reliable and that they do not perpetuate biases or discrimination. The use of AI in legal education can involve processing sensitive personal data, such as criminal records or health data. Legal educators must comply with privacy laws to ensure that personal data is processed lawfully and securely. To address these legal and regulatory issues, legal educators must work closely with legal and regulatory experts to ensure that their use of AI in legal education complies with applicable laws and regulations. They must also ensure that they have the necessary policies and procedures in place to address legal and ethical concerns related to the use of AI. Finally, legal educators must be transparent with their students about the use of AI in legal education, and provide them with the necessary training and resources to understand and use AI tools effectively and responsibly.

4.5 Lack of Standardization

There is a lack of standardization in the use of AI tools in legal education. Different institutions may use different tools, which can create confusion and hinder collaboration. Standardization is an essential element here, as it provides a platform for the industry to discuss and facilitate the development of practical rules and requirements and ways to implement AI-based systems [34].

4.6 Impact on Job Market

The use of AI in legal education may impact the job market for legal professionals. Students may need to be trained in new skills and competencies required in the age of AI. Rapid advances in artificial intelligence (AI) and automation technologies have the potential to significantly disrupt labor markets [35].

Addressing these challenges requires a collaborative effort between legal educators, policy-makers, and industry stakeholders. Legal educators must be willing to embrace change and invest in the necessary infrastructure and training. Policy-makers must guide on the ethical and regulatory issues surrounding the use of AI in legal education. Industry stakeholders must collaborate with legal educators to develop AI tools that are accurate, reliable, and compliant with legal and ethical standards.

5 Future of Legal Education in the Digital Society of AI

The future of legal education in the digital society of AI is likely to be characterized by several significant developments. Some key trends and changes that we can expect to see include Greater integration of AI into legal education, Customized learning experiences, Collaborative learning, Continuous learning, Increased focus on interdisciplinary learning, and Ethical considerations. Artificial intelligence is profoundly changing human social life, and the integration between artificial intelligence and the law continues to deepen [10]. Legal education has to be epistemologically redesigned - leaving the "retrospective" model in a dogmatic past (which applied past solutions to present and future problems, with teacher authorities with all knowledge), and assuming a "prospective/projective" model, with the prioritization of the development of skills for dealing with complex problems and the construction of alternatives that do not exist hitherto. To this redesigned model, an interdisciplinary perspective must be added, including knowledge not traditionally part of the jurist's repertoire. Coding and use of new technologies, in addition to the communicative capacity (working collaboratively), should be the focus of a legal education capable of

offering future professional alternatives and skills to deal with the new technological social reality. The focus on interdisciplinarity must also aim at recent
innovations already put into practice, not only in an explanatory way but also,
in a way in which the development of students' creative, perspective, and pro-
jective skills takes place based on their use and reasoning. Blockchain, AI, smart
contracts, databases, and quantitative methodologies (among others) must be
combined with the training of legal typical skills and capabilities (which continue
to have their importance in the new digitalized world) so that new solutions are
found for new problems [36].

6   Conclusion

In conclusion, the digital society of artificial intelligence is transforming the landscape of legal education, creating new opportunities and challenges for legal educators and students. The use of AI tools in legal education is becoming increasingly common and is likely to continue to grow in the coming years.

However, implementing AI in legal education also faces significant challenges,
such as resistance to change, ethical concerns, and regulatory issues. Legal educators must work collaboratively with policymakers, industry stakeholders, and
legal and regulatory experts to address these challenges and ensure that AI is
used responsibly, ethically, and effectively.

Despite these challenges, the future of legal education in the digital society
of AI will likely be characterized by greater collaboration, customization, and
continuous learning. AI-powered tools can help to create more personalized and
effective learning experiences for students, and enable legal professionals to stay
up-to-date with the latest legal developments and technologies.

As the digital society of AI continues to evolve, legal educators must remain
vigilant and adaptable, continuously seeking new ways to integrate AI into
legal education while maintaining high standards of ethics and professionalism.
The future of legal education in the digital society of AI is bright, but it will
require the sustained effort and collaboration of legal educators, policymakers,
and industry stakeholders to realize its full potential.

To address these challenges, new approaches to legal education are necessary to equip law students with the necessary skills and knowledge to work with
AI. Legal professionals must also understand the implications of AI to create
an appropriate legal framework to reduce potential public risks while avoiding
obstructing innovation. Incorporating AI in legal education can help develop critical thinking and problem-solving skills needed to evaluate the appropriateness
and effectiveness of AI applications in various legal scenarios.

Overall, the emergence of AI technology in the legal industry presents both
challenges and opportunities for law students and professionals. Legal education must be adapted to include knowledge and skills related to technology and
data analytics to effectively work alongside AI. Students must develop a deeper
understanding of AI and its potential uses in the legal industry, as well as the ethical and privacy considerations that must be addressed. In addition to technical

skills, lawyers must possess soft skills such as problem-solving, critical thinking, communication, and collaboration to effectively work in interdisciplinary teams and navigate AI's ethical and legal issues. By adopting legal education and developing the necessary skills and competencies, law students and professionals can embrace the opportunities presented by AI and use it to streamline legal tasks, enhance legal services, and achieve better outcomes for society.

Acknowledgements. The authors are grateful to the Center for information technologies University of Mostar for supporting this research.

References

1. Goldin, C.D., Katz L.F.: The race between education and technology. Belknap Press of Harvard University Press (2008)
2. Kearns, M., Roth, A.: The Ethical Algorithm, the Science of Socially Aware Algorithm Design New York, Oxford University Press (2020)
3. Ashley, K.: Introducing AI and Law and Its Role in Future Legal Practice. In Artificial Intelligence and Legal Analytics: New Tools for Law Practice in the Digital Age, pp. 3–37. Cambridge: Cambridge University Press (2017). https://doi.org/10.1017/9781316761380.001
4. Anderson J., Rainie L.: Artificial Intelligence and the Future of Humans. Pew Research Center **10**(12), 1 (2018)
5. Maharg, P.: Let's get digital. Paul Maharg explores the potential for AI and legal education. New Law J. **167**(7731), 20 (2017). ISSN 0306–6479
6. Susskind, R.E., Susskind, D.: The future of the professions : how technology will transform the work of human experts (First). Oxford University Press. pp. 1 (2015)
7. The AI Advantage: How to Put the Artificial Intelligence Revolution to Work, Thomas H. Davenport 7
8. Ashley, K.D.: Artificial Intelligence and Legal Analytics, New tools for law practice in the digital age, University of Pittsburgh School of Law, 6 (2017)
9. Cerka, P., Grigiene, J., Sirbikyte, G.: Is it possible to grant legal personality to artificial intelligence software systems? Comput. Law Secur. Rev. **33**(5), 685–699 (2017)
10. Ma, B., Hou, Y.: Artificial Intelligence Empowers the Integrated Development of Legal Education: Challenges and Responses. Future Human Image **16** 43–54 (2021)
11. Susskind, R.: Tomorrow's Lawyers: An Introduction to Your Future. 2. ed. Oxford: Oxford University Press, p. 188 (2017)
12. Gurkaynak, G., Yilmaz, I., Haksever, G.: Stifling artificial intelligence: human perils. Comput. Law Security Rev. **32**(5), 749–758 (2016)
13. Sheppard, B.: Incomplete innovation and the premature disruption of legal services. Michigan State Law Rev. **5**, 1797–1910 (2015)
14. Alarie, B., Niblett, A., Yoon, A.H.: How artificial intelligence will affect the practice of law. Univ. Toronto Law J. **68**, 106–124 (2018)
15. The Law Society: Capturing Technological Innovation in Legal Services (2017). http://www.lawsociety.org.uk/support-services/research-trends/capturing-technological-innovation-report/ [Accessed 4 December 2018]

16. Mateus de Oliveira, F.: The impact of the introduction of artificial intelligence in advocacy: skills and professional ethics necessary for the future lawyer. Revista da Faculdade de Direito UFPR, Curitiba, v. 66, n. 2, pp. 69–94, maio/ago. 2021. ISSN 2236-7284. Disponível em: https://revistas.ufpr.br/direito/article/view/73458 Acesso em: 31 ago. 2021. https://doi.org/10.5380/rfdufpr.v66i2.73458

17. Susskind R.E., Susskind, D.: The future of the professions : how technology will transform the work of human experts (First). Oxford University Press. pp. 244 (2015)

18. Davenport, T.H.: The AI Advantage: How to Put the Artificial Intelligence Revolution to Work, pp. 158–159

19. (Dejoux, C.; Léon, E.: Métamorphose des managers.1st edition. France: Pearson. p. 209, 219 (2018)

20. Yoon, A.H.: The post-modern lawyer: Technology and the democratization of legal representation. Univ. Toronto Law J. **66**(4), 456-471 (2016). https://doi.org/10.3138/UTLJ.4007

21. de Oliveira Fornasier, M.: The impact of the introduction of artificial intelligence in advocacy: skills and professional ethics necessary for the future lawyer. Revista da Faculdade de Direito UFPR, Curitiba, v. 66, n. 2, p. 69–94, maio/ago. 2021. ISSN 2236-7284. Disponível em: https://revistas.ufpr.br/direito/article/view/73458 Acesso em: 31 ago. 2021. https://doi.org/10.5380/rfdufpr.v66i2.73458

22. Ivey, M.: The Ethical Midfield in Artificial Intelligence: Practical Reflections for National Security Lawyers. The Georgetown J. Legal Ethics **33**(1), 109–138 (2020)

23. Davis, A.: The Future of Law Firms (and Lawyers) in the Age of Artificial Intelligence. Revista Direito GV. **16**,(2020). https://doi.org/10.1590/2317-6172201945. p. 6

24. Nievelstein, F., et al.: The Worked Example and Expertise Reversal Effect in Less Structured Tasks: Learning to Reason about Legal Cases. Contemp. Educ. Psychol. **38**, 118, 118–19; Melissa Weresh, "Stargate: Malleability as a Threshold Concept in Legal Education" (2014) 63 J Legal Educ 689, 689; Twining and Miers (n 13) 337

25. Santana, M., Díaz-Fernández, M.: Competencies for the artificial intelligence age: visualisation of the state of the art and future perspectives. Rev. Manag. Sci 1–34(2022). https://doi.org/10.1007/s11846-022-00613-w

26. Schultz, N.L.: How Do Lawyers Really Think? J. Legal Educ. **42**, 57, 60. See also Preston, Stewart and Moulding (n 1) 1074–75

27. European University Institute, Badia Fiesolana - Via dei Roccettini 9, I-50014 San Domenico di Fiesole (FI) - Italy (2020). https://aiandlawschool.eui.eu/

28. The University of Michigan Law School. https://michigan.law.umich.edu/courses/artificial-intelligence-and-law

29. Alameda da Universidade, Cidade Universitária 1649–014 Lisboa, Portugal

30. Alma Mater Europaea - ECM (2023).https://almamater.si/uporabna-umetna-inteligenca-c37program

31. Stevens, Two Cheers/or 1870. TheAmerican Law School, in 5 PERSPECTIVES IN AMERICAN HISTORY 403, 511 (D. Fleming, B. Bailyn eds. 1971)

32. Hu, T., Lu, H.: Published by Atlantis Press SARL. This is an open access article distributed under the CC BY-NC 4.0 license http://creativecommons.org/licenses/by-nc/4.0/

33. Holmes, W., Porayska-Pomsta, K., Holstein, K. et al.: Ethics of AI in Education: Towards a Community-Wide Framework. Int. J. Artif. Intell. Educ. **32**, 504–526 (2022). https://doi.org/10.1007/s40593-021-00239-1

34. Szczekocka, E., Tarne, C., Pieczerak, J.: Standardization on Bias in Artificial Intelligence as Industry Support. On: 2022 IEEE International Conference on Big Data (Big Data), Osaka, Japan, pp. 5090–5099 (2022). https://doi.org/10.1109/BigData55660.2022.10020735

35. Morgan R. Frank, David Autor https://orcid.org/0000-0002-6915-9381, James E. Bessen, Erik Brynjolfsson, Manuel Cebrian, David J. Deming, Maryann Feldman, Matthew Groh, José Lobo, Esteban Moro, Dashun Wang, Hyejin Youn https://orcid.org/0000-0002-6190-4412, and Iyad Rahwan Toward understanding the impact of artificial intelligence on labor p.1 (2019)

36. de Oliveira Fornasier, M.: Legal education in the 21st century and the artificial intelligence. Revista Opinião Jurídica, Fortaleza, **19**(31), 1–32, maio/ago (2021)

Author Index

Printed in the United States
by Baker & Taylor Publisher Services